Advance praise for

COMMUNITY-BASED MULTILITERACIES & DIGITAL MEDIA PROJECTS

"By playing at the intersection of the digital literacy and community context, the editors and their co-authors move beyond traditional conversations about the pedagogical and programmatic mechanics of utilizing digital media to the critical examination of digital literacies in specific contexts and the associated challenges that accompany this work. As a STEAM educator and community advocate, I believe that through their work, Heather M. Pleasants and Dana E. Salter have created an invaluable space to interrogate some of the key questions facing those hoping to empower educators and students to utilize digital media to change and improve their world."

—Dr. Brian Williams, Director, Alonzo A. Crim Center for Urban Educational Excellence, and Assistant Professor, Early Childhood Education, Georgia State University

"This is a beautifully conceptualized collection. The result is a nuanced conversation about the intricacies, ambiguities, challenges, and the inspiration of collaborating across boundaries to create media that matter. The editors have invited experienced, self-reflective, community-based practitioners to 'write themselves into the story' of their work. The insights shared and questions explored are invaluably generative. They help us think critically about the ethics, integrity, and purposes of our labor. They remind us that reflection into process is not for the footnotes; rather, it is central to the story of social justice work."

—Darcy Alexandra, visual anthropologist, writer, educator, and documentary practitioner, Centre for Transcultural Research and Media Practice, Dublin Institute of Technology, Ireland

COMMUNITY-BASED MULTILITERACIES & DIGITAL MEDIA PROJECTS

new literacies
AND DIGITAL EPISTEMOLOGIES

Colin Lankshear and Michele Knobel
General Editors

Vol. 63

The New Literacies and Digital Epistemologies series
is part of the Peter Lang Education list.
Every volume is peer reviewed and meets
the highest quality standards for content and production.

PETER LANG
New York • Washington, D.C./Baltimore • Bern
Frankfurt • Berlin • Brussels • Vienna • Oxford

COMMUNITY-BASED MULTILITERACIES & DIGITAL MEDIA PROJECTS

Questioning Assumptions and Exploring Realities

Edited by
Heather M. Pleasants and Dana E. Salter

PETER LANG
New York • Washington, D.C./Baltimore • Bern
Frankfurt • Berlin • Brussels • Vienna • Oxford

Library of Congress Cataloging-in-Publication Data

Community-based multiliteracies and digital media projects:
questioning assumptions and exploring realities /
edited by Heather M. Pleasants, Dana E. Salter.
pages cm. — (New literacies and digital epistemologies; vol. 63)
Includes bibliographical references and index.
1. Computers and literacy. 2. Digital media—Social aspects.
3. Literacy—Social aspects. 4. Narrative inquiry (Research method).
I. Pleasants, Heather M., editor of compilation.
II. Salter, Dana E., editor of compilation.
LC149.5.C63 302.23'1—dc23 2013042399
ISBN 978-1-4331-1976-7 (hardcover)
ISBN 978-1-4331-1975-0 (paperback)
ISBN 978-1-4539-1278-2 (e-book)
ISSN 1523-9543

Bibliographic information published by **Die Deutsche Nationalbibliothek**.
Die Deutsche Nationalbibliothek lists this publication in the "Deutsche
Nationalbibliografie"; detailed bibliographic data is available
on the Internet at http://dnb.d-nb.de/.

Cover design by Becky Robinson

The paper in this book meets the guidelines for permanence and durability
of the Committee on Production Guidelines for Book Longevity
of the Council of Library Resources.

29 Broadway, 18th floor, New York, NY 10006
www.peterlang.com

Printed in the United States of America

—To Ed and Asia: Thank you so much for being who you are, and for all you have done—and continue to do—to make me who I am. I love you! (Heather)

—To my family that I was born into and who has emerged over time and locations: No words can express my thanks for your love and support. And to Dr. O: Thank you for the push(es). (Dana)

Table of Contents

Foreword

The Complicated Work of "Making the Familiar Strange" in Community-Based Literacies Research and Practice

Lalitha Vasudevan

For nearly a decade, I have spent time as a volunteer, mentor, tutor, and researcher involved with a community-based alternative to incarceration program in New York City. This organization provides a range of educational, social service, and therapeutic programming for youth who have been arrested and mandated by a judge to attend. I first met Vicki (pseudonym) when she was a case manager with the organization; she has since taken on the role of senior education specialist within an affiliated afterschool program for younger youth under the auspices of the same organization. In her current role, Vicki must advocate on behalf of the adolescent participants in their school settings and must likewise work with the same adolescents to create connections to school while they are in the charge of the mandated afterschool program. Advocacy, in this vein, requires Vicki to engage in multiple layers of everyday inquiry, data gathering and analysis, interpretation and diverse forms of representation for equally diverse audiences about the meaning making, communicative, and expressive practices of the youth with whom she works. Although she does not identify as a literacy or media expert, Vicki has had to become fluent in the multiliterate discourses of the youth in her charge in order to better represent them in school settings in support of their educational trajectories. This is work that requires translation of the non-school practices and activities for teachers and administrators inside of school.

Vicki exemplifies the ethos of negotiating multiple institutional boundaries in service of social action that is echoed in the work of many of the practitioners and researchers that Pleasants and Salter and the authors in this volume describe and that resonate strongly with discourses currently ongoing among researchers who are committed to participatory, action-oriented, and community-based research. As Lytle and Cochran-Smith (1994) have long advocated, research and practice must be understood not as two sides of a coin or somehow in opposition to one another, but as co-present elements of one's work that feed each other. In Vicki's case, for example, her research into the literate and digitally mediated lives of her youth informs her practice as an advocate and educator with and for youth.

Thus, with the abundance of literacy studies and projects whose contexts transcend school boundaries into the realms of afterschool programs, virtual worlds, community settings, and participants' homes, we have more than ample evidence to support Street's (1993) long-held assertion that we must regard literacies as multiple rather than a singular entity and that literacies vary with context and circumstance. To the calls for action inherent in subsequent sociocultural studies of literacies, and later with the emergence of a multiliteracies framework, there continues to exist, however, an ongoing need to make visible not only the richness and variability of literate traditions in unlikely or not easily accessible contexts; but also to render visible the conceptual and empirical spaces in which these emergent and changing insights about the evolving nature of literacies come to fruition.

In framing this volume, Pleasants and Salter respond to this call by making a simple yet profound assertion: those of us engaged in the community-based, literacy-rich, digitally mediated, action-oriented research –that is, researchers, scholars, and community workers—"have largely written ourselves out of the stories of our work." They set out to make visible the many contours of community-based research and practice that must be negotiated as part of the process, including relationships, beliefs, access to resources, normative practices, institutional policies and more. In doing so, they raise a number of questions about the oftentimes complicated and nuanced nature of multiliteracies research and practice within community settings: What are the rich literacy tapestries that are emergent and flourishing in the communities in which we are working, studying, and conceptualizing literacy shifts? What does the engagement of digital media—as object of inquiry and as medium of investigation—allow us to see about the contexts in which literacy practices flourish? How does materiality shape relationships in community-based digital collaborations?

As a literacies researcher, Kate Pahl has engaged similar questions in her community-based research partnerships in which participatory approaches are central to all stages of the research process (i.e., conceptualization, data collection and analysis, representation), acknowledging, of course, that these are often iterative and overlapping stages. Along with her colleagues and youth participants, she has written about the research process as both a site of discovery and as a sometimes unsettling and uncomfortable place (Pahl & Pool, 2011; Pahl, Steadman-Jones, & Pool, 2013). Whilst engaged in research about young people's everyday literacies and employing a variety of multimodal methods, including photography and video, Pahl admits to important tensions that arise when epistemological ruptures give rise to differences in how, for example, artifacts within a study are interpreted or what meanings are assigned to various social and cultural practices.

Thus, in Pahl's work, we find questions that strongly resonate with others that are called up throughout the chapters in Pleasants and Salter's volume: Whose work is it? What is the impetus behind the engaged scholarship and what are the driving forces that initiate and sustain the work? In what ways do researchers and community workers navigate the tricky shores of power, of letting go of power and institutional privilege and striving to distribute and share power more democratically? What are the temporal bounds of the work—and what traces does a temporally bounded project leave behind? How are we—researchers, scholars, community workers—situated in relation to the communities in which we work? These are fundamental questions to be asking as researchers, community members, youth participants and other stakeholders come together to negotiate both the purpose and promise of projects that seek to enact something rather than merely studying a phenomenon at a distance.

In their framing of this volume, Pleasants and Salter also evoke ethnographic questions wherein they implicitly call into question the challenge laid bare by the simple edict to "make the familiar strange" –how does one accomplish so seemingly straightforward a task when not only one's identity, but also one's livelihood, intellectual pursuits, and personal interests are implicated in the nature of community-based collaboration? Does engagement with digital media further complicate these endeavors? As the editors and their authors suggest, the existence of intangible but shareable artifacts further necessitates communication across project members about who takes ownership and responsibility for the artifacts that emerge from such community partnerships, especially if project partners hope for their work to be sustained beyond the temporal boundaries of a study.

Community-based literacies research and collaborative digital media production are endeavors that necessarily construct new social arrangements within which to interact and allow relationships to form, as researchers do not maintain a distanced stance in relation to the organizations with which they are working, and thus their roles, like the roles of their organizational partners and participants, and ways of interacting are increasingly hybrid and shifting. The authors in this volume reflect a range of these roles and positionalities. Likewise, the youth and community members with whom they work also inhabit myriad social locations and bring with them a wide range of expectations as they engage in visual arts projects, filmmaking, inquiry-based storytelling, and more. These multiple sites and practices allow us to see how the boundaries of literacy and digital media practices are never as clean as our polished analyses may lead others to believe.

Woven throughout the chapters are various responses to many of the questions noted above. Authors tell stories of learning to work together as a project team, of the constraints and affordances of media making and varying access to technologies, and of the at times competing interests between a project's research and pedagogical purposes. These stories of process also are rich with illustrations of curriculum in practice, pedagogical approaches, lessons learned about working at institutional borders, and seeking and gathering resources that add further flesh to the frame that the editors sketch out in their introduction. And what continues to linger after the manuscript comes to a close are the voices of youth, of community members, practitioners, media makers, and of the researchers themselves in which they dare to make visible the vulnerabilities inherent in collaborative work of this kind. Pleasants and Salter have provided a platform for their diverse perspectives, uncertainties, wonderings, and hopes to be taken seriously so that they may inform the practices of and knowledge production that results from future community-based research partnerships.

References

Lytle, S. L., & Cochran-Smith, M. (1994). Inquiry, knowledge, and practice. In S. Hollingsworth & H. Sockett (Eds.), *Teacher research and educational reform: Ninety-third yearbook of the National Society for the Study of Education* (pp. 22–51). Chicago: University of Chicago Press.

Pahl, K., & Pool, S. (2011). Living your life because it's the only life you've got'. *Qualitative Research Journal, 11*(2), 17–37.

Pahl, K., Steadman-Jones, R., & Pool, S. (2013). Dividing the drawers. *Creative Approaches to Research 6*(1), 71–88.

Street, B. E. (1993). *Cross-cultural approaches to literacy*. New York. Cambridge University Press

Acknowledgments

This book is the product of two years and hundreds of conversations, late night phone calls, mid-thought text and email messages, and as many face-to-face meetings as possible with friends, colleagues, and momentary strangers from around the world. These conversations and meetings have pushed our thinking and given rise to even more thoughtful questions about community-based multiliteracies and digital media projects as we conceptualized and edited this project. From the bottom of our hearts, we would like to thank all who have participated in this project in a myriad of ways.

The editors would like to thank the authors of the chapters for being a part of this project (in order of appearance in this book): Lalitha Vasudevan, Amy Hill, Ed Lee, Liz Miller, Pip Hardy (special thanks to Pip for her early contributions to the introduction chapter), Tony Sumner, Diana Nucera, Jeanette Lee, Jason Edward Lewis, Skawennati Fragnito, jesikah maria ross, Rob Simon, Jason Brennan, Sandro Bresba, Sara DeAngelis, Will Edwards, Helmi Jung, Anna Pisecny, Josh Schachter, Julie Kasper, Ouida Washington, Derek Koen, Kofi Larweh, Jonathon Langdon. You all are thoughtful, serious-minded friends and colleagues, who through your work and ways of being were fundamental in helping us push the boundaries of our own conceptualization of this book and the work we all do.

For their thoughtful conversations, insightful examples, expertly timed coffees, and careful reflections on drafts of this book, we thank Aziz Choudry, Sandra Chang-Kredl, Doreen Stark-Meyerring, Anthony Pare, Melanie Wilson, Samah Affan, Delice Igicari M. Mugabo, Rachel Raimist, and Darcy Alexandra, Michael Barrow, and Eduardo Paco Mateo.

From the bottom of our hearts we thank Colin Lankshear and Michele Knobel for their enthusiasm, support and critical affirmations for this book. We held our breath the first time we hit "send" on the email to you that contained the full manuscript for this book. We held it until we got your response and your way of supporting us has served as our model for supporting the authors in this book. Thank you.

We thank Peter Lang Publishing for their patience and guidance through this project. Specifically, we'd like to thank Sophie Appel, Phyllis Korper, Stephen Mazur and Chris Myers for their understanding, support, and perfectly timed input.

I (Heather) would like to thank Dana for collaborating with me to make this book a reality; your creativity, insights and knowledge have been invaluable at every step along the way. I would also like to thank my family—Harley and Merry Mikkelson, Sharon Ransom and Peter Gooch, Michael Ransom, Brian Ransom, Emily Ransom, Daria McMeans, John Mikkelson, Rebekah Mikkelson, Rachel Mikkelson, Nicole Mikkelson, Phyllis Pleasants, Christina Pleasants, Erica Pleasants, and Edward Pleasants and Marcia Pleasants. Finally, I (Dana), would like to thank Heather for trusting me enough to invite me to work with her in growing her initial ideas for this book into the ongoing project it has become. It is a pleasure and honor to work with you. And last but not least, for always putting up with me and letting me stand on their shoulders, I thank my family: Jerrelyn King Salter, Larry Salter, Dollie Salter, Quintal Crawford, Branden Salter, Olivier Darbin, and Maryse and Cojande Francois.

Chapter 1

Writing Oneself into the Story

Heather M. Pleasants and Dana E. Salter

In extending invitations to write chapters for this book, we were initially guided by a single question: within all of the work on community-based multiliteracies and digital media projects that has been written about and discussed, where are the stories of process and the reflections of researchers, scholars and community workers themselves? This book is a response to the call for stories of process as told by those who conceptualize and direct community-based multiliteracies and digital media projects (Walsh, Hewson, Shier, & Morales, 2008). By foregrounding the experiences and perspectives of community activists, project coordinators, scholars, community organizers and funders working across diverse media and geographic contexts, we turn our focus to questions of "why" and "what happened" rather than "how to."

Through the rapidly proliferating means to communicate knowledge about community-based multiliteracies and digital media, we have learned a great deal about contexts, discourses and the multimodal nature of meaning making in producers' multimodal literacy and digital media experiences (High, 2009, Watkins, 2009; Warschauer, & Matuchniak, 2010). However, we have learned very little about how those who initiate, facilitate and/or direct community-based multiliteracies and digital media projects negotiate the issues that arise throughout the process of creating and implementing their work. In fact, when we (the editors) contrast what is being written with what has been said in, for example, informal conversations between conference sessions, Skype chats, Facebook postings, email messages and telephone meetings, what we have noticed is this: we (researchers, scholars, community workers) have largely written ourselves out of the stories of our work.

With this in mind, we were very deliberate in how we framed the book: we wanted it to be a space for a range of voices to talk about issues, challenges and triumphs on personal, local and global levels. Indeed, "levels" is not quite the right word, as it is the intersections of these three spaces that produce implications for practice and theory related to community-based multiliteracies and digital media projects. We asked the contributors to focus on how their frameworks, methodologies, processes and questions "bump up" against the realities of doing their work in contexts that are so often shaped by competing philosophies, interests and conceptual frameworks, as well as economic, geo-political, organizational and community constraints. Through our conversations with community organizations, project participants, researchers, community members and funders, we have seen the need for more discussions of and reporting on actual, on-the-ground activity and the experiences people have had with the process of creating and implementing community projects. This is partially evidenced by the fact that when we explore the literature and research on this work, we don't often see the delightful, frustrating, enlightening messiness involved—the power outages due to unpaid bills, changes in funding that threaten the project altogether, the scavenging for equipment needed for pilot versions of the work, the late night, coffee-fueled conversations about design with our collaborators, the fits and starts involved in getting projects off the ground (see for example Prins, 2010). While we realize that the discursive conventions of reports and articles can limit the content conveyed, we also know that space for exploring the worked-through realities of this work is needed.

Thinking through Community

As a way to set the stage for thinking through and documenting stories of process in community-based multiliteracies and digital media work, we think it is important to begin by discussing a bit about what we mean when we speak of "community" and further, "community-based multiliteracies and digital media." When we speak of a project being "community-based," it is possible to reference a number of definitions of community, simultaneously. For example, in a discursive sense, community can be thought of as the intersection of identity(ies), places, and psychological-social relationships that shape, are shaped by, and give meaning to various interactions that happen in a range of contexts (Cohen, 1985)—this discursive understanding of community has clear relevance for multiliteracies and digital media projects (e.g., Lambert, 2006; Jayasuriya, Weinberg, & Mobile Voices, 2011; Walsh, Rutherford, & Kuzmak, 2010). Community can also be conceptualized as being comprised of organizational entities—colleges and universities, community organizations, non-profits—and the geographic communities surrounding these entities (Pahl, 2010). Communities formed through the process of bringing people together to create digital media and multiliteracies projects and programs are another kind of community, though these may be more provisional or temporary.

As we wrestled with defining community in relation to multiliteracies and digital media projects, we concurrently explored the diverse interdisciplinary research corpus that has, over the last 30 + years, attempted to tease out issues at the intersections of reframed literacy discussions, community-based research and engagement, and emerging technology and digital media uses. One place to begin our definition of multiliteracies and digital media projects is Shirley Brice Heath's 1980 landmark ethnography, *Ways with Words* (Heath, 1983). Heath's study of the literacy learning in the Carolinas is an important marker for this book for three reasons. First, her work was grounded in an ethic of research and pedagogical practice that privileged the experiences and perspectives of individuals (teachers, millworkers, businessmen) who were part of the communities being researched. Second, her work was one aspect of a conversation in which literacy was re-imagined as not just a set of skills to be mastered, but as practices and events that are always mediated by the interplay between local and global social interactions, cultures, assigned meanings and values of communities. Last, Heath's work contributed to linking the personal decisions and identities that we as community members, activists, practitioners and researchers enact and the research we conduct, to the consequences of the community-based ethnographic methodological and project design decisions that we make. Heath also acknowledged the importance of her own lived experience of both the communities she worked with and her own personal history in constructing an account of the out-of-school literacy practices of children and adults.

Using the above three markers as entry points, our working definition of multiliteracies projects refers to focused work around an idea, issue or theme that built upon the concept of multiliteracies (New London Group, 1996; Cope & Kalantzis, 2000; Gee, 2009; Lankshear & Knobel, 2008; Janks, 2010). The idea of multiliteracies shifts the discussion of literacy(ies) from a static print-based discussion to a focus that encompasses the social as well as the multiplicity of literacies and texts used in communication. Accordingly, Cope and Kalantzis (2000) explains multiliteracies as "…a word we chose because it describes two important arguments we might have with the emerging cultural, institutional, and global order. The first argument engages with the multiplicity of communications channels and media; the second with the increasing salience of cultural and linguistic diversity" (p. 5). Multiliteracies discussions emerged out of a perceived need to rethink the demands of kinds of meaning making people make in their "changing public spaces and in the changing dimensions of [their] community lives—[their] lifeworlds" (p. 4).

Indeed, 15 plus years since the New London Group began discussing this term, we are still unraveling the affordances and consequences of multiliteracies and increasing the recognition of cultural and linguistic diversity as it positions and is positioned by historically marginalized communities. Building on our working definition of multiliteracies, our definition of digital media projects draws upon critical digital literacy research—a great deal of this research focuses on youth populations and the education/school context (Jenkins, Purushotma, Weigel, Clinton & Robinson, 2009; Ito, 2010; Pleasants, 2008; Salter, 2012; Vasudevan, 2010). We posit that the digital media projects in this book relate to critical digital literacies in that they are "those skills and practices that lead to the creation of digital texts that interrogate the world; they also allow and foster the interrogation of digital, multimedia texts" (Avila & Zacher Pandya, 2012). This definition of critical digital literacies incorporates Dockter and Lewis' (2009) arguments by seeing community-based digital media projects and critical digital literacies as digitally mediated social practices that envision and frame literacy as a form of critical civic engagement "so that [people] can 'read' [and we would add produce and act upon] the linguistic, visual, and aural signs and symbols that inundate their lives, both public and private" (p.17; also see Merchant, 2009; Mills, 2010).

This kind of community-based multiliteracies and digital media work is being done by media-making organizations such as the Center for Digital Storytelling (CDS, 2012), for example. As an organization whose concept originated almost twenty years ago, CDS has contracted with many universities, and has worked with many different kinds of organizations around the world. CDS is itself a community, and has created a larger digital storytelling community that was at one time partially defined by an annual digital storytelling festival, and is now maintained and very active via social media and an international biannual conference. It is important to note that, as media-making tools become increasingly ubiquitous, it is CDS's ethos and approach to storytelling as life-affirming and transformative as much as it is their technological savvy and expertise that continues to draw newcomers to their approach.

Community-based multiliteracies and digital media work is also situated as an integral component of grassroots community organizations such as the Detroit-based Allied Media Project (Nucera & Lee in this book) and Radio Ada in Ghana (Larweh & Langdon in this book). With media-making as a central and ongoing facet of the life of these communities, these projects embody for us an incredibly rich model of what community-based multiliteracies and digital media has the potential to be.

Institutions of higher education figure prominently within the community-based multiliteracies and digital media work discussed in many of the chapters in this book, whether through developers and staff that are also faculty or graduate students in university settings, or whether the projects described receive direct or indirect funding from postsecondary institutions. ross's chapter in this book (and others) prompts us to seek further discussions of the material and philosophical costs and benefits of university-supported community-based digital literacies and multiliteracies work. Might universities begin to explicitly acknowledge their role in shaping this work, and incorporate that into their vision and mission statements? Many postsecondary institutions have begun to do this through "engaged scholarship"—scholarly activity that links teaching, research and service and that seeks to provide mutually beneficial outcomes to both university communities and those in surrounding geographic regions. However, much of the promise of this strategy will depend on continued exploration of how the goals and outcomes of this work are equitably co-created and determined.

Considering Geopolitical Discourses and Community-Based Multiliteracies and Digital Media Projects

A consideration of the relationships between geopolitical discourses and community-based multiliteracies and digital media projects provides an important frame for broadening conceptualizations and critically reflecting on the process of engaging this work. Briefly, geopolitical discourses (simultaneously local and global—see for example Appadurai, 1996; Creech, Berthe, Assubuji, Mansighn, & Anjelkovic, 2006) can be defined as how we conceptualize relationships between global and local contexts, language and practices in these spaces and meanings derived from these interlocking experiences. More, the actions that produce and are produced by geopolitical discourses are often shaped by the "...negative accompaniments of globalization: displacement, poverty, lack of educational opportunity, and the trauma that sometimes accompanies immigration" (Hull, Zacher, & Hibbert, 2009, p. 145). They are also shaped by region-specific conversations on the proliferation of traditional and digital media, as these are impacted by increased or stagnant infrastructures and network capabilities (e.g., see conversations in Howley, 2010; Lessig, 2008).

As an example, the community-based multiliteracies and digital media projects in this book emerge within contexts shaped by the intersections of geopolitical discourses that Appadurai (1996) outlines as the ongoing global economic crisis exacerbated by changes in the restructuring of capital in global economies; steadily increasing income disparities of individuals, communities and nations; shifting patterns of immigration due to the global economic crisis, and the impact these shifts have on families, and communities (Choudry & Kapoor, 2013; Gee, Hull, & Lankshear, 1996; Castells, 1999). In addition, the exploration of the actions, in the case of our book projects, that produce and are produced by these geopolitical discourses necessarily draw attention to the challenging role of the local in this work. For example, the interplay between local geopolitical discourses such as the impact of schooling practices on teacher pedagogy and student learning; media representations of historically marginalized youth; and psycho-social implications of speaking about trauma stretch the frames we create to conceptualize this work (Herman, 1992; Lauder, Brown, Dillabough, & Halsey, 2006; Stevens, 2011; Vasudevan, Stageman, Rodriguez, Fernandez, & Dattatreyan, 2010).

Multiliteracies and digital media practices cut across these geopolitical conversations; this is particularly apparent when discussing the role of "community" within and across those practices. What is considered a local and global community is dependent on your own position within and/or outside of the community. What that position means, how it is produced and what you can do within that context has consequences on community-based new literacies and digital media projects. For example, despite drawing on varied working definitions of community, each of the authors in the book has been instrumental in creating a community around and through their work, and is connected to a community of practice that supports who they are personally and professionally. Additionally, each author simultaneously reflects in their own way on the consequences of the geopolitical and local community and contexts in which their work rests. Importantly, the authors do not shy away from working through the challenges raised by this way of thinking through community and their work.

Tensions and Challenges in Community-Based Multiliteracies and Digital Media Work

Against the backdrop of literature and theoretical perspectives discussed above, we consider the tensions and challenges in community-based multiliteracies and digital media work, drawing attention to several that cut across our experiences in working on our own projects and the chapters in this book. We see these as falling into the following areas: (1) managing the integrity of process and product, (2) maintaining communication, (3) thinking critically about the concept of "impact" across multiple dimensions and (4) sustaining our work (and ourselves).

Integrity of Process and Product. In any field of work there are links between process and product and corresponding expectations about what the nature of those connections will be, especially in terms of the quantity and quality of what is produced. However, these are more than just simple equations when it comes to community-based multiliteracies and digital media work—the stakes are raised. The stakes are raised because the scholars and program directors of the projects are most often very acutely aware of what reactions to radio programs, digital stories or public art campaigns will be if the work is perceived as being somehow "less than." However, even more at issue is the fact that the stakes are raised because what is produced is directly connected to and representative of people's lives.

In fact, we chose to open this book with chapters that consider the ethical dimensions of community-based multiliteracies and digital media projects precisely because the work done through these projects entails many micro- and macro-level decisions before and during the media-making process, and in sharing multiliteracies and digital media creations publicly. These decisions shape material consequences for all individuals who are directly involved in our programs and projects, as well as others who are indirectly connected to what we do. With the presence of many direct, indirect and potential stakeholders in our work, numerous questions can arise. For example, what is the "right" decision when a community shows more interest in our program than we originally planned or anticipated (Lee and Miller in this book)? What should be said, and to whom, when a digital story is viewed and the audience forms an interpretation of the story and storyteller that is unfavorable (Hill in this book)? When the work of the project is deeply embedded within our livelihoods, how do we balance what might be most helpful for our community media co-producers with the expectations of community members, funders, business people, school personnel, elected representatives and officials regarding the use of the media and art that we have helped others to create (Hardy & Sumner; Washington & Koen; Schachter & Kasper—all in this book)?

These questions may not have straightforward answers. However, through their work, the scholars/practitioners featured within this book discuss both the strategies and practices their work is grounded in, and the "in-the-moment" ethical decisions that necessarily are a part of different social interactions. What has become clear through the chapters assembled in this collection is the extent to which (a) most of these questions arise in the "doing" of the project, (b) the articulation of a priori strategies and practices assist, but do not completely prevent, ethical issues from arising, and (c) openness and honest perspective-sharing are invaluable foundations for community-based multiliteracies and digital media work.

Challenges of Communication. In their chapter in this book on Aboriginal storytelling through digital media, Lewis & Fragnito speak eloquently of the challenges in establishing relationships with—and in some cases being or becoming a member of—the communities central to their work. Folks in specific geographic or cultural communities may have interests that easily match up with what program developers would like to do, but more often, a great deal of time is invested in seeking out connections in which intentions match up. In this case, the Public Programs Supervisor of the Kanien'kehá:ka Onkwawén:na Raotitióhkwa Language and Cultural Center was very excited about the project that Lewis and Fragnito were proposing, but the director of the center had never even seen a video game before, and a great deal of time needed to be spent providing further context for what the project was and why it was important. Additional complexities can arise when staff or priorities change with little warning, as happened twice within Lewis and Fragnito's work. And, as Lewis and Fragnito and other community-based researchers who are also members of academic communities have discussed, community members and organizations may have negative perceptions of program developers' motives, based on past interactions with researchers whose philosophical perspectives do not address how power and status dynamics shape communication, or who may not be cognizant of the "funds of knowledge" (Moll, Amanti, Neff & Gonzalez, 1992) that are already present within specific community contexts. Communication challenges can also arise when we are members of the community in which the work is taking place—expectations can be higher, or simply different, and relationship parameters can be presumed and/or misinterpreted.

Whether we see ourselves as insiders, outsiders, somewhere in-between, or as crossing back and forth between perceived boundaries, it takes time and attention to sustain collaborative relationships built on mutual trust and respect with others within community contexts. Consequently, though most of the authors featured in this collection have been working with and in communities for a number of years, they continue to grapple with how to establish and keep effective communication going throughout their projects, from the very beginning, through the middle and outcomes-stages of projects. In addition to the issues mentioned previously, tensions—or perhaps fine balancing lines—exist between coming in to a project with humility based on one's knowledge of status and privilege, and honoring the fact that people within a community may initially expect us to take authoritative positions in communication and project direction based on social and cultural understandings. Conversely, there may be apprehension or hostility to the positions we occupy based on previous experiences with us or the organizations we represent. Challenges may also exist in helping others to share their experiences and perspectives through using tools and modes of communication that may be unfamiliar to them. How do we help older community members actively take part in the construction of multiliteracies and digital media projects when iMovie, Adobe Premiere and Photoshop may be completely new territories for them (Hardy & Sumner in this volume)? How much and how hard should we push for others to "share their voices" when the social and political context is hostile (Schachter & Kasper in this book)?

As Hill and Hardy and Sumner discuss, it is important to explain throughout a project what permissions media makers are giving when they agree to participate. Procedures borrowed from social science research can be helpful here—particularly those guidelines that make it clear that participation "can be ended at any time without penalty." However, what this means in community-based practices can be difficult to determine. If the project is ongoing—when do we determine that an individual's consent is no longer needed (Hill)? Alternatively, as digital media projects take on a life beyond their creation, in what ways can we continue to credit those who have directly contributed to these projects, such that our involvement with/in communities reaps benefits for those communities (see Lewis & Fragnito)? In representing what we have learned through working in and with communities, what is gained and lost through a unitary (methodological and/or conceptual) narrative and storyline? A polyvocal narrative?

Impact. Though we speak often of the importance of community-based multiliteracies and digital media work reaching diverse audiences, what does this mean in practice? When we speak of "reaching people," does this result in further communication and dialogue within these communities, while also bringing new and diverse perspectives into the conversation? If yes, when and how does this happen? As Washington and Koen in their chapter point out, support for community-based work is often contingent on how well we can articulate the "so what" of our work, or our answers to the question of "why focus on these groups of people?" Whether within the broader public, or within universities, government or private foundation funding, a reality that many community-based media makers and program developers face is one in which they are asked to articulate the Return On Investment (ROI) that will be the result of their work.

While we simultaneously contest the commodification of community-based work (and the people who create it) and acknowledge the ROI contexts in which we often operate, we also actively work toward crafting new understandings of "impact," and new ways of thinking about the differences that make a difference (Nucera & Lee in this book). What might this look like? Further, how can we embed opportunities to show evidence of the significance of our work at various points within what we do? Responses to these questions are critical to changing conversations about impact and an intertwined dialogue about sustainability.

Sustaining Ourselves and Our Work. Successfully addressing how our work creates changes, shows impact, or supports needed community resources (Larweh & Langdon in this book) is a critical component to sustaining the work we do over time. Similarly to questions concerning impact, although questions about sustainability are ones that all community-based multiliteracies and digital media projects must address, the way in which we are seeking to sustain the work links back to our own position within it. If we build or are a part of organizations, our continued existence is contingent on our ability to produce work that meets a community need, resonates with individuals, and is attractive to people (whether within or outside of the community) who can provide resources that enable the work to be done. If we work within a college or university context our work must result in publications and/or be beneficial to students' learning and development. And, whether we work in community-serving organizations, higher education environments, or across both, all of us must at some point communicate the results of our work to various internal and external audiences.

The issue of sustainability is not just relevant to our projects, but to ourselves as well. As mentioned earlier, authors in this book and others doing this kind of work have identities that are necessarily hybridized. It is not by accident that most chapters in this book are authored by more than one person, as the projects highlighted most often demand a team mindset and approach. Even in projects that are led and coordinated by multiple individuals, coordination and implementation work can take a toll on minds and bodies. As a way to manage the multiple stressors that are a part of this work, Nucera & Lee in their chapter suggest that we "just cry," and then "just try," that we directly make fun a part of our work, and that we learn to treat "love as a political concept." In so doing, Nucera & Lee remind us of the importance of remembering ourselves in the process of doing our work and of the significance of being mindful of our emotions and humanity. We have noted that these understandings of what is involved in successfully creating community-based multiliteracies and digital media programs are often obscured in public representations of the work that results, and the authors in this volume have provided important beginning points for dialogues that centralize this fact and help us consider how we can remain personally and professionally healthy.

Overview of the Book

The book comprises five parts. These five parts are, of course, more heuristic than anything else, but they nonetheless help to give shape to discussing the assumptions and exploring the realities of the messy boundaries of the processes of participating in community-based multiliteracies and digital media projects.

The two chapters in Part 1 (Ethics and the Politics of Representation and Doing Good) focus on the ethical dimensions of community-based multiliteracies and digital media projects and the politics of voice, representation, and "doing good." Amy Hill, in her chapter, "Digital storytelling and the Politics of 'Doing Good': Exploring the Ethics of Bringing Personal Narratives into Public Spheres," examines the realities of ethical dimensions of multiliteracies and digital media projects. Hill asks what it means to be an "ethical storytelling facilitator rather than a self-interested story entrepreneur" through exploring her work with community-based digital storytelling. Ed Lee and Liz Miller, in their chapter, "Entry Point: Participatory Media-Making with Queer and Trans Refugees: Social Locations, Agendas and Thinking Structurally" explore the realities of relationships between community-based digital media projects, institutional structures, "doing good" and the politics of representation in their work during a social media project with Montreal-based racialized queer refugees.

The two chapters in Part 2 (Identities and Relationships) deal with how communities of practice and community-based multiliteracies and digital media projects shape and are shaped by identities. Diana Nucera and Jeanette (Jenny) Lee, in their chapter, "I Transform Myself, I Transform the World Around Me" provide portraits of how the development of their personal and professional identities have shaped the goals and purposes they bring to their leadership of the Allied Media Project and to their relationships with others within, and connected to the organization. Pip Hardy and Tony Sumner, in their chapter, "Our Stories, Ourselves: Exploring Identities, Sharing Experiences and Building Relationships Through Patient Voices" discuss how digital stories of patients, "care-ers" and medical professionals reveal commonalities across identities and experiences, and they articulate how bearing witness to stories can create opportunities for more compassionate relationships within and beyond one's experience with health and the health care system.

The two chapters in Part 3 (Methodologies) contemplate community-based multiliteracies and digital media projects methodological considerations and challenges, as well as how buy-in in the community and/or institution-organization can be discussed and conceptualized. Jason Lewis and Skaewnnati Fragnito, in their chapter titled "You Want to Do What With Doda's Stories? Building a Community for the Skins Workshops on Aboriginal Storytelling in Digital Media," discuss the delicate interplay between community identities, methodological assumptions and realities, and conceptualizing the "up take" of digital media projects during the conception, facilitation and completion of their First Nation community-based video game project in a Canada. In the second chapter of the section, jesikah maria ross, in her chapter titled "Adventures in Community Media: Experiments, Findings and Strategies for Change," walks us through the methodological choices she has made in doing environmental justice-oriented community-based media work and the "experiments" that she has completed that have led to important insights about the nature of this work, particularly when done within the context of university-led collaborative projects.

The two chapters in Part 4 (Pedagogies and Knowledge Construction) deal with what happens when pedagogical and knowledge construction experiences bump up against ever-changing contextual realities. The authors in this section also examine how teachers in community-based contexts can resist the dilution and champion the retention of complexity in multiliteracies and digital media projects. Rob Simon, Jason Brennan, Sandro Bresba, Sara DeAngelis, Will Edwards, Helmi Jung, and Anna Pisecny, in their chapter "The Teaching to Learn Project: Investigating Literacy through Intergenerational Inquiry," explore intergenerational inquiry as a means of investigating literacy through new social relationships, new methodologies, and new epistemologies observed during critical incidents in their university-school literacy class. In their chapter titled "Finding Voice: Building Literacies and Communities Inside and Outside the Classroom," Josh Schacter and Julie Kasper use their ongoing visual-photo projects with immigrant youth in Arizona to discuss ways of doing this work in the face of competing ideologies and agendas, and explore what is involved in developing and maintaining both the work and the collaborative relationships that sustain it.

The two chapters in Part 5 (After the Project) reflect on what happens once a community-based digital media project takes on a life of its own and morphs (for better or worse) into a new direction. Ouida Washington and Derek Koen, in their chapter titled, "Visions beyond the Bricks: Reflections on Engaging Communities to Support Black Male Youth," reflect on the development of their initial film into a community-based digital media project with and for black males in five states, and discuss the evolution of their message as it bumps up against funding and engagement realities. In their chapter "Seeing the Synergy in the Signals: Reflections on Weaving Projects into Social Movement Mobilizing through Community Radio," Kofi Larweh and Jon Langdon reflect upon their ongoing work with a community radio station in Ghana that is deeply involved in social movement efforts to maintain communal control over the area's natural resource, salt. They also propose new ways to think about literacy and digital media projects in the contexts of struggle.

Conclusion: Questioning Assumptions and Exploring Realities

As a way to frame an approach to thinking through, documenting, and carving a space for the diverse experiences represented in community-based multiliteracies and digital media work, it vital to name and explore the assumptions and realities faced in doing this work. These assumptions can range from not fully understanding the power of images when working with refugees to create digital stories, to assumptions about the meaning of illness and patient care. These assumptions can be more broadly defined around the current discourses we use to convey our processes as we conduct this work, to assumptions about the impact of funding and the commodification of experience.

Simultaneously, the exploration of the realities of this work helps us document and begin to understand how good intentions intersect with the realities of the contexts in which this work emerges and is enacted. These realities include the skills and abilities that are needed to do this work, for which directors and participants may not have adequate training, to the reality of funding challenges in our current economic state, to the reality of the push for quantitative outcomes for this work, which may or may not include an understanding of the context in which the work is happening. Similar to thinking about assumptions, more globally defined, the realities of this work can also include contextual realities in which these projects may not work.

In this book we invite you to maintain an air of curiosity and ask that you read the chapters as attempts to discuss and question process. To that end, there are two points we'd like you to keep in mind. First, we invite you to question your own assumptions about community-based multiliteracies and digital media projects. Second, we invite you to use this book as a space for reflection on your own work. At the end of most multi-media projects is a product: a film, an audio recording, a piece of artwork, a technological creation, a game, a digital story, a discussion group. These are the artifacts that will, perhaps, be shown or displayed or screened; it is this that will likely attract funding from sponsors, or lead to other projects, or create a movement, or spark a conversation. The goal of many of these projects in community-based settings is to create something tangible: an outcome or an output.

However, the journey from idea to reality can be long, winding, emotionally draining, and fraught with perils of one sort or another. From here a matrix of questions arise. Where do we have conversations about those realities, those perils of this work? Who participates in these conversations? How do the people who create and operate these projects experience their work? What is the impact of their experiences on the ongoing shape of their practice? How do we talk about this work? In the chapters that follow, the authors in this book explore these and other questions as a means to write themselves into their work.

References

Appadurai, A. (1996). *Modernity at large: Cultural dimensions of globalization.* Minneapolis: University of Minnesota Press.

Avila, J., & Zacher Pandya, J. (Eds.). (2012). *Critical digital literacies as social praxis: Intersections and challenges.* New York: Peter Lang.

Castells, M. (1999). *Information technology, globalization and social development: United Nations Institute for Social Development.* Retrieved from http://www.unrisd.org/80256B3C005BCCF9/%28httpAuxPages%29/F270E0066F3DE7780256B67005B728C?Open Document

Center for Digital Storytelling (2012). *The evolution of digital storytelling: An abbreviated history of key moments during the first 16 years (1993–2006).* Retrieved from http://www.storycenter.org/timeline.html

Choudry, A., and Kapoor, D. (Eds). (2013). *NGOization: Complicity, contradictions and prospects.* London: Zed.

Cohen, A. P. (1985). *The symbolic construction of community.* London: Tavistock.

Cope, B., & Kalantzis, M. (2000). Multiliteracies: The beginning of an idea. In B. Cope & M. Kalantzis (Eds.), *Multiliteracies: Literacy learning and the design of social futures* (pp. 3–8). London: Routledge.

Creech, H., Berthe, O., Assubuji, A. P., Mansighn, I., & Anjelkovic, M. (2006). *Evaluation of UNESCO's community multimedia centers: Final report (Report No. IOS/EVS/PA/54).* Paris: United Nations Educational, Scientific, and Cultural Organization.

Dockter, J., & Lewis, C. (2009). *Redefining academic rigor: Documentary film making in the new English/language arts classroom. CURA Reporter.* Retrieved from http://www.cura.umn.edu/publications/ catalog/reporter-39-3-4-6

Gee, J. (2009). Digital media and learning as an emerging field, part 1: How we got here. *International Journal of Learning and Media, 1*(2), 13–23.

Gee, J., Hull, G., & Lankshear, C. (1996). *The new work order.* Boulder, CO: Westview.

Heath, S. B. (1983). *Ways with words: Language, life, and work in communities and classrooms.* Cambridge: Cambridge University Press.

Herman, Judith. (1992). *Trauma and recovery: The aftermath of violence—from domestic abuse to political terror.* New York: Basic.

High, S. (2009). *Telling stories: A reflection on oral history and new media.* British Oral History Society Conference. Glasgow, Scotland. Retrieved from http://digitalhistory.concordia.ca/courses/hist306/wpcontent/ uploads /2009/09/highoralhistnewmedia.pdf

Howley, K. (2010). *Understanding community media.* Thousand Oaks, CA: Sage.

Hull, G., Zacher, J., & Hibbert, L. (2009). Youth, risk, and equity in a global world. *Review of Research in Education, 33,* 117–159.

Ito, M. (2010). *Hanging out, messing around, and geeking out: Kids living and learning with new media.* Cambridge, MA: MIT Press.

Janks, H. (2010). *Literacy and power.* New York: Taylor and Francis.

Jayasuriya, M., Weinberg, M., & Mobile Voices, (June 2011). *Text messaging for grassroots organizers.* Allied Media Conference.

Jenkins, H., Purushotma, R., Weigel, M., Clinton, K., & Robinson, A. (2009). *Confronting the challenges of participatory culture: Media education for the 21st century.* Cambridge: The MIT Press.

Lambert, J. (2006). *Digital storytelling: Capturing lives, creating community.* (2nd Ed.). Berkeley, CA: Digital Diner.

Lankshear, C., & Knobel, M. (Eds.). (2008). *Digital literacies: Concepts, policies and practices.* New York: Peter Lang.

Lauder, H., Brown, P., Dillabough, J., & Halsey, H. (2006). *Education, globalization and social change.* Oxford: Oxford University Press.

Lessig, L. (2008). *Remix: Making art and commerce thrive in the hybrid economy.* New York: Penguin.

Merchant, G. (2009). Literacy in virtual worlds. *Journal of Research in Reading, 32*(1), 38–57.

Mills, K. A. (2010). A review of the "digital turn" in the new literacy studies. *Review of Educational Research, 80*(2), 246–271.

Moll, L. C., Amanti, C., Neff, D., & Gonzalez, N. (1992). Funds of knowledge for teaching: Using a qualitative approach to connect homes and classrooms. *Theory into Practice, 31*(2), 132–141.

New London Group. (1996). A pedagogy of multiliteracies: Designing social futures. *Harvard Educational Review, 66*(1), 60–92.

Pahl, K. (2010). Changing literacies: Schools, communities and homes. In J. Lavia and M. Moore (Eds.), *Cross-cultural perspectives on policy and practice: Decolonizing community contexts.* London: Routledge.

Pleasants, H. (2008). Negotiating identity projects: Exploring the digital storytelling experiences of three African American girls. In M. Hill & L. Vasudevan (Eds.), *Media, learning and sites of possibility*. New York: Peter Lang.

Prins, E. (2010). Participatory photography: A tool for empowerment or surveillance? *Action Research, 8*(4), 426–443.

Salter, D. E. (2012). "They get what they deserve": Interrogating critical digital literacy experiences as framed in a Quebec alternative high school context. In J. Avila and J. Zacher Pandya (Eds), *Critical digital literacies as social praxis: Intersections and challenges*. New York: Peter Lang.

Stevens, L. P. (2011). Literacy, capital, and education: A view from immigrant youth. *Theory into Practice, 50*(2), 133–140.

Vasudevan, L. (2010). Education remix: New media, literacies, and the emerging digital geographies. *Digital Culture and Education, 2*, 62–82.

Vasudevan, L., Stageman, D., Rodriguez, K., Fernandez, E., & Dattatreyan, E. (2010). Authoring new narratives with youth at the intersection of the arts and justice. *Perspectives on Urban Education, 7*(1), 55–65.

Walsh, C. A., Hewson, J., Shier, M., & Morales, E. (2008). Unravelling ethics: Reflections from a community-based participatory research project with youth. *The Qualitative Report, 13*(3), 379–393.

Walsh, C. A., Rutherford, G., & Kuzmak, N. (2010). Engaging women who are homeless in community-based research using emerging qualitative data collection techniques. *International Journal of Multiple Research Approaches, 4*(3), 192–205.

Warschauer, M., & Matuchniak, T. (2010). New technology and digital worlds: Analyzing evidence of equity in access, use, and outcomes. *Review of Research in Education, 34*, 179–225 .

Watkins, C. (2009). *The young and digital: What the migration to social network sites, games, and anything anywhere media means for our future*. Boston: Beacon Press.

Part 1: Ethics and Politics of Representation and "Doing Good"

Chapter 2

Digital Storytelling and the Politics of Doing Good: Exploring the Ethics of Bringing Personal Narratives into Public Spheres

Amy Hill

Introduction

- *A teenager from rural Northern California creates a digital story about his former life as a gang member, which features photos of some of his friends. Though the storyteller doesn't mention the names of these friends, their parents threaten legal action against the organization that sponsored the workshop.*

- *A young woman in Nepal agrees to attend a digital storytelling workshop and share her recent experience of surviving severe abuse at the hands of her husband. After participating for a day, she drops out, claiming that a spirit appeared in her dream and threatened to harm her if she continued.*

- *A man in South Africa creates a digital story about his love and respect for his sister-in-law, who passed away some years prior to the workshop. Viewers at a local community screening condemn the piece for indirectly implicating the storyteller's brother—husband of the deceased—as being responsible for her HIV-related death.*

I come to the world of participatory media—and specifically to digital storytelling—first and foremost as a woman who grew up in a painfully unstable and sometimes abusive family environment. During my early professional career, I sought out new means for shifting public dialogue about violence, and I eagerly took up the tools and practices developed at the Center for Digital Storytelling (CDS). Drawing from well-established methods in facilitative filmmaking, narrative practice, and popular education, the digital storytelling process involves bringing a small group of people together in a workshop setting to share stories from their own lives. Throughout this chapter, "digital storytelling" refers to a workshop process that originated at CDS, in which participants verbally share aspects of their own experiences in a group "story circle;" write and record first-person voiceover narration; select and/or generate still photos and short video clips to use in illustrating their stories; and learn, via hands-on computer tutorials, how to assemble these materials into finished digital videos, or "digital stories." Current CDS practice within custom projects like those profiled here prohibits the use of any copyrighted materials; the chapter therefore does not claim to offer legal advice about rights, royalties, or other similar concerns.

My digital storytelling pedagogy is rooted in a public health approach—one that considers both individual and systemic causes of ill health and inequity. As a middle-class white female engaged in working with individuals and communities who typically possess far less privilege than I enjoy, I work through the lens of cultural humility, which means asking not how others' "difference" from me informs who they are but instead examining how my own location vis-à-vis race, gender, and class influences my perspective and ability to listen, understand, and act (Tervalon & Murray-Garcia, 1998). My allegiance to feminist values leads me to operate from a point of view that "does not intend to speak about, just nearby" (Haraway, 1988) the voices of the oppressed.

In 1999, after making a story of my own, I co-founded a digital storytelling initiative called Silence Speaks (Silence Speaks, 2013), which focuses on how story can inform human rights promotion. Since then, I've led dozens of workshops with women and men from across the United States and in countries around the world. The scenarios presented above are rooted in this direct experience with digital storytelling practice. My initial—and, in hindsight, naïve—desire to surface rarely heard stories in the service of justice has evolved into a much more cautionary stance and a commitment to shedding light on the ethics of bringing sensitive personal narratives into public settings. My hope is that the case studies presented here, of work I've done will spur increased ethical thinking and commitments by practitioners in a variety of participatory media/arts genres.

Responsibility to the Story; Responsibility to the Storyteller

Over the past ten years, improved access to relatively inexpensive digital production tools and an explosion of online media distribution channels has resulted in a dramatic increase in the public circulation of video documentaries (Gregory, 2010), including digital stories. Supporters of the method claim that digital storytelling workshops result in stories that are highly "authentic" and that workshop participants, as they create these stories, undergo a cathartic process of healing and empowerment. But digital storytelling also raises a host of potentially thorny ethical questions. A thorough review of media ethics is well beyond the scope of this chapter, but I want to point to several articles that have spurred my own thinking about ethics.[1]

Renuka Bery (1995) lays out a clear framework for ethical decision-making in the context of participatory media by asking a series of questions about access to and control of production tools and resources; sustainability of projects; ownership of and benefit derived from media products; degrees of media literacy among likely viewing audiences; and, perhaps most importantly, who has the authority to pose and answer ethical questions in the first place. While Bery's writing pre-dates the Internet era, Sam Gregory describes the urgent need for increased discussion of "crucial safety, consent and ethical concerns" raised by the growing online circulation of images of human rights violations (Gregory, 2010; p. 192). He suggests that although the tools of digital video and social media offer intriguing possibilities for action, they also present real dangers, and he pushes for the promotion of "online and participatory cultures that create and share social justice and human rights material in a manner that balances the right to privacy (and the integrity of the person) with the right to freedom of expression" (Gregory, 2010, p. 204).

Finally, a growing literature on the power and politics of listening references what Charles Husband describes as a gap between listening and understanding (Husband, 2009, p. 443). This gap is relevant to a number of important questions that can be asked of digital storytelling workshop facilitation. How are storytellers listened to and understood? What action does a facilitator take, after listening, when it comes to helping storytellers shape their stories? In what ways can the sharing, bearing witness to and shaping of stories be construed as a political act? And when should facilitators or other viewers be compelled to take action as a result of hearing or watching a story?

Case Study Number One: Consent and Its Limitations: Digital Storytelling with Foster Youth[2]

> The most important ethical aim community artists must master is bringing out the full complexity of a situation, including all of its inherent contradictions and ambiguities. The most important ethical self-knowledge community artists need is to know their own values and commitments, to whom they are accountable, why, and how. (Goldbard, 2012)

In the United States, thousands of children and youth end up in foster care each year. Many become part of the system due to physical and/or sexual abuse within their families of origin. Some have parents with severe alcohol/drug problems, and still others have been orphaned by the death of a mother or father. Research and the evolving practices of mental health and community-based practitioners make it clear that long-term healing from the kind of trauma that foster youth often endure is dependent upon creating opportunities for them to make their stories known (Herman, 1992). Traditional one-on-one talk therapy is not always useful for foster youth, who tend to have been interviewed repeatedly—and not always sensitively—by professionals charged with their care. These young people seldom find opportunities to share their stories in safe, supportive and age-appropriate environments.

Since 2001, I've been coordinating a number of digital storytelling projects that aim to provide current and former foster youth with an outlet for constructing narratives about what they have been through and to bring these compelling media narratives into training settings, as tools for educating social workers about the needs and concerns of young people in the system. While the majority of youth who have attended these workshops characterize their experiences as highly meaningful, during informal debriefing activities that take place at the end of the story-making process, I continue to grapple with various ethical challenges related to these projects.

One challenge surrounds the broad issue of consent. For instance, how are young people supported in making decisions to attend workshops and create stories? What information do they receive about potential benefits of participation, and who decides what aspects of the process and its aftermath are or are not "beneficial?"[3] What happens when their energy flags, in the middle of the process, and they become reluctant to complete a script and move into the media production phase of the workshop? How must youth participants obtain consent to use images of other people, in their stories, particularly when doing so may unintentionally implicate those other people in illegal activities? When and how are participating young people briefed on what it means to "release" their stories to sponsoring organizations and funders? And what happens when they change their minds about allowing stories to be shared publicly?

Because many of the staff at my partner organizations are trained social workers, and because some of the staff who assist with digital storytelling have themselves created stories (at CDS, we strongly recommend that partner organization staff attend workshops so that they can experience for themselves the kind of courage it takes to share a personal story within a group process, and we require partners to make staff available during workshops to provide logistical and emotional support), they understand that careful participant recruitment strategies are key. With my support, they design and circulate flyers and email announcements that introduce would-be storytellers to the idea of digital storytelling and explain the purpose of workshops with foster youth.

More importantly, we view the notion of "consent" as a process that begins at this early stage and continues throughout the life of a project and beyond. Partners are transparent, in their outreach, about the fact that the digital stories will be shared publicly. This enables young people to make informed decisions—to the best of their abilities—about whether or not to participate in a workshop. But we understand that youth may need support with the decision-making process, and we ask partners to have multiple conversations with potential storytellers, in order to assess their readiness to function well within a group process, share honest reflections about their lives and feel comfortable making a story that will be seen beyond the confines of the workshop.

In my role as facilitator of these workshops, I take care to stay aware of how power relationships between "staff" or "teachers," and youth participants, can blur the lines between support and coercion. These lines become most obvious during the script-writing process, which can make participants feel alternately empowered and vulnerable as they seek to construct and envision identities for themselves (Brushwood Rose, 2009). In one foster youth session, I worked closely with a young woman named Shelly. She asked me to look at her script after she had written for what seemed like only a few minutes. The basic facts were there, but a sense of her unique voice wasn't. Something about her, as well as my own intuition based on years of experience in supporting youth through the scripting process, told me that she'd be open to honest feedback, and I did something that I don't often do: instead of settling for what I felt wasn't her best writing, I pushed her to reach within herself for a deeper heart to the story. Fortunately, my decision paid off in the form of a revised script full of beautiful metaphor and emotion.

And then there was Rosanna, who attended a session for foster youth that I taught in 2008. Rosanna was initially excited to be participating, but as the workshop went on and she confronted the task of whittling the 1,400-word draft script she had prepared in advance down to a workable length of 300–400 words, she became withdrawn and resistant. She objected strongly to my gentle encouragement that she edit her work. I found myself wondering whether asking her to cut the script was supportive (as we had said the process would be) or cruel, in the sense that I was insisting she revise a narrative about sexual abuse that she had finally, for the first time, been able to write down.

Beholden to the workshop timeframe of four days and to the agenda of the project sponsor and funder, I gently persisted in urging Rosanna to cut her script. We ended up sitting side by side on a couch, sometimes talking, sometimes just staring at her computer screen and sometimes working together on what would become her final script. She continued to express frustration throughout the editing process, claiming that her computer wasn't doing what it was supposed to do and that her story wasn't taking shape in the way she had hoped. I worried…and I did my best to stay present and open and willing to help. I felt like she was expecting me to leave, as every other adult in her life had done, during the years she was describing in her story. Only at the end of the workshop, after the group screening, did she come to me with tears in her eyes and tell me how happy she was with her piece.

The script editing in these foster youth workshops tends to center both on making scripts a manageable length and on the removal of language that may be off-putting to the key audience for the stories: social workers. While digital storytelling at its best allows participants complete and free creative reign over their work, and digital storytelling facilitators must always tread lightly when it comes to offering input, some of my foster youth partners have adopted a strict "sign off" policy that requires a partner staff member to give final approval to story scripts. This means that staff may ask participants to delete or revise overly critical language, factual inaccuracies, material that may incite legal action or details that risk alienating viewers. Youth know before coming into a workshop that their work will potentially be edited in this way, and they know that the goal is not censorship but openness, in terms of a desire that the stories will welcome social worker viewers into a dialogue rather than immediately putting them on the defense. And yet in spite of this transparency, a small number of young people have complained that their words were stifled, their stories silenced.

Foster youth participants have also decided, after releasing their stories (forms are introduced on the last day of the workshop, with time for questions and discussion), that they wish to withdraw them from circulation. While context can be given to a story shown during a training for social workers, the occasionally insensitive responses of viewers can't be controlled. In some cases, storytellers who were present at screenings have been dismayed to hear comments like, "Oh, YOU'RE the one who told the story about…." One young woman said that when this happened, she felt exposed, betrayed, pigeonholed into a past identity that she no longer relates to. What is an ethical response to this scenario? Perhaps adopting a disclaimer to share with viewers, reminding them to respect the dignity of storytellers, who are much more than what their digital stories may reveal. A story can be taken out of distribution at trainings, and it can be removed from a website, but if it has appeared on a DVD that has been made widely available, or if people have downloaded it from the Internet, there are clear limits to the desire that it be removed from the public domain—we make these limitations clear in our written consent documents.

Case Study Number Two: The Right to Privacy versus the Right to Know: Supporting Storytellers in Making Choices about Representation

Nepal has one of the worst records on violence against women in the broader Asian region. According to a report prepared by the Nepal Department of

Health Services (2010), an estimated 81% of women in rural communities face recurring domestic violence at the hands of husbands and in-laws. Nepalese women and girls are also vulnerable to rape, sexual abuse in the workplace and human trafficking. Although caste-based discrimination and the dowry system have been banned since 2009, these traditional practices placing women at risk of harm continue to be widespread throughout the country (*Nepal Bans Dowry System*, 2009).

Political instability and a lengthy civil war overshadowed issues of gender-based violence for many years in Nepal. Finally, in 2009, after a decade of advocacy by women's rights groups, the national government passed legislation designed to protect Nepalese women impacted by domestic violence. While this represents an important step towards justice for Nepal's women, absent effective public education strategies and concerted efforts to push for accountability in enforcement, it is unlikely to make much real difference in their day-to-day lives. With the goal of centralizing women's first-person stories in efforts to raise community awareness about the new law and advocate for timely and effective responses by those responsible for enforcement, I collaborated in 2011–12 on a digital storytelling project called "Voices for Justice."

Designed in close collaboration with the Nepal-based NGO Saathi (Saathi, 2013), the project brought a small group of domestic violence shelter residents together for a four-day digital storytelling workshop in Kathmandu. I traveled there to lead the process—we played games to get to know each other, took photos and video clips, and spent a tearful afternoon bearing witness to narratives that describe the unthinkable: the wife who was beaten almost daily, for ten years; the child bride whose in-laws poured kerosene on her and set her on fire; the young girl lured from the countryside to the capital city by the promise of education, only to be held as a sexual slave for months.

Given the stigma surrounding gender-based violence in Nepal, Saathi staff and I spent many hours prior to the workshop emailing back and forth about ways to protect the safety of the participants. As with my foster youth workshops, all of the women were informed from the outset that their completed stories were likely to be screened in communities, at law enforcement and service provider trainings, and on radio and television to give visibility to the new law. They were offered multiple opportunities to opt in or out of the workshop, as well as multiple opportunities within and after the workshop to decide whether or not to go public with their names and images. They were also reminded of the near-impossibility of complete anonymity when it comes to digital stories—though names can be changed or omitted and images can be blurred, voices are unique and cannot easily be altered without negatively affecting sound quality.

In my work with survivors of trauma, I recommend quite strongly that women who are recently out of abusive situations not be asked to participate. With Voices for Justice, I had to take another approach. Many of the women who were initially asked by Saathi to share their stories declined to participate. They were well established in new lives and careers, with their abuse experiences far in the past, and they did not want to risk being 'outed' as survivors of violence. After much anguished deliberation, Saathi staff and I decided to work with residents of Saathi's shelter. Some of the women had only been there for a few months and continued to struggle with recurring memories and nightmares about what they lived through.

We worked hard to avoid re-traumatizing the participants. I guided movement-based activities and games to create a sense of safety and protection; we took frequent breaks; and Saathi counseling staff helped those participants who occasionally became lost in the past spiral out of their pain and back into the immediate space of caring and attention at the workshop (Hudgins, 2002). Because the workshop took place prior to the important Hindu festival of Diwali[4], we incorporated a candle-lighting ritual into our closing ceremony. During the four days, I was grateful again and again for my own years of training and experience in working with trauma survivors, as well as for the presence of the project's peer translators—all young women with whom the storytellers bonded closely.

Most of the Saathi participants weren't literate, so rather than relying on script writing, I used oral testimony methods that I developed (Hill, 2008) as a way of surfacing stories. And unlike most CDS workshops, the Saathi workshop did not include a hands-on production component. Not only was the project budget insufficient to support equipment rental, most of the participants had absolutely no experience using computers. Teaching them the skills necessary for even the most basic edits of their stories would have required far more time than was available. Instead, Saathi staff helped them before the workshop to take photos and create detailed drawings based on their experiences, and we took additional photos as well as video clips during the days that we spent together. For me, these production strategies raised a number of interesting questions about voice and representation.

A written scripting process allows for the editing of story content—by the participant alone, and/or in concert with a facilitator. It enables storytellers to reflect, reconsider and revise; to take time in determining how they want to describe their experiences; and to deliberate about their choices of words. In some ways, eliminating this process was freeing; I had no choice but to accept the women's testimonies as they emerged—as short, spoken snapshots of what they endured and how they had moved on. I felt that all I could realistically do in the way of offering input was to suggest what could be removed from the oral narratives—advice that I based on conversations with Saathi staff about each woman's status and what might potentially put her at risk of further harm or jeopardize the standing of any legal processes that were in progress. But my guidance about what information not to include clearly gave me an instrumental role in determining final story content. While this made me feel somewhat uncomfortable, I have long been critical of the "invisible facilitator" position from which some practitioners of digital storytelling and other forms of participatory media claim to operate. The reality is that my own sense of aesthetics and technical skills were as essential to shaping the Voices for Justice project as they have been with all of the digital storytelling work that I've done.

Although the women contributed many images for their stories and made detailed storyboards, I was also ultimately responsible for blending their voiceover recordings and visual material into finalized pieces. The challenges of working through interpreters were highlighted when I began to edit: in some cases, women had stated in writing that they wished to be anonymous, and yet they had chosen images or video clips that clearly showed their faces. In other cases, a storyteller stated that she wanted her name and her images to become public, even though Saathi staff and I felt strongly that doing so might constrain her access to legal remedies. The practical solutions were obvious—I was able to blur images and omit names, and Saathi had follow-up conversations with this participant, to help her come to final a decision about the relative degree of privacy she wished for.

But as the memory of the workshop becomes more distant, questions linger for me—particularly questions about the concept of ensuring participant safety. How can I, as an ethical facilitator, best support storytellers in making good decisions about what information to share and what images to show or not show? When are deliberations about safety based on the real possibility of retaliation or harm, and who defines what is "real," in a context where dreams are taken seriously as harbingers of good or bad fortune? When does discussion about safety inadvertently give rise to self-censorship on the part of participants, who may be basing story content decisions on unfounded fears or rumors they've heard about the consequences of speaking out about their experiences, rather than on real risks? And how can I prevent participants from feeling coerced into sharing intimate details from their lives while simultaneously working to establish a respectful environment that encourages freedom of expression? Above all, who is ultimately responsible for ensuring that the storytelling process does no harm—facilitators, partner organizations, or both—and is this kind of assurance even possible?

Questions linger as well about issues of representation. In settings where education levels and literacy are low and funding doesn't allow for extended discussion about the meanings and aesthetics of visual images or the ways in which women survivors of violence are depicted in media, what responsibility do I have to talk with workshop participants about the complexities of representation? How do language, culture, and other aspects of identity factor into decisions (by workshop participants and facilitators) about story content? If a digital story is always in some ways a co-creation of storyteller and facilitator, why are leaders of participatory media projects so often less than transparent about these nuances? Does acknowledgment of having played a direct role in content choices or editing somehow diminish the power or potential impact of the work? Who gets to decide what counts as "honest" and what doesn't? These questions seem rooted in the "politics of doing good."

> *Excerpt from a Voices for Justice story:*
> *I got married at an early age without my parents' consent. I thought that after marriage life would be good, but my dreams were shattered. After the wedding, I found out that my husband was not the person I had thought him to be. ...*
>
> *He would beat me until I was unconscious, and when I woke up, he would say, "I thought you were dead, but you're still alive." I was not allowed to work (outside the home), or tell my story to anyone. I felt so alone. ...*
>
> *Somehow my father knew what was going on. He asked me to come home, but I didn't want to, because I had married by my own*

choice. ...I tolerated all this pain for ten years. My husband threatened to kill me, again and again. I was thrown down to the floor, I had scars and black and blue marks all over my body. ...

Finally, for the sake of my children's future, and for my own safety, I left my husband. I came to Kathmandu and stayed with my sister-in-law. She helped me find the shelter, and the stories of the other women consoled me. Now I'm being trained in housekeeping. I know that one day I will find a job and be able to take care of my children on my own.

Case Study Number Three—From Ethical Facilitation to Ethical Story Sharing: Digital Storytelling with Sonke Gender Justice

HIV and AIDS continue to present significant obstacles to the health and well-being of South Africans. Women and men are vulnerable to the virus in different ways—women, because of their ongoing struggles to achieve gender equality (Amnesty International, 2008); men, because their beliefs about masculinity can often lead them to resist testing or reject treatment (Baker and Ricardo, 2005). Sonke Gender Justice (Sonke Gender Justice, 2013) works in the South African Development Countries (SADC) region to promote gender equality, prevent gender-based violence, and reduce the spread and impact of HIV and AIDS. Crucial to the success of Sonke's work is ensuring a central role for those most directly affected by these issues.

Since 2007, I've been partnering with Sonke on a large-scale digital storytelling initiative that frames personal stories of South Africans as effective "social and behavior change communications" (SBCC) tools for education and awareness, movement building, and policy advocacy.[5] To date, I've conducted a total of eight digital storytelling workshops with urban and rural youth and adults in the country. I've also collaborated with Sonke on the production of four unique DVD story collections, featuring work in multiple South African languages (with English subtitles) and accompanying Teaching Guides. The Sonke stories are being shared widely via educational television and community radio, as well as locally in community settings. Perhaps because the Sonke project has been so successful in creatively distributing stories, it's the site where much of my thinking about digital storytelling ethics has evolved.

When I first traveled to South Africa, YouTube didn't exist, and the mechanics and costs of putting video up online were challenging. At the time, I hadn't done digital storytelling work that had been widely exhibited; my understanding was that two pilot Sonke workshops would serve as a chance for the storytellers to reflect and heal, as much as they would serve as a vehicle for producing media that would be shown publicly. As such, I failed to emphasize as much as I should have, to Sonke staff and partners, the importance of being clear with potential storytellers that the end goal of the workshops was the creation of public stories, not private ones. One storyteller representing a partner organization felt horribly exposed when I shared her story along with the entire collection created in the pilot sessions at an internal screening for Sonke staff—unbeknownst to me, she had not prior to that time revealed her own status as a survivor of sexual abuse. To this day, I deeply regret the assumptions I made about her story and the grave mistake I made, in screening it. Several pilot workshop participants also reported feeling as though they had no choice, at the end of the sessions, but to sign release forms that gave Sonke blanket permission to reproduce and distribute their stories. They felt as though they'd plumbed the depths of their vulnerability in the sacred space of the workshop, and that we as facilitators had somehow betrayed them.

These painful experiences led me to a great deal of soul-searching and to the decision to develop step-by-step guidelines, for organizations that I work with, that explain in great detail how to describe the purpose of a given project to potential storytellers (with special emphasis on disclosing any desires to share stories publicly); how to responsibly screen, recruit, and prepare workshop participants; and how to follow up with them, once they have created digital stories[6]. It also led to many lengthy discussions with Sonke about the need to assess the readiness of potential participants to share highly sensitive stories. We agreed to focus primarily on working with leaders and activists—e.g., people who had already spoken out in a visible, public way, about highly politicized and socially contentious issues like HIV and AIDS and gender-based violence. I labored in the workshops to combine the best in emotional support with the best in production support. As with all Silence Speaks projects, my goal was to shepherd into being stories that would first and foremost have local meaning and relevance—in this case, through their use of South African languages, references to South African places, customs, popular culture, and reliance on images of South African people and locations. That the stories might appeal to a broader regional or global audience was a secondary concern.

I've stumbled more than once, along the way. The notion of story ownership – who within a particular family or community is "allowed" to share what stories and images, about which people and places—emerged early on as a contested topic. At CDS, we frame the notion of "voice" as a way of urging someone to tell a story "that only you can tell"—not as telling a story "about your own life." As a result, CDS workshop participants often make stories about family members or friends. This approach may be appropriate in some environments, but in places where the stigma of HIV and abuse have tangible consequences—where people are routinely shunned, excluded, and alienated if they are known to be HIV positive—questions of who "owns" a story and who is empowered to "give permission" for that story to be shared—can be highly charged.

In one Sonke workshop with rural youth, I reluctantly agreed that a couple of participants could tell stories that were largely about neighbors or family members. These young people used the "I" voice, and I advised them to leave out particular identifying information and images, to protect the privacy of their subjects. Nonetheless, when we showed one of their stories to participants in a subsequent workshop for people affected by HIV and AIDS, the participants reacted with anger, saying that the youth "did not have the right" to speak about other people. In another workshop, an attendant to a Traditional Leader[7] spoke in the story circle about HIV and AIDS within his family. Even though he did not name names, the consensus among the group was that because he is well known in the community, people in the local area would know whom he was talking about, and that the story should therefore not be made.

Sonke workshop participants are not the only ones to have expressed concerns about story content. In one rural area, when Sonke staff made efforts to recruit storytellers who were leaders in local efforts to address gender-based violence and HIV and AIDS, these leaders declined, feeling that the project resembled too closely a qualitative research process they had already consented to, which they felt had offered them no tangible benefits. As a result, the group of people who attended the workshop had not previously been involved in advocacy work, and the stories that came out of this workshop were quite difficult and raw. Several women spoke in detail about ongoing abuse at the hands of their partners, to whom they were still married. I did the best I could to ask them repeatedly about whether they felt safe disclosing certain information, but short of urging them to tell different stories altogether, I felt uncomfortable with the idea of pushing repeatedly for certain script edits. While these women did complete their digital stories and give consent for the stories to be released, I didn't ultimately include their work as part of a compilation DVD that, according to a contractual agreement with the project funder, was to be widely duplicated and distributed (and I didn't ask the funder for permission to exclude these stories, which reveals an imbalance between that contract and my allegiance to community members, to whom I feel I must ultimately be accountable). Clearly, the risk of harm outweighed the women's consent, especially since legal remedies and counseling for domestic violence were in short supply in their area. In this situation, the line between an ethic of "do no harm" and a decision that some might see as patronizing or tinged with censorship was difficult to pinpoint.

These viewer responses to what has been said and shown, in digital stories, point not only to questions about freedom of expression, but also to a need for an ethical approach to story sharing. Such an approach must address questions like, What responsibility do project partners have, to prepare audiences in advance for watching stories that include potentially disturbing topics like sexual assault and child abuse? How should partners go about equipping staff members with the knowledge and skills to sensitively facilitate discussion about these kinds of stories? How can project partners help viewers distinguish between what is educational and what is merely gratuitous, in a social environment where the exposure of young children to media violence—both fictional and nonfiction—is astronomically high? And who gets to determine what contextual information is appropriate, when stories are being presented publicly?[8]

I've conducted several in-service trainings with Sonke staff about effective strategies for facilitating discussions related to the digital stories; authored lengthy explanatory content for the Sonke website pages that feature stories; and written multiple sections for the story Discussion Guides accompanying collections of Sonke stories, each describing how to carry out thoughtful and responsible story screenings. But somehow none of this ever feels like enough. I continue to struggle on a daily basis with how to hold the complexity of taking seriously issues like secondary traumatization and compassion fatigue, while at the same time retaining my passion for individual stories, my belief in their capacity to touch hearts, and my conviction that bringing them forward is vital work in the world—crucial to all efforts to "do good."

> *Excerpt from a Sonke story:*
> *She was young and full of life. She had just graduated from the University of the North West. The worst day was when she agreed to marry my selfish, arrogant brother. He was 17 years older than her...*
>
> *At first, things were great. He was a caring and loving husband ...But after a few months, he changed. He was coming home late, expecting to find everything in place. I covered for her, because she was a good person. But still he would beat her and force himself onto her. Worst of all, he started seeing other young girls. She hung on because our culture taught her never to disobey or challenge him. Our culture says, "Obey your man at all times. Never talk back or question how he comes and goes."*
>
> *By then, I was preparing to register at a college. She was my friend, the closest I have ever had. ...In 2004 she was diagnosed HIV positive. Still he continued to beat her over and over, with no remorse. He expected her to have dinner on the table each night, even when she grew weaker and weaker. She passed away in December of that year. ...*
>
> *I want to share this story with everyone. People don't like to talk about it, but I believe that sexual and domestic violence and HIV/AIDS are everyone's business. ...She died four years ago, but I still ask myself, "How can women, who are the beautiful soul of our nation, also be the nation's victims? Have we learned so little from the struggle our country went through?" Our culture also says, "I am...because of others."*

Conclusion

> ...The new narrative doesn't erase the old one. It stands beside it, a constant reminder of who we were, a never-ending, sometimes painful contradiction...recognizing this requires that we expand our self-story to allow for this contradiction, and that we learn how to live with the unease it can cause us. Such knowledge forces a woman to be compassionate about herself, which, if she's lucky, can lead to an ability to move through the world with that same compassion, as well

> as depth, intelligence, judiciousness, and integrity. This is how I define the beginning of wisdom. (Citron, 1998)

Michele Citron's book, *Home Movies and Other Necessary Fictions* (1998) was one of the catalysts for my own entrée into the world of digital storytelling and the establishment of Silence Speaks. I read it in 2000, before making a story, and her words came with me into the very first workshop I attended. My experience in that workshop mirrors in some ways the trajectory of the ethical concerns I've raised here. Even though I had an intuitive sense of readiness, I felt uncomfortable sharing a story about violence in my family. What happened when I was growing up—the constant and cutting verbal abuse, the physical acting out, the resulting anxiety and hyper vigilance I lived with for many years—was not information I regularly disclosed about myself, at the time, particularly not in professional settings. The terror I felt as I tried to tap into my vulnerability around this material pointed clearly to the need for safe and healing spaces specifically designed to support survivors in sharing their stories.

And, like many Silence Speaks participants, I, too, have struggled with whether or not to show my story publicly. Like many survivors of family violence, I will never forgive particular acts, and yet I didn't, and still don't, see how broad exposure would contribute to anyone's healing. Some might say this perspective is rooted in deeply rooted shame about what happened, in a context where abuse continues to be heavily stigmatized, or that it reflects an unconscious desire to protect the person responsible. Maybe so, and in my reckoning, he has suffered enough from his own self-imposed guilt and remorse. Rather than jeopardizing personal relationships that were—and still are—important to me, I chose to show my first digital story only at contained and somewhat intimate gatherings (for example, at conferences, seminars, or trainings), as a way to make tangible to potential partners and funders the vision I had for Silence Speaks. And I continue to make decisions about where, when, and why to disclose my family history on a case-by-case basis. Sometimes, in workshops, it feels like an appropriate way of making connections with participants–of saying, "yes, I truly understand the courage you are demonstrating and the sacredness of what you are offering, in sharing your story." At other times, it feels as though bringing up my own experience would take away from the space being created for workshop participants and that what is far more important is my ability to extend the kind of unconditional presence that I know from the core of my being is so instrumental to any effort to support their healing (Welwood, 2000).

I also continue to hope that the kind of wisdom Citron describes can lead to constructive and compassionate social and political action, which is the rationale for my work. In the midst of the proliferation of video online, various critiques can be made of participatory media methods like digital storytelling. It purports to elicit direct "experience" and thus may come across to some as an approach that is naïve about the ways in which our experiences are mediated and constructed (Scott, 1992). It makes claims about something called "authenticity," which has always felt suspicious to me. It situates amateurs as media producers and thus results in content that some critical viewers might see as simplistic, sentimental and low quality. At times I agree with these accusations. But ultimately, it's my enduring faith in the value of stories in addition to statistics, in the intimacy of the space where storytellers and their audiences meet, and in the power of honest human connection to do good—that keeps me going.

Digital Storyteller's Bill of Rights, Silence Speaks

In relation to a workshop, you have…

The right to know from the outset why a workshop is being carried out.

The right to assistance in deciding whether you are ready to produce a digital story.

The right to understand what is involved in the process of producing a digital story.

The right to know who might view your finished story, after the digital storytelling workshop.

The right to decide for yourself whether or not to participate in a workshop.

The right to ask questions at any stage of the workshop, before, during, or after.

The right to ask for teaching instructions to be repeated or made clearer.

The right to skilled emotional support, if your experience of making a story is emotionally challenging.

The right to tell your story in the way you want, within the limits of the workshop.

The right to decide whether or not to reveal private or personal information to fellow participants and instructors, at the workshop.

The right to advice about whether revealing your identity or other personal details about your life, in your story, may place you at risk of harm.

The right to leave information and/or photographs that identify you or others, out of your final story.

The right to reject story feedback (about words and images) if it is not useful or offered in a spirit of respect/support.

The right to decide what language to use in telling/creating your story.

The right to be respected and supported by capable workshop facilitators.

The right to a written consent form, if your story will be shared publicly, including a signed copy for your records.

The right to know what contact and support you can expect after the workshop

In relation to sharing your digital story after a workshop, you have…

The right to decide with project partners how your story will be shared.

The right to view and retain a copy of your story before it is shared publicly in any way.

The right to know who is likely to screen your story and for what purposes.

The right to know who is likely to watch or read your story and when (e.g. rough timeframe).

The right to advice about how the process of publically sharing your story may be difficult.

The right to emotional support if you are present when your story is shown in public.

The right to demand that no one should be able to sell your story for profit.

The right to know if any money will be made from your story being shared (e.g., to support not-for-profit human rights work).

The right to withdraw your consent for the use of your story at any time.

The right to information about the limits of withdrawing consent for your story to be shared, if it has already been circulated online or on CD, DVD, etc.

—Special thanks to Aline Gubrium, Lucy Harding, Photovoice UK, and WITNESS for their important contributions to these principles.

Notes

1. Because this chapter is written from my standpoint as a community-based practitioner, it does not discuss additional ethical challenges raised by the use of digital storytelling as a qualitative research method—most notably, the challenge of obtaining approval to conduct research from the appropriate agencies.
2. In the interest of protecting the privacy of storytellers, all names have been changed.
3. Little research has been conducted, to date, about the impact on participants of creating digital stories or allowing them to be shown publicly. A review of the litera-

ture is beyond the scope of this chapter, but anecdotal reports from the Center for Digital Storytelling suggest a range of potential benefits of participation, including but not limited to increased self-esteem, greater computer literacy, a willingness to share and connect with others, and a sense of relief and closure related to having talked about experiences of trauma or grief.

4. Diwali (also spelled Devali in certain regions), popularly known as the "festival of lights," is celebrated between mid-October and mid-December. For Hindus, it is one of the most important festivals of the year and is observed by lighting small clay oil lamps to signify the triumph of good over evil.
5. Recent literature on health communications has documented that storytelling can be a key component of public health communications strategies (Larkey and Hill, 2010), and that SBCC methods are most effective when they employ communication strategies to elicit social change across many levels of analysis, including individual behaviors and social norms (USAID, 2012).
6. For more information about the Silence Speaks approach to ethical practice, visit http://www.silencespeaks.org/about-us.html.
7. South Africa's Constitution establishes the right of communities living under traditional law and custom to influence the way in which the country is run. Houses of Traditional Leaders (known also as Amakhosi, or kings) exist in some provinces to carry out an advisory role in government. Each provincial House nominates three members to a National House of Traditional Leaders, which elects its own office-bearers. The National House advises the national government on the role of traditional leaders and on customary law.
8. For an in-depth exploration of these and other concerns related to notions of participation and benefit, in the context of my work with Sonke Gender Justice, see Hill, A. (2010) "Digital Storytelling for Gender Justice: Exploring the Challenges of Participation and the Limits of Polyvocality." In Berghoffen, D., Gilbert, P., Harvey, T., and McNeely, C. *Confronting Global Gender Justice: Women's Lives, Human Rights.* Oxford: Routledge.

References

Amnesty International. (2008). *"I am at the lowest end of all": Rural women living with HIV face human rights abuses in South Africa.* London: Amnesty International Publications. Retrieved from http://www.amnesty.org/en/library/asset/AFR53/001/2008/en/ebc94db1-f123-11dc-b3df-0fe44bc152bc/afr530012008eng.pdf

Baker, G., & Ricardo, C. (2005). *Young men and the construction of masculinity in Sub-Saharan Africa: Implications for HIV/AIDS, conflict, and violence.* Social Development Papers—Conflict Prevention and Reconstruction, 26. Retrieved from http://wwwwds.worldbank.org/servlet/

WDSContentSerer/WDSP/IB/2005/06/23/000012009_20050623134235 /Rendered/PDF/327120rev0PAPER0AFR0young0men0WP26.pdf

Bery, R. (1995). Media ethics: No magic answers. In R. Slocum, L. Wichart, & D. Rocheleau (Eds.). *Power, process and participation: Tools for change.* Londong: Intermediate Technology Publications.

Brushwood Rose, C. (2009). The (im)possibilities of self-representation: Exploring the limits of storytelling in the digital stories of women and girls. *Changing English*, *16*(2), 211–220.

Citron, M. (1998). *Home movies and other necessary fictions*. Minneapolis: University of Minnesota Press.

Goldbard, A. (2012). *Values and ethics of community arts practice.* Retrieved from http://arlenegoldbard.com

Gregory, S. (2010). Cameras everywhere: Ubiquitous video documentation of human rights, new forms of video advocacy, and considerations of safety, security, dignity and consent. *Journal of Human Rights Practice*, *2*(2), 191–207.

Haraway, D. (1988). Situated knowledges. *Feminist Studies*, *14*(3), 575–599.

Herman, J. (1992). *Trauma and recovery*. New York: Basic Books.

Hill, A. (2008). "Learn from my story": A participatory media initiative for Ugandan women affected by obstetric fistula. *Agenda Feminist Media*, *77*.

Hill, A. (2010). Digital storytelling for gender justice: Exploring the challenges of participation and the limits of polyvocality." In D. Berghoffen, P. Gilbert, T. Harvey, & C. McNeely (Eds.). *Confronting global gender justice: Women's lives, human rights*. Oxford: Routledge.

Hudgins, K. (2002). *Experiential treatment for PTSD: The therapeutic spiral model*. New York: Springer Publishing Company, Inc.

Husband, C. (2009). Between listening and understanding. *Continuum*, *23*(44), 441–443.

Larkey, L. K., & Hill, A. (2011). Using narratives to promote health: A culture-centric approach. In H. Cho (Ed.), *Health communication message design: Theory and practice.* Thousand Oaks, CA: Sage.

Nepal Department of Health Services, Family Health Division (2010). *Nepal maternal mortality and morbidity study 2008/2009: Summary of preliminary findings. Kathmandu, Nepal.* Family Health Division, Department of Health Services, Ministry of Health, Government of Nepal.

Nepal bans dowry system. (2009, January 26). *Pakistan News*. Retrieved from www.nation.com.pk/pakistan-news-newspaper-daily-english-online /International/26-Jan-2009 Nepal-bans-dowry-system

Silence Speaks. (2013). Retrieved April 1, 2013 from www.silencespeaks.org

Saathi. (2013). Retrieved April 1, 2013 from www.saathi.org.np

Scott, J.W. (1992). "Experience". In J. Butler & J.W. Scott (Eds.), *Feminists theorize the political*. New York: Routledge.

Sonke Gender Justive Network. (2013). Retrieved May, 1, 2013 from http://www.genderjustice.org.za/

Tervalon M., & Murray-Garcia J. (1998). Cultural humility versus cultural competence: A critical distinction in defining physician training outcomes in multicultural education. *Journal of Health Care for the Poor and Underserved*, *9*(2), 117–125.

USAID (2012). C modules: *A learning package for social and behavior change communication (SBCC).* Available online at c-changeprogram.org/sites/default/files/sbcc_module0_intro.pdf

Welwood, J. (2000). *Toward psychology of awakening.* Boston and London: Shambhala.

Chapter 3

Entry Point: Participatory Media-Making with Queer and Trans Refugees: Social Locations, Agendas and Thinking Structurally

Ed Lee and Liz Miller

Introduction

Along with the emergence of social media, increased access to digital forms of media making has reconfigured the possibilities for engaging in community-based multiliteracies. As access to digital media forms has increased, so too has the need to incorporate critical notions of literacy. Miller et al. (2012) suggest that to reformulate "notions of literacy and to adapt our curricula and projects...we must develop new tools for critical literacy and for understanding the terms of these tools and platforms. Integrating these tools into the classroom or community group, in combination with personal narratives, is a meaningful way to broaden notions of literacy, to introduce critical social issues, and to raise questions around voice, truth, ethics, history and intellectual property" (p. 7). One avenue for engaging in critical literacy is through collaborative media projects, where directly affected community members can frame their own stories and "reflect on the relationship of their personal narratives to larger social concerns" (Miller, 2010, p. 3).

Through a collaborative creation process, Mapping Memories sought to engage in collaborative media making, in order to engage in developing critical literacy with directly affected community members (Miller, Luchs & Jalea, 2012). Mapping Memories was a government research-funded and university-driven initiative which brought together Montreal-based educators, filmmakers, policy advocates, organizers, students and youth to develop a series of participatory media projects for youth with refugee experiences. This collaborative, multi-media research-creation project aimed to offer individuals a chance to reflect on their unique experiences, to learn new media skills, to work in collaboration with each other, to strengthen peer networks and to express themselves creatively as they shaped their narratives using different sorts of media (Miller et al., 2012). One of these collaborative media projects was with SOY Express, a Toronto-based support group for lesbian, gay, bisexual, trans and queer (LGBTQ) youth with refugee experiences. These collaborations resulted in two multi-media projects (which included photography, creative writing and walking tours) that explored the difficult process of being forced to leave home, as well as the challenges of becoming established in a new place. One of the outcomes of this collaboration was a photovoice exhibit displayed at Ethnoculture, an organisation that presents annual events by and about queer and trans people of colour.

Inspired by the Express photovoice exhibit, AGIR (Action LGBTQ with Immigrants and Refugees), invited Mapping Memories to lead a four-week intensive digital storytelling workshop with queer and trans people with refugee experiences in Montreal. AGIR is an autonomous non-profit organisation whose mandate is to engage in support work and community organizing with queer and trans migrants, including those who are refugees, immigrants and undocumented. In June 2010, AGIR and Mapping Memories came together in order to produce Entry Point: Queer Refugees in Montreal, a collaborative media project by and about 13 queer and trans people with refugee experiences. Having recruited 13 queer and trans refugees, the central goals for this collaboration included: using workshops as a space to bring community members together and tell their own stories, offer an introduction to various media skills and provide opportunities for community members to share their stories to a wider audience. Our project aimed to engage in creating "alternative media in which individual and communities share personal stories and collective experiences...with the goal of raising awareness about a specific issue or challenging dominant discourses in mainstream media" (Norman, 2009, p. 253).

This project was a collaboration between Mapping Memories and AGIR, with one main researcher/media facilitator working with 4 members of AGIR. As coordinators for this project, we all came from different, yet at times overlapping roles as filmmaker, researcher, educator, community organizer, facilitator and community member. Each of us came into the project with the best of intentions, agreeing to adhere to guiding principles of mutual respect and shared ownership (Miller, Luchs & Jalea, 2012). However, these good intentions did not shield us from the realities of participatory and collaborative media making—it is messy with contradictions and inconsistencies and constant negotiations and re-negotiations (Miller et al., 2012). Miller et al. (2012) describe this messy process as the politics of collaboration, which reveal the complicated nature of doing collaborative media projects that oftentimes "bump up" against the reality of doing work that can be conflictual and shaped by competing interests and agendas.

In many ways, the outcomes of the AGIR–Mapping Memories collaboration were multiple and far reaching. As explored later in this chapter, this media project served as a mechanism to deepen relationships between queer and trans refugees, along with allies who were involved with AGIR, in addition to contributing to the longer-term goals for AGIR to engage in community organizing with queer and trans newcomers. In addition, this media project affirmed with AGIR members the central importance of engaging in community organizing that includes participatory media making with directly affected community members.

At the same time, this collaboration also brought up difficulties and tensions during the process of making collaborative media. Certainly, we could simply focus on the positive outcomes of our collaboration, as there were many. However, we felt it was important that we engage in critical reflection in order to examine the micro-processes of how we engaged in collaborative media making. These micro-processes brought us face-to-face with a number of ethical dilemmas. By engaging in critical reflection, we aim to link these micro-processes to the larger social relations that shaped the conflicts and tensions that arose during our process. By critically reflecting upon these complications, our aim is to re-frame "what happened" within the larger social context in order to suggest potential strategies for addressing them.

This re-framing requires that we critically reflect upon the ways in which our social locations, competing agendas and varying forms of institutional power mediated the possibilities and limitations of this collaborative project. Although we will analyze each of these concepts separately, it is important to note that notions of social location, competing agendas and institutional power are in actuality interrelated. Upon examining the tensions and conflict that surfaced, we suggest potential strategies for addressing the various challenges that may arise when doing collaborative media making with marginalized and exploited communities. Although this process can be challenging, it can also shift the terrain of doing collaborative media which can deepen our commitment to reflexive practices and sharing power.

Status Matters

Social location refers to someone's affiliation, self-identified and/or socially imposed, as a member of a group or community based on: race, ethnicity, gender, ability, class, religion, citizenship status and sexual/gender identity and so forth. An individual's social location includes the particular geographic and socio-historical context that one is born into (see Rich, 1984). A person's various group affiliations intersect and operate at the structural/institutional, cultural and interpersonal levels, resulting in differential access to social power and privilege (or penalty), depending on group affiliation. However, although people are influenced by social forces and their various group affiliations, they are not fully determined by them (Baines, 2011). As organizers, we each came into the project with our varied and complicated social locations.

Furthermore, it was important for us to be aware of the ways in which intersectionality lived through our respective social locations. Intersectionality can be understood as when systems of oppression created by categories such as race, class, gender, ability, religion, citizenship status and sexual/gender identity intersect with each other and are mutually reinforcing, resulting in a complex formulation of one's social location and understanding of identity. These intersecting systems of oppression reinforce, multiply or complicate each other, in context and site-specific ways. For example, although all the organizers identified as queer, we all lived varying levels of privilege and oppression, based on our affiliations with dominant and subordinate group status based on race, gender, class, ability and gender identity.

Throughout the life of the project, we carried our social location with us, which influenced our micro-processes, whether we were aware of them or not. A key vector that shaped our process was that of citizenship status. Amongst the organizers, nearly all of us had Canadian citizenship status, with the exception of one organizer, who was also one of the artist-participants. During the initial stages of the developing relationship between AGIR and Mapping Memories, the organizers ensured that directly affected community members, some of whom became artist-participants within the project, participated in the development and organisation of the media project.

Once the project moved forward, various AGIR members volunteered to participate as project organizers. This group included Ivan, who agreed to serve a dual position as both organizer and artist-participant. When organizers developed a structure and timeline for the media project, Ivan provided crucial insights that improved the design and delivery of the media project. Because Ivan had recently gone through the refugee process, he was also able to provide important perspectives regarding the kinds of barriers that some queer and trans refugees could encounter that could jeopardize their participating or completing a participatory and public media project.

Coming from his lived experiences of going through the refugee process, Ivan's suggestions affirmed the kinds of issues that surfaced in previous Mapping Memories collaborative media projects (see Miller et al., 2012). For example, Ivan affirmed the importance that participants be told in advance that the narrative and media creation process may trigger difficult emotional responses and that they should not feel obligated to share traumatic stories if they were not ready to. In addition, Ivan affirmed the benefits of providing paid honoraria and skill-building opportunities for artist-participants.

Because of his ability to reflect upon his experiences as a gay refugee, Ivan had a great deal of insight into the potential issues that could arise during the life of the project. In fact, throughout the media making process, we checked in with Ivan in order to get a sense of how the project was being experienced by artist-participants, so that we could make adjustments based on his feedback. Thus, Ivan 's social location as a refugee shaped the ways in which we developed, organized and engaged with the participatory media project.

However, this also meant that Ivan had to deal with additional pressures at the same time as taking on responsibilities that were above and beyond his fellow artist-participants. For those of us with Canadian citizenship, having this status increased our ability to be involved in the media project, especially as volunteers. Of course, not all citizens have equitable access to life sustaining institutions and social processes (i.e., social services, employment and educational opportunities, health care, etc.). This is especially the case for those citizens who are First Nations, racialized, poor/working class, disabled and/or trans (Galabuzi, 2006; Namaste, 2000; Razack, 2002; Thobani, 2007).

However, as citizens, we certainly did not have to experience the particular kinds of structural violence which queer and trans refugees encounter on an everyday basis (Brotman & Lee, 2011). Varying forms of structural violence are embedded within the refugee process, resulting in economic marginalization, social exclusion and "re-traumatization that is an intrinsic aspect of their everyday realities" (Brotman & Lee, 2011, p. 154). Just as the artist-participants could not come to a workshop and entirely disconnect from the structural violence they encountered on an everyday basis, those organizers with status benefited, both materially and psychologically, from the absence of the kinds of structural violence that shape the refugee process. The stress of the structural violence that Ivan was experiencing due to having gone through the refugee process, meant it was a lot to ask of him to be both organizer and participant.

Although skill building and leadership development of directly affected community members was one of the primary goals for the media project, we realized the important, yet difficult position Ivan was in. Having multiple roles as organizer and artist-participant, combined with his migrant status as refugee, resulted in Ivan contributing greatly to the success of the project. At the same time, he faced additional burdens, precisely because of having multiple roles. As Dean Spade (2011) astutely describes about organizing a conference which centred on the experiences of trans prisoners:

> Some key organizers found the stress of working on the event impacted their mental health… essentially, the very conditions that prompt the need for this work continue to threaten and harm it. The organizing itself can sometimes be a source of support for members during hard times, bringing people together who can offer understanding and share resources. Yet, doing under-resourced work to dismantle massively violent systems can also cause stress and undermine the health of people doing the work. (p. 216)

With respect to the artist-participants, although some of the community members were accepted refugees and/or permanent residents, at least half of the participants were refugee claimants, with one person who was recently refused. Therefore, citizenship/migrant status played a key role not only within the organizing team, but also amongst the artist-participants. For example, the narratives developed by those who were refugee claimants or refused differed from those who were accepted refugees and/or presently permanent residents. Possibly due to the intensive ways in which the refugee process organized the everyday lives of those who were in the refugee claimant process (Lee & Brotman, 2011), their migrant status surfaced more explicitly within their narratives. This was particularly the case for the recently refused refugee who participated in the media project. Therefore, citizenship/migrant status played a key role in shaping the ways in which different artist-participants and organizers experienced the media-making process. Simply put, status mattered.

Competing Agendas

As organizers for this project, we all came from differing, yet at times overlapping educational, professional, and life experiences—as filmmaker, researcher, educator, community organizer, facilitator and community member. Certainly, the diverse sets of knowledge and life experiences that we brought to the project contributed to the many successes of the project. At the same time, it also resulted in tensions and challenges that surfaced throughout the process. Although we were all aware that each of us came from differing educational, professional and life experiences, we never had an explicit conversation about these differences and their potential implications. It is only in critically reflecting back on what happened that we can trace the possible source of some of the difficulties that arose, as resulting from competing agendas that bumped up against each other.

For example, an important decision made near the beginning of this project that had long term ramifications occurred when we decided to accept all of the community members who wanted to participate in the project. During the design process led by the researcher/media facilitator, we took into consideration a number of factors in order to outline the parameters for the project. These factors included the timeframe, budget, workshop model, and amount of volunteer/paid labour. Based on the project design and timeline, in addition to drawing from previous experience, we agreed that having 8 to 10 participants would be ideal.

Because this was the first ever collaborative media project by and about queer and trans people with refugee experiences based in Montreal, there were worries about finding enough community members who would be interested in participating. As we were promoting and bringing queer and trans refugees to the media project, there was uncertainly as to how many community members would actually be recruited. In addition to promoting the project within a number of LGBTQ racialized/ethnic organisations in Montreal, we held a preliminary info session (which included a free dinner).

After this info session and preparing for the first workshop, we realized that there were 14 community members who were interested in being involved. After minimal discussion, we agreed to allow everyone to participate. As the project progressed, one participant dropped out while 13 completed the project. From the perspective (and agenda) of a community organizer, there were many benefits to allowing everyone interested to participate. From AGIR's perspective, this project served multiple purposes, including as an avenue for increasing the membership of directly affected community members. From this vantage point, the more people who participated, the better.

As a community organizer, I also knew what was at stake for many of the community members, especially those who were refugee claimants or recently refused refugees. The structural violence embedded within the refugee policy was being lived out through the lives of these community members and so for many participants, this project served as a potentially life-affirming project to participate in. From a community organizer perspective, the large number of participants was not a huge issue, as it ensured that the participants came from diverse regions (i.e., Africa, Caribbean, Latin America), and social locations (i.e., trans, gay, lesbian, etc.). In fact, some of the community members who arrived later to the project were those who were either less represented (i.e., trans, African disapora, etc.) or the most marginalized (i.e., refused refugees and claimants).

However, the decision to have 13 participants had other ramifications which played out throughout the process of the media project. This is where the differing agendas of various organizers bumped up against each other, resulting in significant tensions. For the project coordinators with experience as educators, a different set of concerns came into view, as a result of having too many community members for this particular project as initially designed. For example, during the first couple of workshops, the artist-participants developed their narratives. Although the organizers spent time working with each community member, it was clear that the artist-participants needed more time to develop their narrative and did not have enough time to dialogue with members of the organizing team.

As the workshops continued, it became more and more difficult to coordinate all 13 community members and link artist-participants with organizers or volunteers who would accompany them through a particular aspect of the creation process. There were times when certain artist-participants either had to wait for an organizer before they could move onto the next step of the process, or they were rushed through an aspect of the media creation process. This resulted in some artist-participants having more time than others to develop various media skills, such as photography, sound making or editing.

From the vantage point of those organizers with filmmaking experience, the consequences of having too many participants for the project played out most significantly during the editing process. There were clearly some participants who had more time to develop editing skills than others, resulting in an unequal amount of time for each participant in editing their short films. In order to meet looming deadlines, a significant amount of the editing ending up being completed by a couple of editors that the researcher/media facilitator hired.

At that time, we were not able to collectively discuss how all of these difficulties were linked to one source and were thus structural in nature—due to having too many participants for the project that was designed. As these concerns were brought up in a follow-up conversation after the completion of the project, one of the sources of the problem began to surface. Although the interests of a community organizer, educator and filmmaker are sometimes aligned, they can also bump up against each other. Even the agendas of two (or multiple) community organizers, educators or filmmakers do not always align.

Certainly no one can ever fully know or think of the possible future implications of every decision being made. However, engaging in a collective reflective process where potentially competing interests and agendas are made explicit from the being of the process may assist organizers in adjusting and proactively reacting to tensions that may surface. Perhaps if we had been able to engage in a collective reflective process of making explicit these different agendas at the outset, we could have been pro-active in developing strategies to prevent or respond to the consequences of competing agendas colliding. In addition, this may allow organizers opportunities to problem solve and make decisions that can address the concerns that arise from competing agendas. This is especially important due to the ways in which tensions between competing agendas can negatively shape how directly affected community members experience and move through the media making process.

Thinking Structurally

In addition to reflecting upon how our social locations and competing agendas shaped our micro-processes, another key site of critical analysis is the ways in which institutional forms of power operated throughout the life of the project. In order to make institutional power visible, Bishop (2005) suggests that we must learn to think structurally, in order to "make our unconscious knowledge of the institution visible" (p. 155). By thinking structurally, we can re-frame our understanding of what happened and link interpersonal interactions with structural causes and the larger social context. In addition, we can begin to identify the link between holding institutional power and how decisions are made and resources distributed. Therefore, this section aims to critically reflect upon what happened over the course of our project in order to reveal the ways in which varying forms of institutional power organized the very possibilities and boundaries of our project.

Mapping Memories was a government-funded research project situated within the university context. By fostering community-university partnerships, Mapping Memories strived to engage in collaborative and participatory forms of research that fostered mutual respect and prioritized shared authority and ownership (Miller et al., 2012). In addition, Mapping Memories sought to ensure that media projects were community-initiated, meaning "community members are involved from the outset in the project design, development of parameters and focus areas, and distribution goals" (Miller et al., 2012, p. 12).

In many ways, this collaborative media project was community-initiated and adhered to the principles of mutual respect and shared ownership. AGIR was involved from the beginning of the process. The project developed over time, with multiple conversations about how to structure the project in a way that would be the most beneficial to AGIR and directly affected community members. As a newly formed non-profit organisation that was entirely volunteer run, this was the first major undertaking for AGIR organizers.

Aware of this context, the Mapping Memories researcher/media facilitator made sure to foster a relationship with AGIR over a period of time, allowing AGIR members and organizers to design a project suited to where it was at. Oftentimes, the timeline for government funded research projects is implicitly driven by already outlined time limitations set out by government funding bodies or the affiliated university. Sometimes, these university or funder-driven restrictions can be in tension with the desire to engage in the principles of mutual respect and shared authority/ownership. In this case, the researcher/media facilitator had a degree of flexibility as the funding timeline was over a number of years. Rather than pressuring AGIR to begin a collaborative media-making project when it was not prepared, the researcher/ media facilitator was able to work within the parameters set out by the funders while at the same time still ensuring the time and space required for the collaboration to be successful. Partly due to this longer-term collaborative process, this project served to deepen the participation of directly affected community members in the everyday organizing and coordination of AGIR over the long term.

Another important question when engaging in collaborative media projects related to the question of funding is how decisions are made to allocate finances and resources. Depending on the source of the funding, there are usually varying degrees to which research dollars are pre-allocated to various aspects of the research project. However, there is usually a degree of flexibility with respect to the allocation of funding dollars, and so this requires negotiation between researcher and community (organisation or members) in order to decide where and how to allocate resources.

At the onset of our collaboration, the researcher/media facilitator made it clear that there was a relatively small budget. It was important for there to be transparency about the budget, as this would inform the decisions that were made related to the design and timeline for the media project. As we were designing the project, one priority for AGIR organizers was to ensure that community members would be provided honorariums for their participation in this media project. In addition, the organizer-community member was provided a second honorarium in order to acknowledge the expertise and labour he was contributing to the project as an organizer, in addition to explicitly acknowledging the particular obstacles he was facing as a refugee that the rest of the organizers did not have to encounter.

These negotiations around budget allocation were a concrete example of how the researcher/media facilitator chose to share the institutional power she had in deciding how to allocate the budget. Alternatively, the researcher/media facilitator could have chosen to withhold information related to the budget or could have been unwilling to negotiate the allocation of funding. If she had chosen to do this, there would have been very little recourse for the affiliated community organisation. This is how institutional power is organized within an academic context—the researcher affiliated to the university has the power to unilaterally make decisions around important areas of the research, including issues related to timeline, budget, project design, etc.—no matter what kind of rhetoric one may speak about related to participation, collaboration or community-university partnerships.

Explicitly identifying that the institutional power resides with the university-affiliated researcher at the beginning of the process can make visible to everyone involved, the unequal power relations inherent within academic processes. By thinking structurally, Bishop (2005) encourages us to ask critical questions about who benefits from community-university partnerships, along with questioning the root causes of these inequalities. If these unequal power relations remain implicit and hidden, then community members can be made to feel like they need to be "grateful" that researchers will collaborate with them—even though the researcher oftentimes requires letters of support from community organisations in order to get the funding in the first place. Revealing these power relations explicitly means that all parties involved acknowledge that the university-affiliated members stand to benefit in ways that community members cannot (i.e., full-time salary, academic prestige and power, etc.). Being transparent opens up space for the researchers to take responsibility for the institutional power they hold and "explicitly acknowledge the degree to which they have access to power and resources from specific institutions while at the same time developing strategies to transfer these resources to community members" (Lee, 2012, p. 89).

Another benefit of thinking structurally is the way in which this analytical approach links individual behaviour to structural causes. Linking individual behaviour to structural causes can be especially useful for organizers when tensions or conflicts surface during the media-making process. This certainly occurred during our media-making process, when community members expressed frustration or outright anger about decisions made by the project organizers.

For example, during our first workshop, the media facilitator presented a short film that a youth had previously completed which described her experiences of persecution while living in Rwanda during the genocide. One of the participants of our media project was from Rwanda and had survived the genocide. After the film was presented, he calmly raised his hand and told the media facilitator that he did not appreciate not being told in advance that they would be watching a film that would talk about firsthand experiences of the Rwandan genocide. He explained that he did not have a desire to revisit his own experiences of trauma. After listening to his reflections, the media facilitator responded by acknowledging the artist-participant by sincerely apologizing for not having informed everyone in advance that the film was going to be about a personal narrative related to the Rwandan genocide.

This example illustrates the subtle ways in which those organizers who are not directly affected and have varying degrees of societal privilege can innocently reproduce oppressive social relations—no matter how well intentioned that individual may be. Rather than responding with frustration or defensiveness, the media facilitator really listened and realized the impact of her decision on that artist-participant. This interaction is a powerful example of how someone in a position of authority and societal privilege can react in ways that take responsibility for the impact of unknowingly reproducing harm.

In a way, this kind of response can be cultivated when individuals engage in ongoing critical reflection of their social location and acknowledge the ways in which they may benefit (knowingly or unknowingly) from the varying positions of dominance they occupy within society. In this case, the privilege of having citizenship status along with not having experienced being a refugee may have prevented the media facilitator from fully considering the potential impact of showing a short film about the Rwandan genocide to a Rwandan genocide survivor, without informing him in advance. Although this may have been considered a rather minor incident, it actually had an important impact on the rest of the process. Furthermore, this interaction occurred in front of the other artist-participants, thereby creating space for the other artist-participants to feel safer in speaking up and communicating their concerns to the organizers.

In fact, a number of community members expressed their frustration or anger and communicated their valid concerns to organizers at various times throughout the life of the project. Certainly this was an indication that certain aspects of the project needed improvement. At the same time, the fact that community members were able to openly speak of their concerns is encouraging because many of the artist-participants had experienced persecution or discrimination at the hands of individuals in positions of authority—both in their country of origin and during their refugee process here. This is one example of how the micro-processes of a collaborative media-making process can have long-term ramifications.

Therefore, thinking structurally can assist organizers to develop strategies that open space for imagining how paying attention to micro-processes can result in longer-term benefits. One final example that demonstrates the powerful benefits of thinking structurally while paying attention to micro-processes reveals what can happen when the research-community collaborators consider the longer-term effects of doing a research project (Walsh, Hewson, Shier, Morales, 2008, p. 388). During the process of the media making, there was an artist-participant, Olivier, who began the project with a shy and timid demeanor. During the process of creating his short film, Olivier began to open up and at some point even brought up some concerns that he had with some decisions the organizers made. During the making of his film, Olivier brought up concerns of the public nature of the short film and the potential consequences of revealing himself.

Paying attention to these concerns, the organizers developed strategies with Olivier to find ways for him to tell his story, while at the same time protecting his anonymity. So his face was not shown in the film and his name was altered. Because this media project fit the longer-term objectives of AGIR, community members were able to deepen their involvement with AGIR, in addition to developing media skills and considering themselves as artists. The short films that were produced ended up being screened at a variety of international film festivals.

Nearly two years after the completion of the media project, AGIR was invited to screen the short films at the Kingston International Queer Film Festival. There were 5 members of AGIR (both organizers and artist-participants), including Olivier, who decided to go to the festival and participate in a Q & A afterwards. Just a month earlier, after waiting nearly 3 years for his refugee hearing, Olivier was accepted as a refugee. During the screening of the films, Olivier began to cry. After the screening, all five of us came to the front and began to answer questions. The first thing that Olivier did was he turned around, with his back facing the audience. He then turned around and said to everyone, "I can finally show you my face and be visible." It was a powerful moment, and one that demonstrates the potential longer term benefits of engaging in collaborative media making where directly affected community members can frame their own narratives.

Conclusion

Although this chapter focuses on the linkages between institutional power embedded within academia and community-university partnerships, there are certainly larger social forces that shape the participatory and collaborative media making process. As organizers, our lived experiences are shaped by our respective social locations that position us within varying positions of dominance or marginalization based on our varying multiple group affiliations (based on race, gender, class, ability, sexual/gender identity, citizenship/migrant status, religion, etc.). Furthermore, examining the varying agendas that the organizing team brought with them reveals the ways in which individuals (along with their complex social locations) bring their access to various educational and professional privileges into the collaborative media-making process.

For the purposes of this chapter, the issues that surfaced during the media-making process related to social location, competing agendas and thinking structurally have been separated. However, as stated earlier, it is important to acknowledge and reflect upon the complex ways in which issues of social location, competing agendas and structural power intersect. Although further examination goes beyond the scope of this chapter, we also cannot ignore the growing influence of neo-liberalism on participatory and collaborative forms of research, as Jordan (2003) cautions "the prevalent discourses of participation that define contemporary approaches to PAR and participatory research are being infiltrated by and appropriated by neo-liberalism." (p. 192).

By reflecting on the micro-processes of this collaborative creation process, our aim was not to immobilize people from pursuing participatory or collaborative media making. Rather, our aim was to critically reflect upon these micro-processes in order to establish linkages between individual behaviour/interactions and structural causes. By clearly identifying these critical linkages, researchers, filmmakers, educators, community organizers and directly affected community members can develop context and site-specific strategies to address these concerns. These strategies promote micro-processes of transparency, sharing power and taking responsibility. By engaging with these strategies, we can move towards developing critical multiliteracies that have multiple and longer-term benefits for directly affected community members.

References

Baines, D. (2011). *Doing anti-oppressive practice: Social justice social work* (2nd edition). Halifax & Winnipeg: Fernwood Publishing:

Bishop, A. (2005). *Beyond token change: Breaking the cycle of oppression in institutions*. Winnipeg: Fernwood Publishing.

Brotman, S. & Lee, E. O. (2011). Sexuality through the lens of intersectionality : Sexual minority refugees in Canada. *Canadian Social Work Review. 28*(1), 151–156.

Galabuzi, G. E. (2006). Social exclusion in historical context. In G.E. Galabuzi (Ed.), *Canada's economic apartheid: The social exclusion of racialized groups in the new century.* (pp. 61–90). Toronto: Canadian Scholars Press.

Jordan, S. (2003). Who stole my methodology? Co-opting PAR. *Globalisation, Societies and Education. 1*(2), 185–200.

Kuriloff, P., Andrus, S., & Ravitch, S. (2011). Messy ethics: Conducting moral participatory action research in the crucible of university-school relations. *Mind, Brain and Education*, *5*(2), 49–62.

Lee, E.O. (2012). Escape, retreat, revolt: Queer people of colour living in Montreal. Using photovoice as a tool for community organizing. In A. Choudry, J. Hanley & E. Shragge. (Eds.), *Organize! Building from the local for global justice*. Oakland, CA: PM Press.

Lee, E. O. & Brotman, S. (2011). Identity, refugeeness, belonging: Experiences of sexual minority refugees in Canada. *Canadian Review of Sociology. 48*(3), 241–274.

Miller, L. (2010). Queer is in the eye of the newcomer: Mapping, performance and place based media. *InTensions Journal*, *4*, 1–23.

Miller, L., Luchs, M. & Jalea, G. D. (2012). *Mapping memories: Participatory media, place-based stories and refugee youth.* Montreal: Concordia University Press.

Mullaly, B. (2010). *Challenging oppression and confronting privilege* (2nd edition). Oxford: Oxford University Press.

Namaste, V. (2000). *Invisible lives: The erasure of transsexual and transgendered people.* Chicago: University of Chicago Press.

Norman, J. M. (2009). Creative activism: Youth media in Palestine. *Middle East Journal of Culture & Communication,* *2*(2), 251–274. doi:10.1163/187398509X12476683126464.

Razack, S. H. (2002). *Race, space and the law: Unmapping a white settler society.* Toronto: Between the Lines.

Rich, A. (1984). Notes towards a politics of location. In M. Diaz-Diocaretz & I. Zavala. (Eds.), *Women, feminist identity and society in the 1980s*. Philadelphia: John Benjamins Publishing Company.

Spade, D. (2011). *Normal life: Administrative violence, critical trans politics and the limits of law*. Brooklyn, NY: South End Press.

Thobani, S. (2007). Compassion. In S. Thobani, *Exalted subjects: Studies in the making of race and nation in Canada* (pp. 105–142). Toronto: University of Toronto Press.

Walsh, C. A., Hewson, J., Shier, M., & Morales, E. (2008). Unraveling ethics: Reflections from a community-based participatory research project with youth. *The Qualitative Report, 13*(3), 379–393.

Part 2: Identities and Relationships

Chapter 4

Our Stories, Ourselves: Exploring Identities, Sharing Experiences and Building Relationships through Patient Voices

Pip Hardy and Tony Sumner

Introduction

> *Storytelling is the mode of description best suited to transformation in new situations of action.* (Schön, 1988)

In a chapter that focuses on processes and initiatives that facilitate reflective exploration of personal and socio-political identity, and then turns those reflections around to illuminate issues and practices in health and social care, it seems only appropriate to begin with a brief exploration of our own personal, professional and ideological identities.

As the millennium turned, we (Pip Hardy and Tony Sumner) breathed a sigh of relief at surviving the "millennium bug," rebooted our PCs and continued our work: developing open and distance learning materials from basic skills to Masters and healthcare to accountancy but, always, remembering that "learning should be delightful."

In the first years of the millennium, we shifted towards the nascent e-learning market, always guided by Pip to deliver transformational learning through emphasizing learners' reflection on their own practice as well as that of others. We had always worked hard at creating educational materials and programs that learners could engage with and relate to. Aware of Pascal's dictum that "we tell stories to entertain, and to teach," we incorporated into those materials and programs textual case studies, stories and vignettes to engage and challenge, as well as the raw knowledge to be transferred.

Then, in 2003, we began developing e-learning materials around what the UK healthcare system called "Clinical Governance"—getting staff to deliver care characterised by safety, quality and integrity, both inherently in its nature and explicitly in its delivery. To do this in the engaging, reflective and delightful way we espoused, via the e-learning platforms and broadband (or not!) connections of the time required something we hadn't yet seen.

Patient Voices

And so it happened. Brendan Routledge, a friend and school educational adviser said, after dinner one evening, "Have you ever seen a digital story?" We watched "Don't judge a book by its cover" (Judd, 2002), and were amazed. Brendan, who described digital stories as "PowerPoint for the soul" had unwittingly shown us what we needed: how to show e-learners the "why" that would compel them to learn the "what."

We hadn't yet discovered BBC Capture Wales, the Center for Digital Storytelling or the concept of the story circle. As 2003 shaded into 2004, we drew on Tony's computer industry experience, Pip's background in lifelong learning, counseling and talking therapies, and helped Ian, Monica, David, Charles, Alison, Emma, Grace and Joe to tell their stories (Kramer, 2004; Clarke, 2004; Allen, 2004; Bruce, 2005; D. Clark, 2004; Desa & 2004; Ryan, 2004a). We intended the stories to be reflective learning objects in learning programs—not realizing that the process would become as important to us, and many others, as the product. Recently, a mental health service user reminded Pip of this…

> *On a rare sunny day in Manchester, England, I (Pip)chat with a storyteller in a peaceful retreat centre garden. Nighat had made her first story a year earlier (Mahmood, 2012). She's back to make a story about how she has changed in that year.*
>
> *"I feel like a butterfly emerging from a chrysalis," she says.*
>
> *She wears bright colours and seems much more confident than a year earlier.*
>
> *I ask her what else she learned from the first workshop. Barely hesitating, she replies: "I learned about empathy."*
>
> *She continued. "I used to be really unsympathetic to homeless people. 'Just get a job!' I would think to myself as I passed them on the street. Then I watched Justin's story (Sharman, 2012) at the end of the workshop. And it made me see homeless people in a different light. He talked about being kicked out by his dad, about living in*

rubbish bins and on the streets.... I hadn't thought about those things. And by the end of the story, he was like a different person."

"So now I see homeless people through different eyes. I understand more about how they might have come to be homeless. I have more empathy for them."

In most health and social care systems, service users are defined more by their ethnicity, age, condition, or culture than by their humanity. The system's "divide and conquer" approach to its service users/clients, customers/consumers results in the labeling and separation of mental health service users, homeless people, patients with arthritis, carers for dementia, etc. *ad infinitum*, creating a mosaic of identities, each representing and reflecting the narrow imposed identity the system allows that particular service user. The same system divides one group of clinicians from another. We have found one of the most powerful tools for breaking down the boundaries that separate and compartmentalize humanity is helping people to share their stories across the borders, the no-go lines, the social and cultural DMZs that societal and structural processes place between them. So we created Patient Voices around a reflective digital storytelling process and we learned, along the way, how much truth and how many truths a brief digital patient story can carry and how it can, if used by a skilful educationalist, illuminate many dimensions of a piece of learning.

Early on, Ian and Monica, our first storytellers, both trained lawyers and passionate patient advocates, told us they had previously felt their experiences had been monopolized and exploited without fair acknowledgement of their contributions, or maximization of the "social capital" they had invested. Their guidance led us towards suitable ethical principles to underpin our work (Hardy & Sumner, 2008). Hence, Patient Voices came into being as a place where the social capital created and donated by storytellers in their stories could become social "seed corn." It aimed to remind those designing and delivering healthcare, proposing and implementing policy, determining healthcare budgets, that inside every patient, indeed, every nurse, doctor, physical therapist or radiographer, is a human being. Not a statistic, a collection of symptoms, a diagnosis, but a person, with a life that is more than their need for medical care. Our hope is that the stories will spread out like Johnny Appleseed's trees—flourishing in pockets of fertile soil and bearing fruits of compassion and understanding that all passing may benefit from. In the rest of this chapter, we will consider how the stories—and the storytelling—offer opportunities to break down barriers by sharing experiences, exploring identities and building relationships, but first we will tell you a little more about what we do and how we do it.

Breaking Down Barriers: What We Do and How We Do It

The first array of barriers to be broken down in any digital storytelling project are those that create a barrier to access to the workshop, followed by those that might place barriers within the workshop to the comfortable, safe and easy participation of storytellers. We had been working with storytellers for several years when, in 2006, we came across CDS, the Center for Digital Storytelling. Pip was on a regular trip to California, her home state, to visit family and, fortuitously, found a place on a CDS digital storytelling workshop that created a state of feeling at home. On her return, we changed the homespun way that we worked so that our current process and, we hope, ethos would be familiar to any who have engaged with CDS.

Our preferred model is a consecutive three-day workshop, centred around a story circle, with between six and ten storytellers supported by two facilitators. To break down barriers to participation in this model we have adapted and restructured the process in various ways over the years with the ease of storytellers' physical, mental, emotional, cultural and (not least!) nutritional needs in mind. In order to care for people's stories, we must care for them first. Table 1 summarizes some of the adaptations we have made to remove barriers to participation by storytellers (beyond normal considerations of accessibility).

Table 1

Storytellers	**Adaptations**
People with early-stage dementia www.patientvoices.org.uk/dc.htm	• Increased facilitator numbers (one to one) • Reduced daily hours (three hours per day, over four days) • Facilitators as chauffeurs, driving computers under guidance of storytellers • Adapting print of scripts to match ability to follow sentences on page, size of print, one sentence per sheet, etc • Recording scripts one sentence at a time • Using "contact prints" of images on paper for image selection by storyteller, rather than on screen • Facilitators "holding the thread" on behalf of the teller of a story that may diverge in an almost fractal fashion • Setting workshop in a familiar physical environment (Stenhouse, Tait, Hardy, & Sumner, 2012)
People with stroke www.patientvoices.org.uk/iowsc.htm www.patientvoices.org.uk/naoconn.htm	• Scheduling workshop for six hours a day, one day a week over four weeks • Minimal writing—use of photos as prompts to record small segments of script at a time • Plenty of encouragement to "take your time" for people with aphasia
Kosovan refugees www.patientvoices.org.uk/newham.htm	• Setting workshop in "safe" environment of community centre • Provision of interpreter support • Allowing a significant break at lunch time for storytellers to create and facilitators to share, traditional food and hospitality
People with disabilities (blindness, Aspergers, quadraplegia, learning disabilities, etc.) re-entering employment www.patientvoices.org.uk/exdra.htm	• Use editing software that can be driven by assistive technologies (speech input, drop-switches, on-screen keyboards, head-tracking mouse pointers)

Table 1 (continued)

Storytellers	Adaptations
Rheumatoid arthritis sufferers www.patientvoices.org.uk/wr.htm	• Adapt schedule to match energy profiles of storytellers: two hours am, two hours pm for four days • Plenty of nourishing food! (O'Neil & Hardy, 2008)
Elderly (ages 72–102) storytellers in care home setting www.patientvoices.org.ukshcj.htm	• Increase facilitator numbers • Technology "chauffeurs" • Use of PA/"karaoke" machine by facilitators and in story circle to aid the hard-of-hearing and the quiet of voice • Large print of scripts for reading/recording
Carers www.patientvoices.org.uk/sheffcc.htm www.patientvoices.org.uk/sheffcc2.htm www.patientvoices.org.uk/hcr.htm	• Provision of respite care • Shortened days to allow travel

In addition, we feel that a convivial setting, nourishment that is more than mere sustenance, and a "human" environment play significant parts in overcoming barriers to the creation of digital stories. Typically, retreat centres, whether of some faith or none, provide conducive settings for effective engagement with and by storytellers.

Like most workshops, ours begin with introductions. We like to get to know the really important things about someone: "Tell us your name, three things you love and three things you really dislike." And so we embark on the exploration of identity, discovering the person behind the condition or the disease or the role.

Exploring Identities *or* Patients Are People Too

Narrative is radical, creating us at the very moment it is created. (Morrison, 1993)

Diagnosed with a rare and terminal disease in her 30s, philosopher Havi Carel began exploring the meaning of illness and how to live well with a life-limiting condition. Her book—*Illness*—relates ways of understanding illness to how we understand our identity (Carel, 2008). The model of illness described offers a way of articulating, perhaps in a language more appropriate to academic/medical audiences, what we have learned about identity from patients and carers for ten years. The *naturalist* or *medical* model regards illness as a collection of symptoms to be diagnosed and, hopefully, cured, often with little acknowledgment or understanding of the person with symptoms. Identity is unimportant: the task is simply to make the patient better. The *normative* or *social* model views illness through the lens of social norms. We express sympathy for a friend with a cold (or avoid him!), look with pity on a man missing a leg, try not to notice a woman with a facial disfigurement, avoid speaking about depression or other forms of mental illness and salute the courage of those "battling" against cancer. Our responses are conditioned by the society in which we live. Some diseases warrant respect, admiration even, others attract disgust and even disapproval. Our language determines and expresses our response to certain diseases (Sontag, 1990).

Neither of these models offers insight into what it feels like to be ill. For this, we need a *phenomenological* model, understanding illness from the ill person's perspective. It acknowledges the changes in the way the ill person feels about him or herself, the ways in which the body lets one down, the physical, psychological, emotional and social changes, the changes in relationships, with oneself, one's family and the outside world. Carel comes to see illness as transformative—there may be negatives in the life-transforming process of illness, but there may also be some good, as many of our storytellers learned, through the process of creating and sharing their stories.

As a patient, Dr. Carel has experienced another phenomenon that we at the Patient Voices Programme have known about for several years. *Epistemic injustice* (Fricker, 2007) arises when the credibility of a speaker (a woman, an ethnic minority member, a patient or perhaps a family carer) is questioned, perhaps as a result of personal prejudice, institutional structures or social norms. In healthcare, patients' testimonies are often regarded as less valid than those of medical professionals—as uninformed, emotional, unhelpful. Words used to describe patient testimonies imply the patient's views are to be disregarded. Patients "allege" or "seem to think" (Gray & Rutter, 2002) while clinicians, experts, "report" or "state." We are guided to believe that the words of the doctor, nurse or other professional carry greater weight than those of the patients they serve. Indeed, in the early days of

Patient Voices a friend, a consultant pathologist, dismissed the stories as "only anecdotal, and with no statistical validity."

However, patients—and family members and friends who care for them—are *the* experts in their own lives. Those with chronic conditions, particularly rare conditions, may acquire knowledge and expertise that exceeds that of the doctor (Gray & Rutter, 2002). Patient Voices storytellers tell of being dismissed, disregarded, unheard, not listened to, often with disastrous consequences. They are often allocated arbitrary (to them) labels by the system, which forces upon them a particular identity, a role in the care process, that they have not chosen, sought or developed, one that may not fit well with their own sense of themselves and their own experiences. When epistemic injustice devalues first their own identity, and then even the identity applied to them by the system, tensions, conflicts and crises (both internal and external) may occur. This can be particularly painful for those "invisible" carers with day-to-day responsibilities for their loved ones, as described in several carers' stories.[1]

Being dismissed as ignorant, ill-informed, emotional, anxious or distracted rarely helps patients or their carers feel better. Often storytellers say we are the first people to listen to them, that the simple act of being listened to helps them feel better, to feel human again. Below is an excerpt from one digital story that Jean created, about her experience of living with arthritis:

> *Let us imagine a young woman. Beautiful, intelligent, full of energy and vitality. In the prime of life, she discovers that she has rheumatoid arthritis, a crippling disease causing extreme exhaustion, stiff, painful joints, and sometimes heart disease. Surgery may restore some mobility, but often the joints become so deformed they cannot perform their usual functions.*
>
> *We can read textbooks detailing symptoms, diagnosis and treatments of rheumatoid arthritis. We can review statistics, graphs and charts about how many people are affected, and their likely progression and prognosis. We can study pictures of deformed thumbs, misshapen wrists and ankles. We may be able to gain some objective understanding of the disease.*
>
> *However, try to imagine...*
> *... having wrists that do not bend*
> *... giving up work*
> *... using a wheelchair*

> *... being in constant pain*
> *... having to ask someone to wipe your bottom because you cannot do it*
> *... the impact on your identity, self-esteem, relationships, social and economic status*
> *... the challenge to your values, hopes, vision of the future, identity.* (Bailey-Dering, 2007)

Many medical professionals see people like Jean as a bundle of physical symptoms: a patient. They are not interested that she can't work in her garden any more, can often barely walk and relies on her husband for almost everything. They are not interested in the person who, often unexpectedly, usually unwillingly, assumes the identity of *patient*. They don't see the perilous descent from good health and capability to helplessness and disability. They don't share the remarkable courage and resilience in her recognition that she is still the same person.

We began the Patient Voices Program to address precisely this issue, to remind clinicians that patients are people first, that "the patient journey is only one aspect of the life journey" as storyteller Ian Kramer reminded us. We wanted clinicians to see patients as human beings with lives, wives, husbands, parents, children, hobbies, likes and dislikes that all affect their response to illness, their motivation to get well, the likelihood (or otherwise) of "compliance" with treatment. We wanted clinicians to realise that the people they see as patients are also experts—experts in their own lives. We hoped that, by sharing these short stories of experience without judgment (though often with an invitation to reflect on their own practice or personal experience) that viewers would be reminded of our shared humanity.

No Longer Suffering in Silence

> *One of the hardest things in life is having words in your heart that you just can't utter.* James Earl Jones (n.d.)

In over 100 workshops, working with over 700 storytellers, we have observed that, almost without exception, the people who sit with us in a story circle, whether patient, carer, doctor, nurse, midwife, physiotherapist, hospital administrator, old, young, rich, poor, educated or not, are experts in another very human experience: suffering. Suffering knows no boundaries, is no respecter of class or race. Suffering is universal. Suffering makes us human: it is an inherent part of the human condition. Yet many of the individuals and groups we meet are convinced that they have the monopoly on suffering. However, many people lack the opportunity, the environment or the support to make sense of their own experiences—or those of others. One of the key tasks of a Patient Voices reflective digital storytelling workshop is to create a place of tranquillity where storytellers can recollect and reflect on their experiences and try to make sense of their suffering.

Suffering is not something that we can learn from books, movies, courses, training programs or other people; it is something we know about from our own experience. We have to experience it—and wc do. And those experiences are the very stuff of stories, as Flannery O'Connor, in likening the progression of a story to the task of confronting a dragon, reminds us:

> *No matter what form the dragon may take, it is of this mysterious passage past him, or into his jaws, that stories of any depth will always be concerned to tell....* (O'Connor, 1970)

Every storyteller is unique. Every story is unique and, at the same time, every story links us to our fellow human beings. One of the challenges for us, as digital storytelling facilitators, is how to help people tell that phenomenological story of their experience without imposing yet another set of structures, systems, norms or language; how to help them tell the story they need to tell in order to see themselves as who they really are. Another, far greater, challenge is to enable others to realise that, by sharing these important stories, each individual story is, in fact, the whole story; that my story is also your story and your story is also my story.

Sharing Experiences: A Transformative Act?

> *Each affects the other and the other affects the next and the world is full of stories, and the stories are all one.* (Albom, 2003)

Just as suffering is part of the human condition, so is the ability—and the desire—to tell stories. As human beings, we celebrate our joys, grieve for our losses, test our strengths, accept our weaknesses, learn about ourselves and others, share our experiences and rejoice in our common humanity through stories. In doing so, we learn a great deal about ourselves, about our capacity for courage and our ability to bear pain, about how to show kindness to strangers as well as ourselves; about the ways in which we change and the ways in which we remain resolutely who we are.

We hear stories of illness and accident, birth and death, tragic mistakes and unexpected miracles; unbearable loss and unexpected jubilation, of anxiety and relief, agonising pain and, sometimes relief from pain. Woven through these stories is the theme of changing identity: from health to sickness, from able-bodied to disabled, from carefree to carer, from despair to recovery, from student to nurse, from junior doctor to registrar/resident, from immigrant to healthcare assistant. As we move through life, the changes in our identity can be so subtle that they are barely noticeable, or so enormous that they challenge our very notion of ourselves. Suffering, and our response to it, is part of our identity. Stories act as a bridge, allowing us to cross the barriers between one person and another, offering us the opportunity to share our understanding of suffering, of humanity, and reminding us that we are not alone. Stories allow us to share our experiences of being human.

Passing Dragons

When we reflect on what these stories and storytellers have in common, we have realised that they all involve a dragon—or two.

> *Eva is also one of our oldest storytellers. We first met Eva on a beautiful summer day. She was sitting in our conservatory, so it was difficult to tell quite how small she was. She had been "volunteered" by other members of her community to take part in a workshop as part of a project to let the world know about the extraordinary work being done by the even more extraordinary women in her order of nuns, the Sisters of the Holy Child Jesus.*
>
> *As is our custom, we spent the first hour of the workshop trying to put people at their ease, helping them feel at home, introducing ourselves to one another, talking about what makes a good story and showing some digital stories that we think are good examples of the genre. Two sisters had been to a previous workshop, and we showed their stories.*
>
> *As soon as we broke for coffee, Eva came up to Pip. Her white hair, soft voice and diminutive stature belied the strength of her character, as Pip was about to find out.*

"I think I've been sent here under false pretences!" she said, "I don't think I belong here and I'm not sure I want to stay."

Pip was stunned. What had gone wrong? She had spoken to each of the participants on the phone to introduce herself and brief them about the workshop, suggesting ways of preparing, talking through their ideas for stories, so Pip tried to reassure her.

"Eva, we are not going to force you to stay! In fact, I don't think anyone has ever done a Patient Voices workshop under duress. Perhaps I could make you a cup of coffee and we could have a chat about your concerns."

Eva softened. A little. "Could you make me a cappuccino?"

We could. Aware of the gravity of the situation, Pip even sprinkled chocolate on the top. Pip and Eva adjourned to sit in the shade of an old apple tree. Eva sipped her cappuccino.

Her concerns were similar to the concerns that most people have before the story circle. "What story shall I tell? Will it be too personal? Will I reveal too much of myself? What on earth am I doing here with all these strangers?"

Pip reiterated that she need stay no longer than she was comfortable but that we were looking forward to hearing her story. We agreed that she would stay for the next session and make a final decision about the rest of the workshop at lunchtime.

Eva stayed for the story circle. She stayed for lunch and for the afternoon script-writing session. She stayed for dinner and returned the next day. She grappled with her story. She spent a lot of time under the apple tree thinking, remembering, writing, re-writing. We talked about her story. She chose her pictures. She worked with another facilitator to put together her digital story using Premier Pro. She joined us for 4th of July celebrations. She enjoyed a glass of champagne when we premiered the stories. She watched each story attentively and made loving and appreciate comments about each one.

And then, this 82-year-old nun said, "These three days have been more like a retreat than any retreat I can remember. I can't remember ever having this level of genuine mutual support. I've learned about the value of combining words, music and art. I've learned that fear can be diminished through this process."

Eva's story, "Standing on My Own Two Feet," can be seen at the Patient Voices website (Heymann, 2008). Eva has been back three more times and has made three more stories. Mostly, they follow the course of her increasing dementia, facing painful memories and coming to terms with both the darkness and the light in her past and in her future. She has talked to me about how important it was to her to discover the joy of sharing stories with others and that being part of a group could be both wholesome and enjoyable! As a writer, photographer and music lover, the possibility of combining all these elements in her digital story was a revelation for Eva. She says that it has helped her to recognize and express things about herself that she couldn't do in any other way. We laugh about how both of our lives might have been very different if she hadn't enjoyed that cappuccino quite so much! Eva is living testament to the words of Jean Vanier, sent to us by another storyteller after the creation of a particularly painful story:

> People reach greater maturity as they find the freedom to be themselves and to claim, accept and love their own personal story, with all its brokenness and its beauty. (Vanier, 2004)

And all of the people who have sat in a story circle with Eva remember her with gratitude and delight for her wisdom and insight, her depth of understanding, her appreciative comments and her unexpected creativity.

Over the years, we have, inevitably, developed great attachment to and identification with our role as digital storytelling facilitators, as well as to the workshops, the stories and the storytellers. We remember Eva with gratitude as well. In our case, gratitude for challenging, questioning and, ultimately, helping us improve our understanding of how the many identities in a storytelling workshop interact and engage, of what our identity as "facilitator" means and requires of us. It is worth taking a few minutes to watch Eva's other stories and decide for yourself what she has learned—and what we, in turn, might learn from her, and from her series of stories (links are in the references): From Darkness into Light: New Worlds (Heymann, 2009b), A Chocolate Watch (Heymann, 2009a) and The Sun Also Rises (Heymann, 2010).

Was Eva transformed by her experience of creating a digital story? We cannot speak for her, though she tells us that the experiences of creating her stories have been crucial for her in thinking about herself in new and different ways.

Were we challenged and transformed by meeting Eva, working with her and sharing her stories? Unquestionably and permanently.

We believe that the transformative potential of digital storytelling relies on the creation and maintenance of a safe space in which stories can be shared.

Safety Within and Without

Just as there are challenges of telling stories, there are also challenges to assisting others in completing the process of telling a digital story. A vulnerable and damaged facilitator cannot, with storytellers of this nature, be as capable of creating and holding what Jung referred to as *temenos* (Jung, 1968), the "sacred space" at the centre of the workshop that is needed by potentially vulnerable storytellers. To do this, and to manage the issues of transference, projection, identification, etc. that we have observed occurring in the process, we have learned to value ourselves and our profession as facilitators. We strive to do this through professional values and practice that includes:

- having clinical supervision with an experienced supervisor of counsellors every few workshops to ensure we are emotionally and psychologically healthy
- having at least two facilitators at every workshop, so that we can provide mutual support and grounding and so that, if a storyteller needs more intense support, other storytellers will not be vulnerable or neglected
- limiting workshop size so that the story circle, which forms its heart and provides the safety of the group, does not grow beyond the management of the facilitators and split, amoeba-like, creating divisions and barriers within the group.

In our own reflections and conversations, we sometimes talk (half jokingly) about the work of facilitating a Patient Voices workshop as feeling like running the proverbial "three-ring circus." In our model the rings contain the technological, emotional/personal, artistic and narrative hurdles that we must jump ourselves, and help others to jump also. We often experience feelings of elation when a storyteller creates a powerful and important story; of identification when a story resonates with our own experiences or those of close friends or family; of responsibility when a storyteller commits their emotional, physical and intellectual strengths and energy to a story. Around this are our experiences of transference from storytellers and of how walking in their shoes with them through their pasts and presents for the three days of a workshop can leave us with emotions and experiences that we need to reflect on and process in a separate, safe and supportive environment. We do this on a regular basis with a qualified and experienced supervisor.

Building Relationships, Embracing Identities

When service users, patients and carers—when any of us are divided—we may be conquered. When we join together in sharing stories, we are able to understand our commonality and community of experience and able to understand that as Pip regularly reminds us "no one—and no one group—has the monopoly on suffering" (Hardy & Sumner, 2010). Our identity is constructed, expressed and shared through our stories; what changes our engagement with others from being one based on monologues that are merely transactional exchange of information to having a real relationship with them is the sharing of stories that allow us to construct a dialogue of identities. Our understanding of our own identity is defined by self-awareness of our stories. Our relationships with others can only be effective relationships if we have shared, heard, and reflected on both our own stories and the stories of the other.

Just as the storytelling process has helped many patients, carers and professionals to reflect upon their own stories and identities, creating the story of the Patient Voices Programme itself over this decade has shaped our own identities in varied and, sometimes, unexpected ways. We have learned unexpected things about ourselves. Tony, the technical one, turns out to be a master at remembering exactly what a storyteller said in the story circle that could become that perfect last sentence to leave the viewer amazed, stunned or reaching for a Kleenex. Women (including nuns!), who represent the majority of our storytellers, love him. They are surprised by his empathy and emotional intelligence, and by his unerring ability to cut right to the heart of a story. And he has learned to listen differently—according to the guidelines of our story circle, he is not allowed to interrupt!

Pip, the shy, quiet one, has, on the other hand, discovered that it is possible to talk to more than a handful of people without being overwhelmed by fear and nausea—especially if there is a decent microphone! As well as standing up and talking to large groups of people, she has grappled with some serious technology and can hold her own with any techie debating the merits of Premier Pro or Final Cut, the relative merits of .wmv or .mov files and instructing others in the finer points of showing digital stories within PowerPoint presentations. She has conducted research, completed a Masters and is working on a PhD so that she can evaluate, assess and share the benefits to a large mental health care organisation of embedding story-based work and "the evidence of experience"—in their core processes.

We have discovered that, together, we are a formidable team of *story midwives*—or *doulas*—facilitating and celebrating the birth of stories that may be long overdue and in need of careful nurturing. Our complementary skills seem to offer just the right degree of safety, competence and nurturing so that people can give themselves to the emotional labour of creating a story with authenticity and love.

Conclusion

> *Statistics tell us the system's experience of the individual, whereas stories tell us the individual's experience of the system...* (Sumner, 2009)

Many of our storytellers keep in touch with us. They tell us that, after sitting in a story circle, they have greater empathy and understanding for others—like Nighat at the beginning of this chapter. They tell us that the experience of creating a digital story has changed them, enabled them to see themselves differently, with greater acceptance "for all their brokenness and beauty" (Vanier, 2004). They tell us that they are happy to have met others like them.

When we recorded the very first Patient Voices digital stories way back in the distant past of 2003, we had a dream. Our vision was broad and ambitious: we wanted to transform healthcare so that patients would feel they were being treated like people. We wanted to counteract what we saw as the increasingly toxic culture dominated by targets, tick-boxes, questionnaires, audits, statistics and outcome measures. We wanted evidence-based healthcare to include the evidence of experience and not only the evidence of randomised control trials. We wanted to hear about—and to experience—healthcare encounters that were relational and not merely transactional. We wanted to be part of a healthcare culture characterised by humanity and compassion, where every person was valued and every voice mattered.

There is still much to be done. Along the way there have been challenges and upsets, uncertainties and anxieties and not a little heartache.

But facilitating truly reflective digital storytelling workshops is, as Joe Lambert (founder and executive director of CDS) says, the best job in the world. We have met incredible people, heard amazing stories, been to places—both physical and experiential—we'd only dreamed of. We have made wonderful friends and our lives have been enriched beyond measure by the stories they have shared with us.

We have laughed and cried, rejoiced and sympathised with our storytellers, celebrated births, mourned deaths and, sometimes, helped people who know they are going to die share their most important stories while they still can.

What Have We Learned?

We have learned to negotiate the delicate balance between our commitment to helping the storyteller tell the story he or she needs to tell, while keeping the sponsors happy by ensuring that the stories will fit comfortably with their project goals. We have pushed ourselves to do things that have not always been comfortable and certainly not easy—and discovered that we were capable of things we had never dreamed of. We have watched our income drop year-on-year—and hired a new accountant. We have been anxious, exhausted, stressed and wondered whether we would have to find another way to earn a living—but something always seems to turn up. We have learned about faith—and hope.

Often we see a group of disparate storytellers share their stories, break down barriers between themselves and make lasting connections. Sometimes that community becomes something tangible and humbling. In 2009 we ran a workshop in Sheffield. A diverse group of people came—a roofing contractor, a council manager, mothers, carers, mental health service users—created, shared and heard each other's stories. All told deeply affecting and powerful stories about injury, loss, caring, being cared for.

We kept in touch with members of the group, and they kept in touch with each other. Then, ten months later, we got a call. One of the storytellers had been diagnosed with an aggressive and terminal cancer. While the drugs could keep the pain at bay, she wanted to make another story for her family. Could we help?

We all did. Everyone came, including the man who had commissioned the first workshop! One storyteller made her house available for the workshop, everyone brought food and drink, we brought our skills and laptops—

gave our time. Everyone dived into the process, and all, including the storyteller we had come together to support, made stories. At the end of the workshop the story premiere was more poignant than usual.

A few months later we took one of those stories, sadly and also joyfully, to show at a memorial ceremony—and all of the storytellers came to hear that one story again.

Over the past year, the term "compassion" has become very popular in the UK National Health Service and "the patient experience" is now recognised as being an important part of every healthcare encounter. Everyone is talking about stories. Researchers are using the Patient Voices stories as qualitative data to find out what really matters to patients. Where we have been involved in long-term projects with organisations, they are beginning to see reductions in the number of complaints in relation to poor communication, lack of dignity and respect—the very themes of the stories they have created. And then, recently, this happened.

> *At the Royal Society of Medicine in London, Pip shows a group of newly qualified doctors Jean's digital story.*
> http://www.patientvoices.org.uk/flv/0110pv384.htm (Bailey-Dering, 2007)
>
> *She invites the audience to respond. One young doctor has this to say:*
>
> *"The story made me really aware of the impact of the disease on their relationship. I guess I had never really thought about how Rheumatoid Arthritis could have such a huge impact on their physical relationship, their emotional relationship, the economics and practicalities of their relationship (because she obviously can't work) and the pressure her husband must be under caring for her 24/7."*
>
> *"So, how might that affect your practice?" Pip asks.*
>
> *"I hope that, the next time I meet someone with RA, I won't just talk to them about their physical symptoms. I hope I would ask them about their relationships, what support they have and be more aware of the impact of the disease on partners and other members of the family—the psychological and social aspects of the disease as well as the physical ones."*

So, things are changing, albeit not quite as quickly, or in quite the ways we wished.

Margaret Mead encourages us to remember that:

> *A small group of committed, thoughtful people can change the world—indeed, it is the only thing that ever has. (Mead, 1964)*

And so, as the Patient Voices Programme moves into its second decade, we (Pip Hardy and Tony Sumner) breathe a sigh of satisfaction at completing the latest workshop, at helping another small group of committed and thoughtful people to vocalise, reflect on, distil and share their stories. We reboot our PCs, and continue our work. What, above all, we have learned was best articulated by Gandhi:

> *We must be the change we want to see in the world.*

Note

1. My Michael http://www.patientvoices.org.uk/flv/0088pv384.htm (Spurden, 2007) Why am I not the expert? http://www.patientvoices.org.uk/flv/0086pv384.htm (Currie, 2007) Who cares? http://www.patientvoices.org.uk/flv/0003pv384.htm (Ryan, 2004b)

References

Albom, M. (2003). *The five people you meet in heaven* (1st Ed.). New York: Hyperion.

Allen, E. (2004). Emma Allen's stories. *Patient Voices*. Retrieved July 17, 2013, from http://www.patientvoices.org.uk/eallen.htm

Anderson, E., Hardy, P., Kinnair, D., Sumner, T. and Thorpe, L. (2011). They just don't get it: Using digital storytelling to promote meaningful undergraduate reflection. *Medical Teacher, 34*(7), 597–598.

Bailey-Dering, J. (2007). Getting to the bottom of things. *Patient Voices*. Retrieved July 18, 2013, from http://www.patientvoices.org.uk/flv/0110pv384.htm

Bruce, C. (2005). Charles Bruce's stories. *Patient Voices*. Retrieved July 17, 2013, from http://www.patientvoices.org.uk/cbruce.htm

Carel, H. (2008). *Illness*. Durham, NC: Acumen.

Clark, D. (2004). David Clark's Stories. *Patient Voices*. Retrieved July 17, 2013, from http://www.patientvoices.org.uk/dclark.htm

Clarke, M. (2004). Monica Clarke: Stories. *Patient Voices.* Retrieved July 17, 2013, from http://www.patientvoices.org.uk/mclarke.htm
Currie, J. (2007). Why am I not the expert? *Patient Voices.* Retrieved July 17, 2013, from http://www.patientvoices.org.uk/flv/0086pv384.htm
Davitt, J. (2004, June, 7). Used in class. *The Guardian.* Retrieved from http://www.guardian.co.uk/education/2004/jun/08/elearning.technology16
Desa, G. and. Desa, J. (2004, 2007). Grace and Joe Desa's stories. *Patient Voices.* Retrieved July 17, 2013, from http://www.patientvoices.org.uk/gjdesa.htm
Fricker, M. (2007). *Epistemic injustice: Power and the ethics of knowing.* Oxford: Oxford University Press.
Gray, J. A., & Rutter, H. (2002). *The resourceful patient.* Oxford: eRosetta.
Hardy, P., & Sumner, T. (2008). Digital storytelling in health and social care: Touching hearts and bridging the emotional, physical and digital divide. *Lapidus Journal, 3*(3), 24–31 .
Hardy, P., & Sumner, T. (2010). Humanizing healthcare: A conversation with Pip Hardy and Tony Sumner, Pilgrim Projects/Patient Voices. In J. Lambert (Ed.), *Digital Storytelling: Capturing Lives, Creating Community* (3rd ed., pp. 143–156). Berkeley, California: Digital Diner Press.
Heymann, E. (2008). Standing on my own two feet. *Patient Voices.* Retrieved July 17, 2013, from http://www.patientvoices.org.uk/flv/0249pv384.htm
Heymann, E. (2009). A chocolate watch. *Patient Voices.* Retrieved July 17, 2013, from http://www.patientvoices.org.uk/flv/0412pv384.htm
Heymann, E. (2009). From darkness into light: New worlds. *Patient Voices.* Retrieved July 17, 2013, from http://www.patientvoices.org.uk/flv/0345pv384.htm
Heymann, E. (2010). The sun also rises. *Patient Voices.* Retrieved July 18, 2013, from http://www.patientvoices.org.uk/flv/0517pv384.htm
Jones, J. E. (n.d.). Retrieved from http://www.success.com/articles/766-finding-his-voice-james-earl-jones
Judd, J. (2002). *Don't judge a book by its cover.* Retrieved July, 2013 from http://clips.e2bn.org/view.php?id=110
Jung, C. G. (1968). *Psychology and alchemy* (R. F. C. Hull, Trans.) New York: Routledge & Kegan Paul.
Kramer, I. (2004, 2013). Ian Kramer: Stories. *Patient Voices.* Retrieved July 17, 2013, http://www.patientvoices.org.uk/ikramer.htm

Mahmood, N. (2012, 2012). Loneliness. *Patient Voices.* Retrieved July 18, 2013, from http://www.patientvoices.org.uk/flv/0598pv384.htm

Mead, M. (1964). *Continuities in cultural evolution.* New Haven, CT: Yale University Press.

Morrison, T. (1993). *Nobel Prize speech.* Singapore: World Scientific Publishing Co.

O'Connor, M. F. (1970). The fiction writer and his country. In Fitzgerald, S. & Fitzgerald, R. (Eds.), *Mystery and manners: Occasional prose.* New York: Farrar, Straus and Giroux.

O'Neil, F., & Hardy, P. (2008). Designing patient-shaped healthcare: Hearing Patient Voices. *White Rose Health Innovation Partnership Technology Bulletin.* Retrieved from http://www.whiterose.ac.uk/sites/default/files /Patient%20Shaped%20Healthcare.pdf

Ryan, A. (2004). Alison Ryan: Stories. *Patient Voices.* Retrieved July 17, 2013, from http://www.patientvoices.org.uk/aryan.htm

Ryan, A. (2004). Who cares? *Patient Voices* Retrieved July 18, 2013, from http://www.patientvoices.org.uk/flv/0003pv384.htm

Schön, D. (1989). Coaching reflective teaching. In P. P. Grimmett & G. L. Erickson (Eds.), *Reflection in teacher education* (pp. 19–29). New York: Teachers College Press.

Sharman, J. (2012). Skip rat junkie. *Patient Voices.* Retrieved July 17, 2013, from http://www.patientvoices.org.uk/flv/0597pv384.htm

Sontag, S. (1990). *Illness as metaphor and AIDS and Its metaphors* (1st Anchor Books Ed.). New York: Doubleday.

Spurden, J. (2007). My Michael. *Patient Voices,* Retrieved July 18, 2013, from http://www.patientvoices.org.uk/flv/0088pv384.htm

Stenhouse, R., Tait, J., Hardy, P., & Sumner, T. (2012). Dangling conversations: Reflections on the process of creating digital stories during a workshop with people with early stage dementia. *Journal of Psychiatric and Mental Health Nursing, 20*(2), 134–141.

Sumner, T. (2009). *Inspiring innovation through Patient Voices.* Paper presented at the Innovation Expo.

Vanier, J. (2004). *Drawn into the mystery of Jesus through the Gospel of John.* New York: Paulist Press.

Chapter 5

I Transform Myself, I Transform the World Around Me

Diana J. Nucera and Jeanette Lee

Introduction

It took me about five years to really understand the complexity of the statement "I transform myself, I transform the world around me." Detroit Summer and Allied Media Projects recruited me to bring my media and technology teaching knowledge to Detroit in the summer of 2008. I left several lives behind me to start what seemed to be a dream job of building media labs and teaching media arts with people who saw the holistic potential of media and technology. At the time, it was rare that I came across people who wanted to use media and technology to foster healing, build relationships and bridge communities, so I jumped at the opportunity. I saw it as a chance to rest from the relentless struggle of climbing non-profit ladders that could not hold my creative weight to begin with. This was also an opportunity to heal from the scars that working in academia had left on me. I remember feeling I had everything I needed and nothing at all.

The process of brainstorming the contents of this chapter conjured up old emotions from my first days at Allied Media Projects. A memory of intense, and what felt like unexplainable feelings were triggered. I blindly searched for something tangible that would reveal the significance of this memory. I sifted through old documents, calendars, and emails. I found an email sent 08/08/08 addressed to my dear friend and companion, Felice Archbold. I shared with her the chaos my mind was experiencing as I started my new life in Detroit; attached to the email was a poem. After reading the poem I could clearly remember August 8th, 2008, the day I locked myself in the first media lab I built in Detroit and set out to understand my future, my agency, and the tumultuous sea of emotions flooding my body. Five years later, I find myself circling back to what I can now describe as documentation of my self-transformation. The memory of writing the poem is just as profound and timeless as the text that poured out of me that day.

When Jenny Lee and I sat down to write this chapter, our intention was to interview each other, pull threads from our conversation, and then write about those threads. After reading the transcript of our conversation I realized that the poem I wrote 5 years ago and our dialogue carried the same content. I scattered the poem throughout our conversation and found that the text seamlessly wove together, and gracefully uplifted, our thoughts. It became obvious that understanding transformation was the thread we were searching for and the poem served as the needle stitching it all together.

I strongly believe that personal transformation is at the heart of social change. Fostering spaces that allow transformation to emerge is how I choose to approach community organizing, my music and art, and how I choose to approach teaching media and technology. I've learned along the way that the conditions that allow transformation to occur are rarely the same and transformation is most certainly not something you can force out of someone. It is summoned. It must be desired. Each person must approach self-transformation in their own way. It is not a cookie cutter or a blanket solution. It is as complicated and as simple as life itself. It can be a painful. Transformation is an unpredictable, emergent process.

The question I have carried with me from the moment I heard "I transform myself, I transform the world around me," is: What conditions allow our full potential and self-determination to emerge?

—Diana J Nucera

I have come to learn that life is best spent allowing life to thrive around me. My heart has learned to foster love and let it go, so new life can spring from it. My brain has learned to carry every piece of myself along the way, leaving trails of bits that didn't quite work in my wake (in case I forget my path). My soul has learned to move fearlessly with excitement and to understand the possibilities of existence.

Jenny: What has brought you to this work?

Diana: What has brought me to this work... so when we say "this work," are we talking about AMP? Or...

Jenny: The work of community-based media.

Diana: Ok, so should I give the timeline? Or more, my heart...

Jenny: Your heart's journey.

Diana: Ok, well... I consider myself a digital baby which means that TV and the Internet played a big role in my adolescence. I recall in high school needing to have at least one Internet source for a term paper and looking up raves on a Yahoo search engine when the Internet finally made it to the computers in my school library. Even before that, I remember watching profound moments of history on TV, like the fall of the Berlin Wall. I stood in the middle of my green-carpeted living room in Frankfort, Indiana, in front of the TV and felt the power of media as the Berlin Wall fell in front of me. I remember being astounded by witnessing such a historic moment happen before my eyes but also being confused because I had no idea this wall existed. I remember asking my father, "Why didn't they teach me about the wall in school?" His response was "They didn't teach me either." I was 8 when that happened and I never really looked at TV or school the same after that.

Growing up in a small town in Indiana meant that there was not a whole lot of things to do, so naturally, TV was my babysitter, where my cool friends lived, my escape. I had a relationship with television. Around the time I was in middle school, I got fed up with it. As I grew into my creative self, TV all of a sudden seemed terrible and cheesy. I could see through entertainment's silver lining and started realizing that these people weren't my friends, they were just trying to sell me stuff. I would get so angry. I developed a habit of screaming at the TV. I would yell at the characters then yell at the actors playing the characters, criticizing both of them for willingly sucking. I still do that to this day. It just feels so satisfying. So, from the age of 12 on I grew up deconstructing media.

My family was one of five families of color in Frankfort's population of 15,000, so I was hyper aware of racism at a very young age. I always wondered why there were no Latinas on TV and why there was no one I could relate to. I could only find them on Univision, the all-Spanish station my mom had to pay extra for. I didn't speak Spanish and barely understood it because if I did, I would get bullied. Univision meant nothing to me, even though it was the only station that had people on it that looked like me. I was so confused. I remember feeling lost in my own skin, unsure if I was supposed to be on earth. In hindsight I was having what I call now a mixed girl identity crisis. My mother was like the people on Univision and my father was like the people on every other station, but I couldn't relate to either. The more I grew into my own identity, it became clear that I was different and that that was something I was going to have to deal with. Sometimes it felt good to be different, almost like a relief. Sometimes it felt depressing and lonely, especially as I entered into my adolescence. To this day I still oscillate between those two worlds, insecure that I am being dismissed because I am different but proud that I am a unique creature on this earth.

Luckily Punk Rock was alive and kicking and those that were also different wore it all up and down their bodies with no shame. I started hanging with the punks and rockers. We joined forces and followed bands to find others. We threw shows to draw others to us. We questioned everything—capitalism, media, gender, sexuality, education, politics. Music literally saved my life. I was so relieved when I found others that were "different." The bands we followed and the crowds that joined us were my community. We traveled all over the Midwest to be with each other.

The most significant trip I went on was an adventure to Ohio to see some bands in 1999. That was the trip I stumbled upon the Underground Publishing Conference, which is now the Allied Media Conference. That trip changed everything. I saw people using their "differences" to carve new paths for possibilities. I saw zines that questioned media, capitalism, sexuality—everything my friends and I did—and when you are isolated by living in rural areas, that was a major discovery! What stood out the most to me was the way people were taking action—by making and distributing their own media. Seeing others do it themselves made me realize I could too. Something sparked in me. I craved more after that. I quickly came to realize that the only way out of small-town Indiana was college. After my trip to Ohio, I decided I was going to move to San Francisco, to let the gay in me out and go to art school so I could finally fix all the crappy TV out there. Haha.... I was young and naive, but passionate. I guess that is all that matters in the long run.

Art school made me even more critical about art, media, and diversity. It baffled me that I was in a big city full of all kinds of people and I was *still* one of few people of color. I was also one of few people that worked while going to school. San Francisco didn't make sense anymore. I was sick of juggling jobs to pay for rent that kept rising and I couldn't stand the unintentionality behind the art that surrounded me. So I moved to Chicago, which seemed like a more affordable city, to be closer to family and go to grad school. When I landed a job at *Street Level Youth Media* as a video instructor I started to realize the possibilities of life as a media artist. I found a group of artists that had similar experiences. We were young people of color making media and teaching other young people of color to make media. I was like, "this is it, I'm going to teach others how to make videos and together we're going to fix all of the crappy TV! I'm going to make media that has real representation of people and diversity!" So all of those crazy experiences as a young person in small-town Indiana and all of my wacky moments in San Francisco came to a head at Street Level. I found this job, via craigslist btw, where I was able to put my ideas into practice and my experience to good use. *Youth Media* led me into community media organizing.

My journey to community media is rooted in understanding my own struggles, understanding my own place in this world. I also recognized that without the process of making media, or access to making art and music, I don't know that I necessarily would have made it out of Indiana alive. It was such a depressing place that left me thinking there was no place for me. At least no place that was *worth* something. The punk rock music scene and the DIY movement opened my mind to new possibilities of life. Now my work, in whatever form it takes, revolves around bringing arts into the schools and unleashing the creativity in others because having art class and orchestra in school gave me the tools I needed to deal with my oppressive environment. To this day I still play the cello and to this day it still balances me. I know how powerful creativity and the media-making process is because it literally saved my life. I feel so compelled to share that with others.

> *And now I stand in front of you with only my findings to cover my scars.*

Jenny: Thinking about the way that you told your story makes me think about my own. So, you talked about being a digital baby.... We were born roughly around the same time. In the way that you described your relationship to digital media and TV, my relationship was definitely formed around writing and books. I remember having a really deep connection to stories and storytelling. My family had a dog, which was this dachshund-terrier mix and looked like a rat—a really unattractive dog. But I had this deep connection with the dog and would make up these stories about the dog's origins and I would tell my family that the dog was communicating with me the adventures of all its past lives. My mom was a writer, and she was a really good listener. Growing up, she would spend almost every morning alone, writing. I started doing the same thing when I was about 7 when someone had given me a journal as a gift.

There were politicizing moments for me, threaded throughout childhood, leading up to one moment that's really clear in my mind, when I was in high school, and I realized—everything I've been told is a lie. I was in 10th grade and in my world history class the teacher gave us excerpts from Howard Zinn's *A People's History of the United States* (2005) to read and it was the first chapter of the book where they're talking about the arrival of Columbus and the Jamestown Colony, the true story of Thanksgiving. At the time I was in love with this English boy. I flipped out on him for his complicity in colonization.

I think leading up to that point, the thing that shaped my relationship to the world and the concept of social justice, was the experience of growing up in Metro Detroit, which is one of the most racially segregated regions in the country. My family lived in Detroit when I was born, but moved to the suburbs when I was growing up. So I still had relationships in the city and would spend a lot of time traversing the border of 8 mile (the East-West road that separates the city from the suburbs). But in the city where I grew up, a lot of my friends' parents wouldn't let them go into Detroit because they were afraid. This was an entirely white, predominantly Jewish community. A lot of their perceptions of the city were shaped by a reality of danger, but so much of it was shaped by the way the media portrayed the city, and Black communities in the city specifically. So that was how I began to understand racism, and how fear played into racism, and how the media contributed to that fear.

Seeing how racism operated on that level within that community also impacted the way I understood the experiences of being a part of a mixed race family there. My dad was a Chinese immigrant who moved to Detroit in the 70s to go to school at University of Detroit. During that time period there was a lot of anti-Asian racism in Detroit, marked by the murder of Vincent Chin on June 22, 1982 (incidentally, the day I was born). My Dad never experienced that kind of violence, thankfully, and I never experienced anything more than the mildest forms of racism. But our "otherness" was tangible. My family moved to China for three years when I was in high school, and that added another layer to the experience of being an "other." In that process I really learned how, as a mixed person, there's no place where you're ever "home" in your identity, where everything is affirmed and makes sense. But at the same time, there are so many people who share that feeling of "otherness"—whether because they're mixed-race or adopted, or just "weird" in the context of where they were raised. I've been so fortunate to grow community and a sense of home with other others.

The experience of growing up mixed-race also shaped my relationship to media—this idea of complexity that pervades the way I think about media and storytelling now. I have a level of comfort with discomfort and a way of seeing that allows for ambivalence. I remember when I learned what ambivalence meant. I was like, this is an interesting word. I always thought that it meant wishy-washy but it actually means two really strong feelings held at the same time that something can be yes and no powerfully at once. Later, I started thinking about it as the spectrum of color that exists between black and white. If you zoom in close enough on a photograph, that border isn't grey, it's actually every color.

When it comes to the work that I'm doing now, I have a desire for that level of complexity, for there to be space for that complexity. I had to move through phases of being more oppositional, seeing things more as stark binaries, before I grew into that desire.

> *We find each other, we lose one another, we redefine each other, we take on different forms. We disguise ourselves; as songs, as art, as animals fragmenting to cover more ground. Our thoughts fall from the sky. We move faster and faster colliding particles as we sprint through the air. We send ripples of our voices to catch someone's listening ear. The process repeats, each time different.*

Diana: It is interesting that we met when we did to do this work together. I think we both had to deal with really intense feelings and confusion of being mixed raced and somewhat of an outcast growing up. We both experienced being the "other" and walked a similar line that bordered various social worlds. No wonder when we first met it felt so familiar, so comfortable. I think when "others" find each other we no longer feel isolated, we become "another" with "others." I remember feeling that the first time I saw you talk at the AMC, about grassroots fundraising. I remember feeling that when I first walked into the Underground Publishing Conference/midwest zine fest. That feeling of not feeling alone had such a profound effect on my life.

My mission in any work I do is to use my "other" perspective as a means of shaping spaces that allow "others" to find "another." To use my struggles as a privilege that supports the growth and potential around me. I AM the person that we strive to work with, the person that we theorize about and build practices for. I vision a world that is different than the one I was forced to grow up in out of necessity, not philosophy. I vision a world that accepts the whole self as well as others, one that can hold the complexities of the emotions that flow through my body and make up who I am. It is funny when I hear people say stuff like, "wow they are magical unicorns coming up with such innovative ways of organizing" etc... When really, we are processing our struggles trying to understand why we've been handed the cards we have and how to best play them. We are carving out a place for our histories to exist in this world while simultaneously making sure none of it gets erased.

I often think about the museum complex and how museums are places where the history of creativity is stored. Outside of that space, if you don't make it in there, artists are not remembered. Processes are not archived and in time they are forgotten. I also think that DJ's are music historians. Record collections are like mini music museums. Each holding a set of emotions and memories of an era. I think records have lasted such a long time because they are tactile preservations of sound and culture. I think as humans, we have an inherent desire to be remembered and to leave a legacy behind. I think this desire comes from an internal understanding that time and life is cyclical. We leave clues that help us approach the future in ways that allow our current struggles to shift so we may find ourselves in a more joyful place.

The mission I have in the work I do at Allied Media Projects is as a Herstorian, as an archivist, as a facilitator. I strive to facilitate the preservation of stories from 'others'—those who have been marginalized, oppressed, and/or who have experienced social exclusion—to ensure they thrive and support the journey of "others" to find one another. I see the Internet as the "museum" that archives these stories. The relationships we build in the process of telling these stories allow us to heal from our struggles, gain strength and move forward with the confidence that we deserve a joyful world. Our lives are precious and our stories hold solutions for complex problems.

Slowly, surely, a pattern forms.
Slowly, surely a pattern breaks.

Jenny: There's been a lot of discussion about how, when people have the ability to radically extend their lives through technology, only the privileged will be able to afford it, and what impact that will have on the future. In so many ways, that's what's been going on already, if you think about language as a technology, or music as a technology. Look at people like Shakespeare and Beethoven—their lives were "radically extended" through the reproduction of their theater and music. Who were all the other people living at their time, who had that creativity, who had these gifts to offer, but didn't have access to the technology of language or music, and now they don't live in our memories as a result?

Diana: Right, right right! Yea, wow... so this desire to share my creative process, to share everything I've learned around making media—of course part of that is, yes, let's fix the crappy TV—but it also comes from, you never know who is going to be the "Shakespeare or Beethoven" of our time. The more you make the technologies of our time accessible, and the more diverse the pool of people who use them is, the greater the chances are—maybe it won't be just some privileged white dudes.

Jenny: It's part of the process of creating a world in which everyone can reach their full potential. But also remembering, as we often say, "together we are a genius." So much of our work is about creating structures in which genius emerges from a collective effort.

> *We dance new cells to birth changing ourselves, changing each other. The light dies throwing our newly imprinted bodies back to our shadows. The cycle begins again.*
> *The process is rigorous. It pulls at my skin and pierces my soul. I am exhausted. The languages I am forced to use are skewed from those my ancestors embedded in me. My findings are hidden and death lingers in the background.*

Diana: In reaching your full potential there are so many blocks along the way. Sometimes I sit at AMP and I'm like wow, I should never take this for granted because I've been given the opportunity to live out my full potential. I am surrounded by people who want my full potential to thrive. There are not many places I've come across this planet that care about my potential, or others for that matter.

Jenny: But then you think of all the points where you were thwarted along the way. You had all of these things happen, but they were essential parts of you becoming who you are, of you reaching your full potential...

My skin is bruising.

Diana: Yea, I think the problem with media is that it makes life seem really easy. I think people expect life to be easy and when it gets tough, they quit and move to the next thing that offers pleasure. In the process of living to your full potential you have to learn from your mistakes, understand the difference between reaction and action and take responsibility for them. Transformation is not usually pleasurable until you've come to the end and are able to articulate how you've changed, well after the struggle. You have to want to transform and I don't think it is something you can do alone. Transformation is rooted in the relationships you carry. I believe the path to reaching your full potential starts with first understanding your relationship with yourself, then your relationships with others, and finally your relationship to the world as whole.

When you're considered a monstrosity, ugly, poor, different—you hold so much complexity and such valuable perspectives of how the world works, but you don't know that unless you have something to draw it out. The bruises struggle leaves behind condition us to shut down and allow self-doubt to define us. This creates a disconnection from our self-love and the love surrounding us. This disconnection keeps us from being vulnerable and we lose the opportunity to build deep relationships with others as well as ourselves without this vulnerability. We disconnect because we are afraid of summoning the feeling of failure which then makes love a very scary emotion to project and intake. Life is definitely not easy, and loving life is just as hard.

My truths live in love and my life relies on them to thrive. I have no choice but to imagine the boxes around me as gifts. I sift through my shadows in search of the spark. I search for my future self and others who are brave enough to find the same. My fingers are numb from digging.

Jenny: I think it relates to leadership too. The moment that I felt like I had found my "others" was when I started working with Detroit Summer. I had been part of community media and activist organizations that took a more superficial, fast-paced approach to change. They were focused on "winning" and they were totally dominated by white men. Within that space, all I could do was be reactionary against the things I experienced as oppressive or problematic. I was participating in a call-out culture, which doesn't fundamentally change things. I became really drawn to women of color feminist thinking and practices (Lorde, 1995; Smith, 2000). Within some of those spaces, I sometimes found myself at the margins as well, never knowing if I was "woman of color" enough. But ultimately, what I appreciated about radical women of color organizing, more than being at "home" in my identity, was that the strategies were so much more holistic and effective.

Finding *Detroit Summer* was like coming home. But it was also scary because it wasn't like an instantaneous feeling of "oh, this is my community." It was an instantaneous feeling of "I *want* this to be my community." Then it was a process of allowing myself to feel uncertain and uncomfortable as I figured out what was my place within *Detroit Summer*, and within the city in general. Part of that was a process of understanding the privilege I carried, having grown up in the suburbs, in a middle-class family, being mixed, able-bodied, "pretty," all of those things were forms of privilege.

When I was thrust into this leadership position in *Detroit Summer* after two years and they were like, "Well, the people who grew up in the organization and have been leading it are all leaving now. You're here and you have some competencies, why don't you run this." I spent the next five years figuring out how to lead in a way that would diminish my leadership and make it unnecessary, and that would build up leadership in the youth who were at the heart of the program. There were all of these other dynamics of *Detroit Summer* having dealt with a lot of college students and they were overrunning the whole thing. So my first impulse was—I need to lead in a way that allows me to get out of the way so that youth who were born and raised in the city can run it.

But then at a certain point, that approach didn't make sense either. How can you pass on leadership that you haven't fully claimed? Coming out of the experiences of feeling marginalized within other organizing spaces I was hyper sensitive to dynamics of power and privilege. But in some ways that hyper-sensitivity only reinforced my internal self-doubting arguments about why I wasn't skilled enough, radical enough, smart enough, or whatever, to be in a leadership role. I realized I had to re-think what leadership even meant.

So then when *Detroit Summer* went through this shift of starting a collective leadership structure the question became, what does collectively held leadership look like? And that was when I started really feeling the importance of having a balance between autonomy and collectivity—not giving up your own voice in order to lift up other people's voices, but not letting your voice become a "spokesperson" voice either—not letting privilege determine whose voices are ultimately heard.

I think that comes through in the type of work we're doing here at AMP and the kind of media that we value—the thing that you always say, D, about how you need to know your own voice in order to deeply listen, and value the voices of others. We think about the role of media makers as using their visions to facilitate the visions of others. That's the kind of leadership we're trying to project.

I offer my love to you.

Jenny: D, what are some of the BIG IDEAS that guide who you are and what you do?

Diana: FUN, FUN, FUN. Seriously! "If I can't dance, I don't want to be part of your revolution" (Goldman, 2011). Change doesn't have to be an awful experience, hard maybe, but not awful. Going back to what we were saying before about how in order to reach your full potential, you have to go through these struggles to understand what you're fully made of, yes...but we don't HAVE to suffer in the process of ending suffering. I understand and feel complexities through fun and joy too. I strive to keep my childhood innocence throughout adulthood. I hope I can hold onto that for as long as possible. I deeply fear my mind becoming jaded.

I am inspired by fun and beautiful things, whether the fun and beauty is obvious or something I have to reveal. I feel like I may have brought the value of fun and beautiful things to AMP.

Jenny: Absofuckinlutely

Diana: In social justice work people are so fucking serious—and they should be, there are lives at stake. I have the desire to hold that seriousness and joy together, creating more of an accessible work environment that allows for a multitude of perspectives to work on issues, not just the serious critical perspectives—which is what I tend to run into more. I think life is meant to be joyful even in the rough parts. How can we learn from our mistakes if they trigger pain and suffering? To me, the popular education movement embodies the idea of education through play which is a guiding principle for how I approach education and organizing.

Vulnerability is another guiding principle in my life. I've learned this principle through playing cello. In my early years of playing I realized I have the ability to make people cry. At first it was weird, I thought I was hurting people, but now when I see people wipe their eyes, I realized it is a gift. I'm actually not that good at playing the cello, technically. Hell, I've been playing for twenty-three years and don't know much about music theory, but I play with my soul. It is my main piece of technology. If Shakespeare's was language...mine is the cello. The cello undresses my soul as I play. I understand now that nakedness opens a space for others to be naked, to be vulnerable and this is why others would cry...because I was crying too.

Jenny: I cried the last time I heard you play cello. It's weird, the vibrations or the sound. It touches you.

Diana: Each one of my cello strings feels attached to my heart, they are my heartstrings. As I pluck my heart strings, I pluck yours as well. When I play I try to communicate a feeling rather than entertain. Manipulating emotions, connecting strangers and revealing the unknown are all powers artist have. Artists have more responsibilities than we give them credit for. So when I step into a space to teach, facilitate, speak, or play the cello I realize that I have the power to move through and create emotion so I approach this responsibility in the most respectful way I know, through being as vulnerable and real as I can. This is my way of being transparent. I want others to trust me, trust the space I create and join me in being vulnerable. I truly believe vulnerability is a deep form of intelligence and a brilliant teaching tool.

Creativity is also a major guiding principle in my life. I do not think I would be alive right now if I did not take the time to understand my creativity. There were definitely times where my creativity made me the "other." It is bittersweet to carry the gift of creativity. Whatever the challenge in front of me I always had the ability to make anything out of nothing. I know this skill came from being "the other." I think creativity naturally emerges when you have nothing to support you. When you are trapped and have the desire to change conditions you are stuck in. Creativity is also an emergent process. It is a human survival strategy.

So yea the big ideas that guide me are—fun and beautiful things, vulnerability and creativity. OH—and "just try," which is pretty self explanatory....JUST TRY!

Jenny: What about the AMP principles? (http://alliedmedia.org/#!/amp-network-principles)

Diana: I've learned those though...for instance I don't think I would have assumed that there are people already working on problems that are significant to me, because I didn't grow up around that.

Jenny: But it's interesting with that one...even if people aren't working on problems in productive ways, they're still working on them. If the problem is depression because there are no jobs, and the way people deal with that is by being addicted to drugs, you still need to understand that as a reality of how people are "acting on a problem in some fashion." Because if you didn't and you just brought in a "solution" that would create more jobs but not deal with the fact that people were addicted to drugs as a result of the economy being so shitty, then that solution would fail in the longrun. So just understanding what people are doing around these problems first, even if they're not healthy things, is important.

Diana: I can't say that I felt the AMP principles throughout my whole life... like "I presume my power and not my powerlessness."

Jenny: I was actually thinking about that one when you were talking about laughter and fun. Because in a sense when you're dealing with the shittiest possible reality and your choice is to laugh in the face of it, that's totally a form of presuming your power. It may be the only form of power you have in that instance is to choose if you're gonna be defeated by it or choose your own response.

Diana: It's true, I mean, now that I think about the AMP principles within my whole story, I think they were present in clandestine ways, just never articulated. Four years later to this day, I read them and feel fulfilled. The timelessness of these principles amazes me. So yea, I am most certainly guided by the big ideas of the Allied Media Projects Network Principles.

Do as you will, be who you are, take care of what you need.
We will work to regain our ground.

Diana: What about you? What are the big ideas that guide you in your work/life?

Jenny: I'm kind of fixated on the AMP Principles lately. The one that I was thinking about the most was "we begin by listening." I feel like for a lot of my life—I mean, I've gone through different phases—but a lot of my life has been as a "quiet person," kind of slipping in and out of situations and having to deeply read them and understand them first before saying anything or acting in any way. That comes out of a fear of my own voice at times or a fear of not doing the right thing. But it instilled in me this default to listening. A big part of the process of figuring out my role in *Detroit Summer* was about listening too. My role was to provide a lot of support to people, especially young people who were processing so much. All they really needed was someone to listen to their process unfolding, but to have it be real listening, where they would know that their story wasn't being judged, and was making sense to someone.

The skillset I built in that process carried over into my approach to making media and my belief in media as a transformative tool. The power in making our own media is so often framed as a power in the act of speaking. But then there's this whole other side of it, which is the power in the act of listening. And being able to really understand the world through people's various forms of communication.

That continues to guide the work that I do. Even just in terms of what makes for effective organizing. A lot of organizing "begins by talking." It assumes that if we give people the right analysis about the oppression they've experienced, then that will be transformative. Most people know when someone is listening with the goal of making your story support their analysis, and when someone genuinely cares about the complexities of your story. In my experience, when you begin by authentically listening, you build trust. Especially for people who are traumatized by a lifetime of not being heard. Oppression fuels a culture of bullhorns, where we have to inflict our voice on others. When you can arrive at a place where you actually are heard and you can just speak in a normal voice, then you can start listening to other voices. You never want to let go of that. That's so much a part of the relationship-building we do.

And it's really about what kinds of relationships we need in order to fundamentally transform the world. What you said about vulnerability is totally true. I think relationships rooted in deep listening would be another component of it.

Diana: Imagine if people regularly cried in public with each other, how different the world would be.

Jenny: Everyone is basically walking around with the desire to cry at any given moment, and it's taking so much strength to hold that in.

Diana: I think that's what oppression is, right? Not having the ability to fully feel yourself and being forced to be someone who you're not. Humans embody complex systems. We are complex life forms. When you take away the tools and practices of self-expression, violence happens.

Jenny: You forget that you're human and then you treat other people like they're not human.

Diana: YES! I'm gonna start tagging "safe crying zone" around the city.

Jenny: "Just Cry."

Diana: HAHA, "Just Cry" and then "Just Try."

> *I will work knowing that you work with me. That we work together. I will know that in working towards something incredible my part is as crucial as yours.*

Jenny: So the other "BIG IDEA" for me, is Love as a Political Concept.

Diana: Yes, I was hoping this would come up!

Jenny: This concept has guided my work since I watched Michael Hardt talk about it on YouTube (2007) and realized the extent to which relationships that are rooted in love have been the sites of transformation for me. It's in the act of loving someone so deeply that I've fundamentally changed as a person over and over again. So when we think about these new kinds of relationships that we need to undergird a new society or a better world, a more just, creative, collaborative world—it's like we don't know what those relationships look like other than what we experience. And of course when we think about our relationships with our families and to the extent that those model shitty examples or just brokenness, then it becomes all the more important that we become active in building the relationships that we want.

Just looking at the way patterns of love play out generationally and in the world. Perpetuated in many ways by our family stories but also by the cultural stories we consume through media. They create patterns of love that limit the field of what we're even capable of imagining in terms of relationships—intimate relationships—but then that in turn ends up informing what we're capable of imagining in terms of political relationships. If we never learned how to deeply trust, or listen or be vulnerable within our families, then we never learn how to do that in our romantic relationships or our friendships, and then how could we ever do that within the culture, or our political relationships?

So thinking about love as this starting point for how we relate to ourselves and our histories next to each other, and then next to the world as a whole as a political entity. It's so important...but it also makes it feel so good when we feel like we're breaking patterns. It lets you look at a beautiful relationship, not just for what it is, but as a little opening into what is possible.

> *We harvest the emotions from our shadows and teach them how to be dreams. We blink and a flame catches. A bright burst swallows the sky and light is allowing us to find each other once again.*

Diana: Love is not insular to that relationship or confined within a specific box, it is a ripple effect. The act of genuinely loving has the ability to change the way the world works. Which is probably why so many people within our community and generation are rejecting the marriage complex and looking for alternative ways of having relationships. We are looking for ways to genuinely love each other that allows for the ripple to flow.

To be vulnerable and trustworthy within love requires deconditioning as you mentioned. When loving, you are at a risk of falling into the patterns of how love was handed to you. Confronting these patterns of destruction is a type of commitment—when you commit to loving in that way, you commit to yourself not just to someone else. You are committing to practicing love in a way that's sincere and powerful.

Diana: Jenny, I love you.

Jenny: D, I love you too.

May life never stop us from asking of it.

Conclusion

The AMP Network Principles came up a lot for me in the course of this conversation, which makes sense, because they come up a lot in everyday life. Even though we wrote these principles in 2009, they grew from the previous 10 years of listening and learning through the Allied Media Conference. Like, Diana's poem, they are also a "living document," a set of ideas that people were embodying through their lives and work, which we crystallized into a set of words. They take on more and more of a "life" each year at the Allied Media Conference, and through our local programs, Detroit Future Media and Detroit Future Schools, as we continually ask ourselves what these principles look like in practice.

We return to them for guidance when faced with hard organizational questions, like, "What does 'scaling up" mean to us? How will we sustain the work? And what is our role in our local political "ecosystem?" But they've proven just as helpful for me, and I think a lot of other people too, as guidance for personal questions like, "How do you break up with someone and still work with them?" and "What's the point of self-care?" "What are all the possible shapes that 'family' can take?" and "How do I nurture my own creativity while nurturing it in others?" We've learned that there's a fractal relationship between the personal, the organizational and the social. The principles are part of the equation that holds the pattern together.

—Jenny Lee

The Allied Media Project's Network Principles

We are making an honest attempt to solve the most significant problems of our day.

We are building a network of people and organizations that are developing long-term solutions based on the immediate confrontation of our most pressing problems.

Wherever there is a problem, there are already people acting on the problem in some fashion. Understanding those actions is the starting point for developing effective strategies to resolve the problem, so we focus on the solutions, not the problems.

We emphasize our own power and legitimacy.

We presume our power, not our powerlessness.

We spend more time building than attacking.

We focus on strategies rather than issues.

The strongest solutions happen through the process, not in a moment at the end of the process.

The most effective strategies for us are the ones that work in situations of scarce resources and intersecting systems of oppression because those solutions tend to be the most holistic and sustainable.

Place is important. For the AMC, Detroit is important as a source of innovative, collaborative, low-resource solutions. Detroit gives the conference a sense of place, just as each of the conference participants brings their own sense of place with them to the conference.

We encourage people to engage with their whole selves, not just with one part of their identity.

We begin by listening.

The Living Document: By Diana J Nucera

I have come to learn that life is best spent allowing life to thrive around me. My heart has learned to foster love and let it go, so new life can spring from it. My brain has learned to carry every piece of myself along the way, leaving trails of bits that didn't quite work in my wake (in case I forget my path). My soul has learned to move fearlessly with excitement and to understand the possibilities of existence.

And now I stand in front of you with only my findings to cover my scars.

We find each other, we lose one another, we redefine each other, we take on different forms. We disguise ourselves; as songs, as art, as animals fragmenting to cover more ground. Our thoughts fall from the sky. We move faster and faster colliding particles as we sprint through the air sending. We send ripples of our voices to catch someone's listening ear. The process repeats, each time different.

Slowly, surely, a pattern forms.
Slowly, surely a pattern breaks.

We dance new cells to birth changing ourselves, changing each other. The light dies throwing our newly imprinted bodies back to our shadows. The cycle begins again.

The process is rigorous. It pulls at my skin and pierces my soul. I am exhausted. The languages I am forced to use are skewed from those my ancestors embedded in me. My findings are hidden and death lingers in the background.

My skin is bruising.

My truths live in love and my life relies on them to thrive. I have no choice but to imagine the boxes around me as gifts. I sift through my shadows in search of the spark. I search for my future self and others who are brave enough to find the same. My fingers are numb from digging.

I offer my love to you.

Do as you will, be who you are, take care of what you need. We will work to regain our ground.

I will work knowing that you work with me. That we work together. I will know that in working towards something incredible my part is as crucial as yours.

We harvest the emotions from our shadows and teach them how to be dreams. We blink and a flame catches. A bright burst swallows the sky and light is allowing us to find each other once again.

May life never stop us from asking of it.

References

Allied Media Project Network Principles (2013). Retrieved on June 24, 2013 from http://alliedmedia.org/#!/amp-network-principles

Goldman, E. (1931). *Living my life*. Alfred Knopf: New York.

Hardt, M. (2007). *About love*. Retrieved on June 24, 2013 from http://www.youtube.com/watch?v=ioopkoppabI&list=PL4ADA3C3A5F727C98.

Lorde, A. (1995). Age, race, class, and sex: Women redefining difference. In B. Guy-Sheftall (Ed.), *Words of fire: An anthology of African-American feminist thought*. New York: The New Press.

Smith, B. (Ed.) (2000). *Home girls: A Black feminist anthology*: New Brunswick, NJ: Rutgers University Press.

Zinn, H. (2005). *A people's history of the United States: 1492 to present*. New York: Harper Perennial Modern Classics.

Part 3: Methodologies

Chapter 6

You Want to Do What with Doda's Stories? Building a Community for the Skins Workshops on Aboriginal Storytelling in Digital Media

Jason Edward Lewis and Skawennati Fragnito

Who We Are and How We Came to Be

Aboriginal Territories in Cyberspace (AbTeC) is a research network of artists, academics and technologists centrally concerned with Indigenous representation in, and production of, digital media (AbTeC, 2008). AbTeC investigates and identifies ways for Indigenous peoples to tell our stories via networked technologies, and in so doing, strengthen our communities while proactively participating in shaping cyberspace. We are based at Concordia University, in Montreal, Quebec.

We had been thinking, talking and making artwork about Aboriginal representation in webpages, virtual environments and software for years when, in 2004, the Social Science and Humanities Research Council (SSHRC) offered a new grant program focused on creating and supporting Aboriginal research networks (SSHRC, 2011). This program was unique in several ways that were key to AbTeC's launch. First, it provided a concrete framework within which to articulate the conversations we had been having with colleagues within both the academy and the Aboriginal arts community regarding the lack of Indigenous characters and stories in popular media in general and in cyberspace in particular. We had been engaging a wide range of people on this topic, with the seminal conversation taking place in 2003 at the Skinning Our Tools symposium (Banff Centre for the Arts, 2003) with Celia Pearce, a "Serious Games" designer, researcher and teacher (Pearce, 2009; Pearce, Fullerton, Fron & Morie, 2005). After seeing Skawennati give a presentation about "Aboriginalizing" a commercial chat space (Fragnito, 1997), Celia, who had spoken about "modding," or customizing, video games (Pearce, 2002), asked her: "How would you like to see some Aboriginal characters in video games?" Skawennati and Celia's subsequent dialogue oriented us toward considering video games as a potential medium through which we could address some of our concerns about representation and participation.

Second, the new SSHRC program was the first federal grant available to us that allowed us to list community members as co-investigators. Not only did this recognize the integral role played by those community members in conducting the research, it also meant that Skawennati's central role in the project could be formalized within the university context and she could be compensated for the time she spent on it.

And so AbTeC grew, as we gathered Native and non-Native North American Serious Game advocates, games studies academics and game designers as well as artists with practices in New Media, activism, education and/or storytelling. If you were interested in exploring issues surrounding Indians in cyberspace, we were interested in you.

The Skins workshops took shape during two AbTeC Network Meetings, the first held in November of 2006 and the second in November of 2007. The first meeting brought together the research network in order to hold a wide-ranging discussion about how to identify, encourage and support Aboriginal new media creators. We came out of that meeting with a rough consensus on several strategies, one of which formed the seed of the Skins concept. We had concluded that the most effective means for strengthening the Aboriginal presence in cyberspace was to train and mentor young digital media creators within a context that emphasizes the value and richness of stories from their community (Dillon, 2006a). Our hope was that, in a learning environment, such an emphasis would encourage participants to look to those stories as inspiration for the work they would create. This would meet two of our goals simultaneously: promoting more Aboriginal creators working in cyberspace, and promoting more Aboriginal content in the domain.

The second AbTeC Network Meeting was focused on developing a plan for executing that strategy. To that end, we ran a mock game design workshop with the attendees. Our goal was to test the curriculum we had developed in the year between meetings, as well as to shake out issues of timing, resources and personnel. We then used the results of that trial run to rewrite the curriculum and prepare to introduce it into the classroom the following fall, in September 2008, as the Skins Workshop on Aboriginal Storytelling and Video Game Design (AbTeC, 2010).

The Skins strategy would be to target young people, engage them in a context that valued their communities' cultural heritage, and motivate them by working in a medium they know well as consumers. We envisioned a video game workshop for youth preceded by a Storytelling Series in which traditional stories, myths, legends and histories would be relayed by elders in public presentations. The youth would pick a story and, with the Elders' guidance, would transmediate it into a video game. It sounded so elegant, logical and simple. As it turned out, we were right on two out of three counts.

Challenge One: Grand Theft Rez?

Our first major challenge arose early in the process, during the first AbTeC Network Meeting. Many of our members were researching and designing Serious Games as well as other socially responsible alternatives to the popular shoot-em-ups that dominate the popular imaginary (Isbister, 2009). We had brought the members together to brainstorm a curriculum. First we needed to decide what kind of game we planned to assist the participants in making. Would it be 2D or 3D? A platformer or a role-playing game? On a console, or on the web, or on the desktop? And then came the question: "What if they want to make the Native version of Grand Theft Auto?" one AbTeC researcher asked, citing the violent open-world action-adventure/driving franchise (Grand Theft Auto, 1997–2011). We all realized that we had assumed that these youth, none of whom we had yet met, would want to make a happy, peaceful, culturally meaningful game, ideally one that taught a lesson about colonization or oppression. A long discussion ensued, one that included a series of jokes about Indians and the broken-down cars one often finds on the reservation. The car from *Smoke Signals* (Eyre, 1998) that only drives in reverse was referenced as a canonical image that would fit perfectly into such a scenario. We even gave our imaginary game a title: "Grand Theft Rez." The term neatly encapsulated a core thread of our conversations about descriptive vs. aspirational representations of culture, and how to balance the one against the other.

The AbTeC research team brought a huge diversity of intellectual, social and aesthetic agendas to the conversation. Given the cultural politics of the project, it was no surprise that a substantial portion of those involved felt very strongly that we should steer the curriculum—and the participants—away from game genres that tended towards violence as well as gender- and race-stereotypical character design. In short, they had concerns about engaging in a process that might end up producing Grand Theft Rez. Such a game would run counter to the focus they had in their own work on promoting the production of video games that embodied arguments for positive social change. Many had joined AbTeC precisely because of our interest in effecting positive change within the Aboriginal community, and providing avenues for the representation of non-mainstream cultures within the video game medium. They questioned how effective such attempts at change would be if the outcome was Grand Theft Rez.

We addressed this challenge by reiterating our belief that the best way to effect long-lasting change was to teach the participants the methods and tools for creating whatever it is that they wished to create, and that the best way to engage the participants in this effort was to do it within the context of a medium and genres that they loved. It would be counter-productive—not to mention deeply patronizing—to say to them, "Well, you shouldn't love those kinds of games; you should love these kinds of games. We're only going to help you if you like the right kind of games."

A related concern of many on the AbTeC team—which we realized was a derivative of the Grand Theft Rez problem—was related to team members' interest in creating a game that was in some way innovative. Different AbTeCers were interested in different sites of innovation: narrative, gameplay, aesthetics, characterization, etc. Many of their academic or creative practices were based on experimenting with one or more of these aspects. Often, they held a critical outlook that considered the game industry's conservative tendencies as discouraging of much-needed experimentation (Isbister, 2006; Pearce et al., 2008; Dillon, 2007). Their normal response was to actively work to counter that status quo, by producing or helping produce games that broke industry conventions in one way or another.

When, later, we actually started working with Skins participants, however, we found they were very much interested in creating video games along the lines of those that they played. These were games such as Halo (2001–2011), Call of Duty (2003–2011), and The Legend of Zelda (1986–2011), all of which faithfully recapitulate the conventions of their genre (first-person shooter, platform adventure, fantasy-adventure, etc.) The participants loved these games, and were not interested in embarking on a quest to find new structures and new approaches. They wanted games "just like we play on the Xbox" (Williams, 2011), but which told their stories.

Over the years of the project, our use of Grand Theft Rez expanded to become shorthand for the variety of cultural, conceptual and aesthetic contradictions we faced in the project. We wanted to entice youth to participate by using video games…but many of the video games popular with our target ages of sixteen to twenty-five are incredibly violent and misogynistic (Dillon, 2010b). We wanted the youth to work from within a framework of sensitivity to and pride in their culture…but video games, like many forms of popular entertainment, rely heavily on cultural stereotyping (Dillon, 2004; Dillon, 2006; Langer, 2008). We wanted to use stories that are important to the community while remaining respectful…but popular media—such as video games—tend towards an irreverent attitude towards original source material (Dillon, 2008). The AbTeC research team members were committed to creating games that pushed on the norms and conventions of the games industry…but the participants were overwhelmingly interested in games that fully embraced them.

The Grand Theft Rez conceit focused our planning on the fact that the participants themselves were our concern, not the game. As we wrote the curriculum and conducted the workshops, Grand Theft Rez reminded us to work where the students were already, rather than force them to come to us; to concentrate on giving them the skills to make the games they love; and to familiarize them with what it takes to make a career in the games industry. And we needed to do so even when it might rub against the intellectual or social agendas of research team members.

Interlude: The Mechanics

While we were developing the Skins workshops, we were often frustrated by how descriptions of projects that contained similar components left out most of the nitty gritty (Parker & Becker, 2005; Parker & Becker, 2006; Wyeld, Leavy, Carroll, Gibbons, Ledwich & Hills, 2007). Papers about these projects tended to be useful for understanding the goals of the project, the outcomes and an idealized structure for how to connect the two. We found details about how projects grew, what resources they required, and how they changed over time to be sparse.

Yet, it was precisely such detail we needed in order to build our own project. We do not want this chapter to leave the reader with similar questions; to that end we will provide here the sort of details we think would be useful to other people who are interested in not only in understanding such projects but also in building something similar. As of the time of this writing, we have held three major Skins workshops. Each workshop used the same curriculum, but were structured quite differently. First we will describe the curriculum, and then discuss the evolution of the structure. This section will necessarily be brief; please see AbTeC's previous publications (Dillon & Lewis, 2011) for a much more in-depth discussion of the curriculum.

Curriculum

We began Skins 1.0 with the draft curriculum we wrote and revised during, in-between, and after the two AbTeC Network Meetings. The curriculum was designed to encourage participants to be creators of media—not just consumers of it—and to empower them with the skills to tell their own stories, and better inform the stories told by others. We divided the curriculum into four sections: Storytelling, Play, Design and Production.

Like many video-game-creation workshops, our curriculum included lessons in storyboarding, sketching, paper and physical prototyping, game design, level design, 3D modeling, animation, and sound design (Figure 1).

Figure 1. Skins Workshop 1.0 participants, instructors and mentors creating physical prototype of game level.

What makes Skins unique is the central role given to Aboriginal storytelling. The Storytelling component focuses on how stories are told in Aboriginal communities as well as on the stories themselves. We discussed what that actually was, and we showed examples of how Aboriginal people have been represented in stories—negative and positive, stereotypical and individual, and authored by Native and non-Native creators. We explained how and why some choices are made and we told many stories ourselves, especially traditional legends and myths.

We wanted participants to be immersed in stories at the same time they were being asked to think about structure, meaning and performance. We used this component to begin conversations with the students about what sorts of stories they would like to see made into video games. Those ideas became the basis for brainstorming sessions aimed at defining a story that they would develop into a game. The final portion of this component was to then write a game treatment, outlining the basic concept, the narrative, and important design and gameplay elements.

The Play component set aside time throughout the workshop for participants to explore existing video games, board games, etc., together. These activities provided us with material for discussions about how games are structured, and how to think about and imagine new kinds of gameplay. We also included screenings of movies made by Native creators that served to enrich our Storytelling conversations about Aboriginal story approach and structure.

The Design component focuses on how to move from the game treatment to the actual design of the game. This component included lessons in game-specific script writing and storyboarding, character design, level design, audio design and exercises in sketching and paper prototyping.

The Technical component focuses on realizing the design. This component included lessons in 3D modeling and animating, image processing for texture creation, character and level building, programming the game engine, and audio processing.

We prioritized software that was free—or had a free version—wherever possible. Building the curriculum around such software enabled participants to continue with game creation and skill-building at home and after the workshop concluded. This meant using the Unreal Development Kit (Epic Games, 2009) for Skins 1.0 and Unity game engine (Unity Technologies, 2011) for Skins 2.0 and 3.0 for building the game environment, Blender for modelling and animation (Roosendaal, 2002), and Audacity for audio processing (Mazzoni & Dannenberg, 2011). A major exception to this approach was our use of Adobe Photoshop (Adobe Systems, 2012) and Adobe After Effects (Adobe Systems, 2012) for image and cut-scene processing, as these are standard tools used across the creative industries which have no suitably powerful free analogues.

Structure

All of the major workshops drew participants from Kahnawake, who ranged in age from 16 to 44 (with a median age of 20.) The three workshops varied in terms of schedule, sequencing and location.

We held Skins 1.0 at the Survival School, the Kahnawake high school, over 9 months, from September 2008 to June 2009 (Lewis & Fragnito, 2011). We were invited by Owisokon Lahache, an arts and culture teacher, to integrate the curriculum into her arts class. We met with the class two hours every ten days, and held one two-day intensive every month. The intensives were made possible by the fact that Survival School schedules one pedagogical Friday every month, allowing us to use that Friday and the next Saturday for all-day sessions. We were with the students approximately 198 hours, and taught the curriculum sequentially. They created the prototype Otsi:! Rise of the Kanien'keha:ka Legends. (2009). For Skins 2.0: Skins Summer Institute, we moved our location to Concordia University (Figure 2). We made the move in the hope that working there would familiarize the participants with the university setting, demystifying it and make enrolling seem more possible. We also wanted to simplify management of people, space and technology by holding it in our space.

The 2.0 workshop was conducted over fourteen days in July, 2011 (Lewis & Fragnito, 2012c). The compressed schedule meant that we had 112 hours of classroom time with the students and the three curriculum components were taught in parallel. In that time, the participants produced another prototype, this one called The Adventures of Skahion:hati: The Legend of the Stone Giant (2011).

Skins 3.0: Extended Play was also held at Concordia. From March through August, 2012, we ran bi-weekly four-hour classes as well as two one-week all-day intensive sessions. 3.0 focused on production, and we were again with the students for 112 hours. As the workshop focused on production, we were able integrate characters and events from Skins 1.0 and Skins

2.0 as well as create additional content to finish a fully playable game: Skahiòn:hati—Rise of the Kanien'kehá:ka Legends (2012). See Figure 3 for screenshot from this game. The structure of the workshops evolved in an attempt to find a schedule that worked well with staff and participants' work and family obligations. In Skins 1.0, the integration of the curriculum into Owisokon's regular course syllabus meant that we were guaranteed an attendance of between ten and fourteen students in those sessions, and the monthly two-day intensives provided a regular, focused block of time to cover much ground. However, her class was on a ten-day schedule, meaning that the day of the week it occurred varied from meeting to meeting. This made for a serious staffing challenge for us. Our research assistants all studied on a regular 5-day schedule, and sacrificing a Saturday every month was difficult domestically for us personally as a couple with young children.

We addressed these issues in Skins 2.0 by moving to a fourteen-day intensive schedule in mid-summer. This schedule made things considerably easier for our research assistants, as they were not enrolled in classes during the summer, and for our domestic life, as it allowed us to have a relative stay with and provide childcare for the duration. This schedule was quite productive, as we were able to move the participants through the entire curriculum and into production within the time period.

However, fourteen days straight was too intense. Going eight hours a day, seven days a week burned everybody out, and still caused problems on everybody's domestic front as staff and participants saw very little of their children, spouses and friends during the workshop.

For the third iteration, we split the difference between 1.0 and 2.0. We began the workshop in late March, meeting with the participants every other week for 4 hours, supplemented with a one-week intensive in May and another intensive in July to finish the workshop. Another big change we implemented after 2.0 was deciding to continue working with the same group of students, rather than bring in a new cohort. We felt this was the best way to focus on production and reach the goal of finishing a truly playable game (the 1.0 and 2.0 games were more prototypes than finished experiences).

The time spent in Skins 2.0 and in Skins 3.0 turned out to be about the same as Skins 1.0: 224 hours vs. 198 hours. We would like to claim that neat near-correspondence as part of the master plan, but we decided to conduct 3.0 with the 2.0 group only several months before the start of the last workshop. The 3.0 schedule turned out to be a great schedule for balancing peoples' availabilities and energy levels.

The bi-weekly sessions kept production moving along while providing time for participants and staff to develop the game in-between sessions. The intensive sessions focused everybody's attention for a week, and resulted in substantial progress each time.

Figure 2. Skins Workshop 2.0 recruitment poster depicting Flying Head, Village and Hunter assets from Skins 1.0 game.

Figure 3. Screenshot from Skins 3.0 game: Skahiòn:hati—Rise of the Kanien'kehá:ka Legends, showing the protagonist being pursued by a Stone Giant.

Resources

The Skins workshops required significant resources. We obtained multiple rounds of support from both federal (Social Sciences and Humanities Research Council: two grants totaling $660,000) and provincial (Fonds de recherche sur la société et la culture: one grant totaling $149,000) academic funding bodies, as well as a significant matching grant ($100,000) from Concordia University.

Up-to-date physical facilities were key to conducting such a technology-heavy workshop. For Skins 1.0, we were fortunate that Kahnawake Survival School had just moved into a brand new facility, including a state-of-the-art teaching computer lab. For Skins 2.0 and 3.0, Jason's Fine Arts faculty provided us with computer labs and lecture rooms (Concordia University, 2012a), while the Hexagram Research Institute (Concordia University, 2012b), in which his studio is located, provided us with all the audio/visual equipment we needed. All of these resources were provided free of charge.

We deployed a considerable amount of skilled human resources. We employed three to four research assistants ten to twenty hours per week year-round to work on the curriculum and develop the workshops. Their hours would expand to full-time and their numbers to seven to ten several months prior to, during and one month after each workshop. These students would create teaching material for the curriculum and teach sections of the workshop itself (Lewis & Fragnito, 2012b). The fact that Jason's program, Computation Arts (Concordia University, 2012c), operates across the full range of digital media production expertise required—from concept development to design to implementation—was key in our ability to properly staff the workshop.

We also brought in two to three established Aboriginal artists and designers as mentors. They would lead some of the instruction as well as serve as models for the students for what it meant to be a successful artist within the community (Lewis & Fragnito, 2012a). Additionally, we invited industry guests to attend select workshop sessions. They would give presentations about their role in the video game industry (art director, producer, lead programmer, etc.) and talk about their professional development (Lewis & Fragnito, 2012d). Finally, we had an assessment and documentation team that consisted of one camera operator/editor, two participant-observers and an additional person who helped formulate the assessment plan and questions.

Challenge Two: Anybody Wanna Dance?

From the beginning of Skins, we felt these workshops could be interesting to many different Native communities, from rural reserves to urban Friendship Centres. But we needed a place to start. The obvious choice was Skawennati's home community, Kahnawake, located across the St. Laurence river from Montreal.

Understanding the challenges we faced in finding a community partner requires a bit of context on Skawennati's relationship to the community. Skawennati was born in Kahnawake and lived there for the first three years of her life. Her mother is "full-blooded" Mohawk while her father is non-Native. Many readers may recall that the Indian Act (1876), before it was amended, caused Native women who married non-Native men to lose their Native status. The children of these unions were also refused recognition as Indians. Meanwhile, non-Native women who married Native men gained Indian status, and their children did inherit status. In 1984, Bill C-31 attempted to rectify this sexual discrimination (Indian Act, 1985). However, Kahnawake was one of just two reserves that chose to not restore band membership to their women or the children of those women. Skawennati thus grew up knowing that she was Mohawk and having close relationships with her Mohawk family on the reserve, yet she did not participate in daily reserve life. This history resulted in her always having a slight feeling of being unwanted by the community. When we started looking for collaborators in Kahnawake, these feelings affected her confidence in seeking out potential partners. Looking back on this time, she realizes that she was fearful of further rejection and this slowed her efforts considerably.

Complicating our efforts was the contentious history of academic engagement with Aboriginal communities, where Aboriginal people are often treated more as research objects than as human beings, and where the research is done primarily to benefit the academics involved rather than the community. As Linda Tuhiwai Smith observes, "[I]ndigenous peoples are deeply cynical about the capacity, motives or methodologies of Western research to deliver any benefits to indigenous peoples whom science has long regarded, indeed has classified, as being 'not human" (1999, p. 118). Often community members see such projects as more helpful to the project creator than to the group they are aiming to help. One potential collaborator told us, 'We get called all the time, by the universities or some research institute, wanting us to get involved in one study or another." As well, they find that when they do allow researchers on reserve, the researchers often need help themselves—information, education, direction (and directions!). Then, when the project is over, the researchers leave, often never to be seen again. If the community is lucky, it gets a copy of the paper (Wilson, 2004; Little Bear, 2000).

Once we focused on Kahnawake, we knew we would be looking towards traditional Iroquois stories for inspiration. This led Skawennati to what she thought would be the perfect institutional partner: the Kanien'kehá:ka Onkwawén:na Raotitióhkwa Language and Cultural Center (2012). Established in 1978, the Cultural Centre's mandate is to preserve and enrich the language and culture of the Kanien'kehá:ka (Mohawk) of Kahnawà:ke.

Skawennati had worked with the Cultural Centre years earlier, as a member of Nation to Nation, a First Nations artist collective which did a series of exhibitions at the centre. She felt she knew the institution and that they knew her. Even though they had changed directors since the Nation to

Nation events, she expected to find like-minded individuals there who would be interested in a project that would preserve and promote Kahnawake stories. Additionally, Skawennati felt confident that AbTeC had much to offer to the Centre: instructors, research assistants, other human resources, equipment and a fully-funded budget. We were interested in collaborating on curriculum development, and were flexible about location as we had excellent facilities at Concordia but were eager to travel if they wanted the workshops held on-reserve. We thought they would be well-positioned to identify community members—elders, storytellers and participants—who would be suitable for the project.

It took some time to arrange a meeting with the Centre's Director and the Public Programs Supervisor. When it finally did take place, we experienced an unexpected major obstacle: the Director had never seen a video game. She had no context in terms of the medium for evaluating our proposal. Thus we spent much of our time trying to illustrate to her what video games were, how they could be used in cultural projects, and what kind of games we were interested in seeing produced.

The Public Programs Supervisor, on the other hand, had some experience with video games and seemed quite enthusiastic. We believe that his enthusiasm, plus our own sincerity and certainty that we would make a great fit, eventually led the Centre to agree to partner with us. We were elated.

However, the letter of support (required for the first grant for which we were applying) they wrote was terse and provisional. It read "I am pleased to inform you that our organization would like to express an interest in exploring this proposed project titled 'Skins' with you. Please note that in no way does this letter reflect any legal or binding commitments of our organization to your project."

The letter was not a ringing endorsement of the project, but it was an expression of support. We submitted the grant application. Fortunately, we were awarded funding.

Unfortunately, shortly after we contacted the Cultural Centre to deliver the good news, we received a letter from them stating that they did not wish to partner with us after all. No reason was given and Skawennati, her fear of rejection realized, was too stricken to dig more deeply into their change of heart.

Back to square one we went, following up on other leads. Kahnawake had just a few years earlier opened up a library, and Skawennati was acquainted with its director (Kahnawake Library, 2012). The two had taken a Mohawk language class together in the early nineties and had run into each other over the years. The director was an artist herself, and Skawennati thought she would find interesting the idea of the library supporting a video game workshop within the context of a storytelling series. The director loved the idea, saying that the Library had been looking for something just like it.

Again, we were elated. And again, shortly thereafter, we were left bewildered and disappointed. The director had taken the proposal to her board, and the board had refused to collaborate. They offered us the use of the library's space, which was kind, but they were not interested in actively working with us on the workshop or on finding elders for the storytelling series. As the space they had available was quite small, we did not see how such an arrangement would substantially benefit the project. We began our search anew.

In June 2008, with only one year of the SSHRC funds remaining, we finally had a little luck come our way. Skawennati's cousin, an elementary school teacher, organizes the annual science fair at her school every spring and asked Jason to be the judge. He accepted, and we attended a celebration dinner afterwards. We happened to sit with another cousin, Owisokon Lahache, the teacher at Kahnawake Survival School introduced in the workshop description above. In casual conversation we told her about the Skins concept as well as our difficulties in finding a partner on the reserve. Owisokon's reply was welcome and straightforward: "I'd like to do that with my class! Come and meet with the guidance counselor and we'll see if this is possible."

During that meeting the counselor and Owisokon asked all the right questions: Who is your audience? What do you want to teach them? What resources are you providing? They understood the concept, appreciated its educational potential, and liked our answers. Owisokon was vocal in her enthusiasm for the vision we presented, and made it clear that she was very interested in acting as our liaison and host at the school. By October, we were in her Survival School classroom. Owisokon has since become a full collaborator on the project, acting as co-investigator on further funding applications and playing a central role in all of the Skins workshops.

The success of Skins 1.0 helped us considerably when we went looking for additional funding and partners. Kahnawà:ke Ionterihwaienstáhkwa Ronaterihwahtentià:ton, or the Kahnawake Education Center (2012), which oversees the high school, was receptive. We had several productive meetings with Kahnawake Education Center (KEC) staff, and the Director in particular was enthusiastic about how the Skins workshops could be extended to engage reserve youth other than high school students. She agreed to become a formal partner and provide assistance in recruiting students for the workshops. She even assigned us an official liaison. They wrote a great letter of support for the grant applications. Again, we were fortunate and were awarded funding. We started working with Owisokon on the next workshop. But....

Six months later, our liaison, with whom we had developed a great relationship, left KEC and was not replaced. Shortly thereafter, the Director became embroiled in reserve politics and was fired for unexplained reasons. An interim Director has been appointed. We remain hopeful that our partnership with KEC will continue despite this, but, as of this writing, we have not had meaningful conversations with them in almost a year.

Finding a partner took several years, and several disappointments. At the time, the process was frustrating. But it was also productive, as talking to people and organizations about the Skins project helped both of us develop relationships in Kahnawake. The process helped Skawennati gain confidence about her place within the community—she was often asked who she was, and grew accustomed to naming her mother, grandparents and other relatives as a means of firmly locating herself within the cultural geography and history of the reserve. It gave us time to repeat and reinforce the fact that we were doing the project in no small part because of our dreams of the world we want our own (Mohawk-Cherokee) children to inherit.

Finally, we believe no substitute exists for pure perseverance. As we have written elsewhere (Lewis, 2012):

> We were clear about how we would use the outcomes to advance our research projects. We participated at multiple levels in the community, from attending the annual pow wow to volunteering as judges for the district science fair. We spoke often about the multiyear nature of our funding, as well as how we were setting in place mechanisms, personnel, and financing to work with community members at the high school and university levels and were developing ideas to find ways for those students to bring their technical skills back to the reserve. In short, we showed in multiple ways that our commitment to the project, and to the community, was not just professional but also personal, and not just opportunistic but essential to who we were and wanted to be.

Challenge Three: You Wanna Do What with Doda's Stories?

> We've been translating the stories, the native traditional stories into a video game in order to intrigue the youngsters to remember the stories, and it keeps the story alive. If interaction will do that, then that's the avenue we need to take. (Towana Miller, Skins 2.0 and Skins 3.0 participant)

> Our community needs to know that our young people learn different today, our young people do things differently with the digital—we are in the digital age. And we need to create our own things. (Owisokon Lahache, Lewis & Fragnito, 2012c)

> There's a story I know. It's about the earth and how it floats in space on the back of a turtle. I've heard this story many times, and each time somebody tells the story, it changes. Sometimes the change is simply in the voice of the storyteller. Sometimes the change is in the details. Sometimes in the order of events. Other times It's in the dialogue or the response of the audience. But in all of the telling, of all the tellers, the world never leaves the turtle's back and the turtle never swims away. (Thomas King)

We are interested in the ways in which the stories central to Aboriginal communities can be passed down to the next generation using new modes of storytelling. These stories form the spine around which our communities maintain their identity, yet many communities report difficulties in getting youth to pay attention to them (Archibald, 2008). This grounds our motivation for bringing the stories into focus for the youth by remediating them into the form that, by most accounts, gets the most attention from youth (Seif El-Nasr & Smith, 2006; Kafai, 1995).

The Skins workshops entailed Kahnawake youth engaging with stories from the community, but the stories had rarely been told in interactive media, and, to our knowledge, never in a video game. When we told community members we thought video games might be a fruitful medium for telling some of the old stories, we were met with a barrage of questions: Which stories? Who would be telling them? Who would see them? How would they be distributed (DVD, Internet, console)? Would somebody who owned the game then think they owned the story?

In addition, there are stories that are only told in certain societies. Some stories can only be told under certain conditions, such as specific times of year or day (King, 2003). Some stories are sacred, or simply sensitive in some aspect such that people do not want them remediated in any way, much less into a video game.

Our primary means for navigating these issues was to rely on Owisokon as our community liaison and mentor. Owisiokon is well-known and well-respected in the community. She is "longhouse," or a person who strives to live in accordance with traditional culture. She has worked at the high school in the community for twenty years, and in that time she has taught a significant portion of the community's youth. She is an artist herself, and invested with encouraging future generations to express themselves and their culture.

Owisokon was central in our discussions during the workshop about what stories we might consider remediating and how. The participants themselves also exhibited a strong sensitivity for such issues, with many of them possessing some knowledge about both the stories and what it was appropriate to do with them.

As stories were brought to the group for consideration, we went through a standard sequence of questions:

1. **What stories could we tell?**
   Stories in the community are embedded in a complex web of shared understandings about to which society within the community a story might belong, who may tell the story, when the story might be told, etc. (King, 2003). The result is that the participants could not simply identify a story they thought interesting and then go about remediating it. Participants brought story ideas to class, as did Owisokon. Our visiting mentors also told stories from their home communities. We would have discussions of how the person knew the story, if other people knew it, and if anybody knew of the constraints—if any—normally imposed on the telling of it. (Stories not meant to be told in that context simply were not discussed.)

2. **What stories should we tell?**
   Even with having to discard some material in the first step, we were left with a wealth of interesting stories and characters. At this stage, we would revisit the story and ask a series of questions to better understand it and to think through how it might be remediated. Such questions include:

   - What is the purpose of the story?
   - What makes the story interesting?

- Can those things be captured in an interactive experience?

3. **How would we tell the story?**
Once we had worked through the questions in the second step, we were down to a handful of stories. We then spent considerable time discussing which of those stories to produce, looking for answers to the following questions:

- What game genre would serve this story?
- What visual and gameplay style would be appropriate?
- What parts of the original story needed to be retained, and what parts could be modified or dropped to make an engaging game experience?

At the end of this process, we had decided on the story and produced a treatment that outlined how the story was going to be "game-ified." The treatment then served as the starting point for the design sessions.

Future Work

We are in the process of deciding what we will do for Skins 4.0. As discussed above, the schedule for 3.0 worked best out of the three iterations. The challenge is to see if we can squeeze the full workshop into that timeframe. We also must decide if we want to propose to new participants that they add a third level to the current game or develop something completely new; if we want to stick with the same technology; if we want to restrict or expand the age range of the participants; etc.

We also have substantial amounts of assessment data from Skins 2.0 and 3.0, including hundreds of hours of video, entrance and exit interviews, ethnographic observations, etc. We are slowly processing and interpreting all of that data to turn into journal articles, as well as actively recruiting for more graduate students to help us with assessment the next time. We would also like to devise a plan for supporting a long-term assessment of the impact of the workshop on the participants. One of our disappointments is that we have not found somebody to take over leadership of the project. We had hoped to groom a graduate student or two who could assume leadership of it for a few years after graduating. We wish to do this in order to move on to other items in the AbTeC agenda.

A number of other strategies for understanding and promoting Aboriginal new media production came out of the Network Meetings, as well as in the years since; we have to decide whether to pursue those other avenues for reaching our goals, or continue leading Skins ourselves.

If we do continue producing the Skins workshops, we will most likely expand the participant pool to include Natives from other reserves as well as urban Aboriginal people. We remain convinced that the Skins model could be of benefit to other Native reserves. To that end, we have written the curriculum up, with hour-by-hour instructions, content and teaching aids, and made it available for download from the AbTeC website (Lewis et al., 2010). In the fall of 2012, we presented the game made at the Skins 3.0 workshop to the Kahnawake community. (Figure 4)

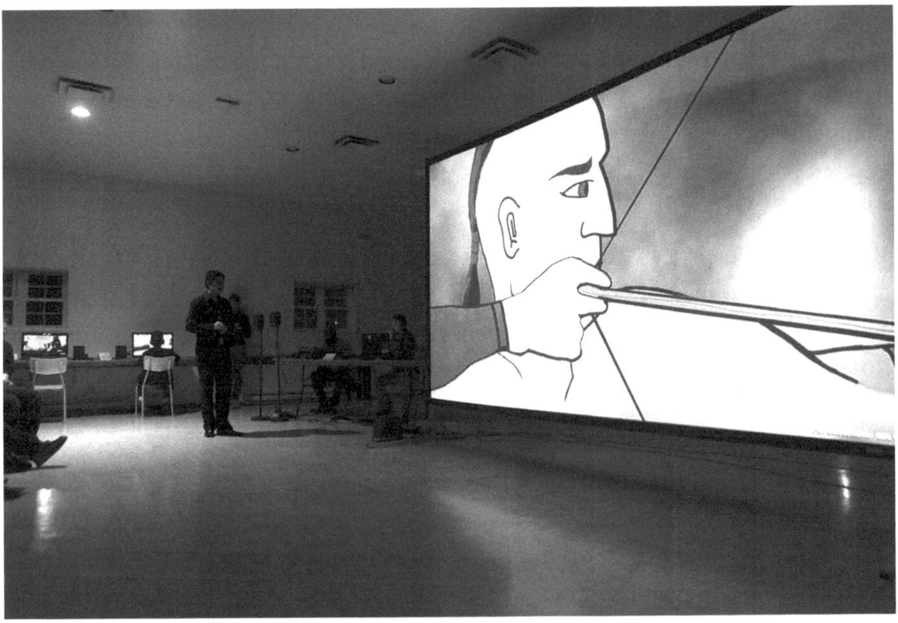

Figure 4. Tehoniehtathe Delisle, participant in Skins 1.0, and junior mentor in Skins 2.0 and 3.0, presents Skahiòn:hati—Rise of the Kanien'kehá:ka Legends game made in Skins 3.0 at the game launch on the Kahnawake reserve.

The event was well-attended by band members and officials, and received significant coverage from numerous local radio and television stations. The strong attention paid both within the community and from outside of the community provided us with one strong indicator that the effort is worthwhile and worth pursuing further.

Conclusion

One fact that we have not yet mentioned, and that most observers of the project do not realize: neither of us are game designers. We have creative, intellectual and technical practices that range across the field of digital media, but we have never created a game ourselves and have no plans to do so. Yet, because of Skins, we have chosen to spend the last six years and may spend many more with game production at the center of our professional lives. We talk often about how it might be easier, and less costly, to build the Skins workshops around some other form of digital media which is more central to our personal practices, such as video or machinima or interactive artwork. But Grand Theft Rez always comes back. Would any of those media be of sufficient interest to the youth to induce them to commit the necessary time, work, and passion? We do not know. Perhaps someday we might find out.

Whatever form future AbTeC adventures take, we do know the following. We need to address a need of the community in the way that coincides with its interests. We have to ensure as well that it meets our goals, or we will burn out. We need to persevere in our attempts to form productive partnerships. It will be difficult, as most individuals and institutions trying to effect positive change on reserves are already overloaded. Even if they subscribe to our vision, they may simply not have the time or bandwidth to take it on—now. But later that may change. And we need to understand how the value of the cultural property in that community has many valences and uses, many owners and subscribers, and many histories and versions. This must all be respected, yes, but if our communities are to evolve, the stories we tell and they way we tell them must also evolve to reflect the concerns and worldviews of new generations.

The Skins experience has provided many secondary dividends, some unexpected. A small group of Kahnawake youth are now familiar with and comfortable at Concordia. They know a few faculty and staff members personally, and several former participants have enrolled in the university for further study. The game produced in the first Skins workshop went on to win a major award at the imagineNATIVE Film and + Media Arts Festival, validating the participant's hard work and newly formed skills on an international stage. Multiple generations of non-Native Concordia research assistants have been deeply immersed in the richness and complexity of Iroquois culture in general and the Kahnawake community in particular. We cannot help but think that, as they go out into the wider world after graduation, they will have a greater sensitivity towards, understanding of, and sympathy with First Nations issues. These are no small victories. We close with an early conversation between Owisokon and Skawennati, as told by Skawennati:

> Owisokon at the very beginning…of the Skins process…she was asking these questions: what is this project, what are you going to do, what are you going to be teaching them? Finally, she says, "and what do yous want anyway? Why are yous doing this." And because it was Owisokon, who I have known for many years, I felt free enough to say, "well, we want to change the world." (Lewis & Fragnito, 2011)

This remains just as true today. Changing the world is hard work. It happens one small step at a time. It will be a long time, perhaps decades, before we know if Skins was successful. Perhaps the most important lesson we have learned is to accept that fact—and to keep on steppin'.

References

AbTeC (2010). *Skins 1.0.* Retrieved from http://www.skins.abtec.org/skins1.0/

AbTeC (2008). *AbTeC - About.* Retrieved from http://www.abtec.org/

Adobe Systems. (2012). *Adobe After Effects* [Computer software]. San Jose, CA: Adobe Systems Incorporated.

Archibald, J. (2008). *Indigenous storywork: Educating the heart, mind, body, and spirit*. Vancouver: University of British Columbia Press.

Banff Centre for the Arts. (2003). Retrieved from http://www.banffcentre.ca/bnmi/programs/archives/2003/skinningourtools/default.aspx.

Call of Duty [Computer software]. (2003–2011). Santa Monica, CA: Activision.

Canada, Indian and Northern Affairs Canada, Indian Act, QS-3621-020-BB-A2, Ottawa. Retrieved Oct. 5, http://lois-laws.justice.gc.ca/eng/acts/I-5/index. html.

Concordia University (2012a). *Welcome to the Faculty of Fine Arts.* Retrieved September 2, 2012, from http://finearts.concordia.ca/

Concordia University (2012b). *Hexagram—Concordia.* Retrieved September 2, 2012, from http://hexagram.concordia.ca/

Concordia University (2012c). *Homepage – Design & Computation Arts.* Retrieved September 2, 2012, from http://design.concordia.ca/

Dillon (Lameman), B. A., & Lewis, J. E. (2011). Skins: Designing games with First Nations youth. *Journal of Game Design & Development Education, 1*(1). Retrieved March 3, 2011 from http://www.rit.edu/gccis/gameeducationjournal/

Dillon (Lameman), B. A. (2010, April 23–24). *The good, the bad, and the sultry: Indigenous women in video games.* Paper presented at Unpacking the Indigenous Female Body, Vancouver, British Columbia.

Dillon, B. A. (2008). Signifying the west: Colonialist design in Age of Empires III: The WarChiefs. *Eludamos: Journal of Computer Game Culture, 2*(1), 129–144.

Dillon, B. A. (2007, November 14–18). *NDNWN: Designing games with Aboriginal stories.* Paper presented at FuturePlay 2007, Toronto, Ontario.

Dillon, B. A. (2006, October 10–12). *North American Indigenous imagery and identity in the game world.* Panel held at FuturePlay 2006, London, Ontario.

Dillon, B. A. (2006, September 21–24). *Odaminodaa: Game education for Indigenous youth.* Paper presented at the Canadian Game Studies Association Symposium, Toronto, Ontario.

Dillon, B. A. (2004, May 5–9). *Native Americans in the gaming age.* Paper presented at the 2nd Annual Cultural Studies Association Conference, Boston, Massachusetts.

Epic Games (2009). *Unreal development kit* [Computer software]. Cary, NC: Epic Games, Inc.

Eyre, C. (Director). (1998). *Smoke signals* [Motion picture]. United States: ShadowCatcher Entertainment.

Fragnito, S. (1997). *CyberPowWow.* Retrieved March 4, 2011, from http://www.cyberpowwow.net/

Grand Theft Auto [Computer software]. (1997–2011). New York: Rockstar Games.

Halo [Computer software]. (2001–2011). Redmond, WA: Microsoft Studios.

Indian Act (1985). RSC c I-5. Retrieved September 2, 2012, from http://canlii.ca/t/l0hh

Isbister, K. (2009). Step two: Understand social play. In C. Bateman (Ed.) *Beyond game design: Nine steps toward creating better video games*. Newton Center, MA: Charles River Media.

Isbister, K. (2006). *Better game characters by design: A psychological approach*. San Francisco, CA: Morgan Kaufmann.

Kafai, Y. B. (1995). *Minds in play: Computer game design as a context for children's learning*. Hillsdale, NJ: Lawrence Erlbaum Associates.

Kahnawake Education Center (2012). *Home*. Retrieved September 2, 2012, from http://kec.qc.com/

Kahnawake Library (2012). *Skawenniio Tsi Iewennahnotahkhwa KAHNAWAKE LIBRARY*. Retrieved September 2, 2012, from http://www.klibrary.ca/

Kanien'kehá:ka Onkwawén:na Raotitióhkwa Language and Cultural Center (2012). *Home*. Retrieved September 2, 2012, from http://www.korkahnawake.org/

King, T. (2003). *The truth about stories: A Native narrative*. Minneapolis, MN: University of Minnesota Press.

Langer, J. (2008). Playing (post)colonialsm in World of Warcraft. In H. G. Corneliussen & J. W. Rettberg (Eds.), *Digital culture, play, and identity: A World of Warcraft reader* (pp. 87–110). Cambridge, MA: The MIT Press.

Lewis, J. (2012). Time travelers, flying heads, and second lives: Designing communal stories. *Interactions, 19*(2). Retrieved September 2, 2012, from http://doi.acm.org/10.1145/2090150.2090157

Lewis, J., & S. Fragnito. (2011). *Skins 1.0 documentary*. Retrieved September 2, 2012, from http://vimeo.com/6909022.

Lewis, J., & S. Fragnito. (2012a). *Skins 2.0: Mentors*. Retrieved September 2, 2012, from http://vimeo.com/42707251.

Lewis, J., & S. Fragnito. (2012b). *Skins 2.0: Research Assistants*. Retrieved September 2, 2012, from http://vimeo.com/41441111.

Lewis, J., & S. Fragnito. (2012c). *Skins 2.0 documentary*. Retrieved September 2, 2012, from http://vimeo.com/47593267.

Lewis, J., & S. Fragnito. (2012d). *Skins 2.0: Industry guests*. Retrieved September 2, 2012, from http://vimeo.com/41441108.

Lewis, J. E., Fragnito, S., Dillon (Lameman), B. A., Parsons, B., & Lahache, O. (2010). *Skins 1.0: A workshop in Aboriginal storytelling in game de-*

sign. Montreal, QC: Obx Labs. Retrieved September 2, 2012, from http:// www.obxlabs.net/docs/skins_1.0_curriculum.pdf

Little Bear, L. (2000). Jagged worldviews colliding. In M. A. Battiste (Ed.), *Reclaiming indigenous voice and vision* (pp. 77–85). Vancouver, BC: University of British Columbia Press.

Mazzoni, D., & Dannenberg, R. (2011). *Audacity* [Computer software]. Pittsburgh, PA: The Audacity Team.

Otsi:! Rise of the Kanien'keha:ka Legends [Computer software]. (2009). Montreal, Quebec: Aboriginal Territories in Cyberspace.

Parker, J. R., & Becker, K. (2006, March). *Games for encapsulation and promotion of native cultures.* Paper presented at IMAGINE Network Symposium, Banff, Alberta.

Parker, J. R. & Becker, K. (2005, October). *Teaching Aboriginal language using GameBoy*. Paper presented at FuturePlay 2005, East Lansing, Michigan.

Pearce, C. (2009). *Communities of play: Emergent cultures in multiplayer games and virtual worlds.* Cambridge, MA: MIT Press.

Pearce, C. (2002). Emergent authorship: The next interactive revolution. *Computers and Graphics*, *26*, 21–29.

Pearce, C. (aka Ludica), Fron, J., Fullerton, T., & Morie, J. (2008). Getting girls into the game: Towards a virtuous cycle. In Y. Kafai, C. Heeter, J. Denner, & J. Sun (Eds.), *Beyond Barbie and Mortal Combat.* Cambridge, MA: The MIT Press.

Pearce, C., Fullerton, T., Fron, J., & Morie, J. F. (2005, December 1–3). *Sustainable play: Towards a new games movement for the digital age.* Paper presented at the Digital Arts and Culture Conference, IT University of Copenhagen, Denmark.

Roosendaal, T. (2002). *Blender* [Computer software]. Amsterdam, Netherlands: Blender Foundation.

Seif El-Nasr, M., & Smith, B. (2006). Learning through game modding. ACM *Computers in Entertainment, 4*(1). Retrieved September 2, 2012, from http://www.sfu.ca/~magy/conference/LearningByBuilding-SeifEl NasrSmith.copyed.pdf

Skahiòn:hati—Rise of the Kanien'kehá:ka Legends. [Computer software]. (2012). Montreal, Quebec: Aboriginal Territories in Cyberspace.

Smith, L. T. (1999). *Decolonizing methodologies: Research and indigenous peoples*. London; New York: Zed Books.

SSHRC (2011). *SSHRC – Aboriginal Research Pilot Program.* Retrieved September 7, 2012 from http://www.sshrc-crsh.gc.ca/funding finance-ment/programs-programmes/aboriginal-autochtone-eng.aspx

The Adventures of Skahion:hati: The Legend of the Stone Giant [Computer software]. (2011). Montreal, Quebec: Aboriginal Territories in Cyber-space.

The Legend of Zelda [Computer software]. (1986–2011). Kyoto, Japan: Nintendo.

Unity Technologies. (2011). Unity [Computer software]. San Francisco, CA: Unity Tcchnologies.

Williams, A. (2011). *Skins 2.0 Assessment Report.* Internal AbTeC document. Montreal, Quebec.

Wilson, A. C. (2004). Reclaiming our humanity: Decolonization and the recovery of indigenous knowledge. In D. A. Mihesuah & A. C. Wilson (Eds), *Indigenizing the academy: Transforming scholarship and empowering communities* (pp. 69–87). Lincoln: University of Nebraska Press.

Wyeld, T. G., Leavy, B., Carroll, J., Gibbons, C., Ledwich, B., & Hills, J. (2007, September). *The ethics of indigenous storytelling: Using the Torque game engine to support Australian Aboriginal cultural heritage.* Paper presented at the Digital Games Research Association International Conference, Tokyo, Japan.

Chapter 7

Adventures in Community Media: Experiments, Findings, and Strategies for Change

jesikah maria ross

Introduction

I picked up my first video camera in 1986 during my junior year of college. It was a portapak, a clunky configuration of equipment comprised of a huge video camera connected by a cable to a separate recording deck, all of which seemed to weigh just short of a ton. The weight didn't bother me though; I was too excited by the training workshop I was in at the local public access television station. I could hardly believe that a television channel was offering the equipment and technical assistance I needed to learn how to document and broadcast issues that were important to me.

As a college student, I was heavily involved in a number of social action groups working on issues ranging from solidarity with the Sandinistas in Nicaragua to alleviating hunger in the United States, from divestment in South Africa to environmental protection in Northern California. Young and idealistic (not to mention quite strident), I jumped at any opportunity to "tell our story" and get as much press as possible. Consequently, I ended up on various commercial radio and television programs as well as in many newspaper articles. But each encounter with mainstream media left me puzzled, shocked, and even mortified at how my ideas were framed, my comments quoted out of context, and my efforts downplayed or lightly ridiculed. I realized that if the groups I worked with wanted to get our message out or convey our point of view, we would need to take the media into our own hands and make it ourselves.

That's the short story of how I became deeply involved in community television production and independent documentary filmmaking. Alternative media (Sholle, 1995) was the perfect match for my goals and interests: it could be used to disseminate information, create art, offer self-representation, mobilize activist efforts, and validate people's real lives and experiences. It provided a concrete avenue for communities to speak out and to each other in order to facilitate ground-level change. I was hooked (ross, 1999).

For the next decade, I worked in community television as a media trainer and project director. After hours, I worked on social issue documentaries (as the indie documentary field didn't offer many paying day jobs). Community media seemed like my calling; I felt so at home facilitating dynamic and supportive spaces for community members to discover the stories they wanted to tell and then learn how to utilize media tools to do it. But I also craved the creative practice and higher production value that came with being part of a professional documentary production team. I also recognized that while community media had deep resonance for participants in localized areas, professionally produced media had the ability to reach much wider audiences. I puzzled many a night over how I might bridge those realms.

I continued to muse about how to link community and public media through graduate school and beyond, as I forged a career over the past twenty-five years that has included being a community media facilitator, project director, and documentary media-maker. I've bounced among these three roles through various gigs—from teaching community video to directing international participatory media projects to making NPR and PBS documentaries—and although this variety of jobs was both interesting and challenging, I longed to integrate the different types of work I loved. In 2008, I managed to do just that by launching the ART OF REGIONAL CHANGE (ARC), a community engagement program at the University of California, Davis. The four years I spent directing ARC did not live up to my hopes and expectations. But it did give me an incredibly useful laboratory to test out new approaches to creating community media. In the process, I learned important lessons in how to effectively wear multiple hats and navigate the university system, even when the odds were stacked against me (more about that later).

With this backstory in mind, this chapter sketches out my approach to implementing ARC, including some of the pitfalls I encountered and a productive experiment I conducted to address emerging personal and institutional challenges. I'll also highlight some of the surprising lessons learned from the ARC experience along with a few unresolved issues. As I discovered, universities are fantastic sites for doing community media projects, but these projects need to be designed in ways that are legible to administrators and that dovetail with university teaching and research agendas. If not, you run the risk of marginalization and, ultimately, the kind of invisibility that leads to program closure.

Creating My Dream Job

The big idea behind the ART OF REGIONAL CHANGE was that it would bring students, scholars, and artists together with local groups to collaborate on media arts projects that strengthen communities, generate engaged scholarship, and inform regional decision-making. These university-community engagement projects would take place in UC Davis's home region: Northern California's Central Valley and Sierra Nevada mountains.

> **ARC Program Approach**
>
> - **Interdisciplinary**: Bringing together different disciplines and experiences leverages perspectives to better identify issues and develop solutions for the places we live.
> - **Place-based**: Having a geographic location gives us a container to focus our efforts.
> - **Storytelling**: Drawing on a skill and process we use daily while valuing distinct forms of knowledge and self-expression.
> - **Media Arts**: Utilizing tools that are engaging and relevant to stakeholders and generating products that can be distributed through multiple platforms.

As ARC's founding director, I had three main objectives. First, the program would integrate my favorite professional roles within one job: artist, teacher/facilitator, and project director. Second, it would tap into the arts, humanities and social sciences to effectively enable communities to identify and document their assets, issues and creative solutions.[1] Finally, the program would produce both community media and public media so that residents could create and use their productions to meet local needs and generate stories that could then, through more professionally crafted productions, reach wider audiences and decision-makers, who sometimes live outside of the communities they govern.

I designed ARC's approach to community engagement as interdisciplinary and place-based with a focus on storytelling using the media arts. Why?

To me, the interaction of humanists, artists, social scientists, and local residents generates the kind of knowledge and alliances necessary to really effect ground-level change. Examining a place and what that place means to residents and academics alike creates common ground for all participants, enabling communities to reflect on their history while involving scholars in collaborative research. A focus on storytelling acknowledges diverse ways of communicating experiences—literature, drawings, maps, photonovelas, comic books, quilting—while valuing different kinds of expertise. And media, whether it's video, audio, photography, or web-based, is an incredibly versatile storytelling tool. It can be used to document processes, conduct research, and communicate findings in creative and compelling ways (e.g., photo-blogs, do-it-yourself google maps, audio slideshows, video documentaries). Mediamaking is also engaging to wildly diverse groups—youth, community leaders, academics, organizational representatives—who have something to say and generates products that can be distributed through multiple platforms such as radio, television, the web, exhibitions, DVDs, and community screenings. In terms of a program model, I crafted each ARC project to address a community question, need, or aspiration and planned and implemented the effort in partnership with a community organization. The projects generated community media (public access TV, community audio tours, local screenings/dialogues), social media (YouTube, Facebook) and public media (NPR and PBS programs, museum exhibits) to reach different audiences. They also produced educational materials, essays, or research papers based on the project. I aimed to co-direct the projects with a community partner or university scholar, though sometimes I ended up being the sole project director. I always formed a community advisory group, facilitated the media production and distribution efforts, and served as the project artist-in-residence. This multilayered collaboration among myself, a

ARC Program Model

- Design projects around a community question, need, or aspiration
- Implement projects in partnership with a community organization
- Involve faculty, artists, and students alongside community members
- Generate community, social, and public media productions
- Produce essays, studies, & educational materials in conjunction with media work

co-director, a group of advisors, and an organizational partner generated a lot of moving parts which required more time and attention than all of us were used to from previous collaborative efforts. As a result, I needed to allocate more of my time to project management and had to counsel prospective advisors and partners to be prepared for more meetings and emails, often giving them an estimated amount of time they might spend per week on the project. The upside of this complex project architecture is that ARC projects tended to have lots of community buy-in and meaningful outcomes. The downside, of course, is that it was more demanding in terms of communication and decisionmaking across project stakeholders.

Learning by Doing

Judging by participant satisfaction, local impact, and the number and reach of media productions generated through ARC (Chavez-Garcia, 2011), the program excelled in community media projects that involved a group of residents in learning how to make pieces that addressed local needs and interests. Despite the solid inroads into the communities we worked in, ARC didn't seem to gain much traction within the institutions the program depended on: the university which, in part, sponsored the program, agencies and foundations we needed to attract for additional funding, and the press, which plays a big role in garnering the kind of high profile attention needed to interest academic and non-academic funders alike. Although UC Davis is a land grant college with a well-touted public benefit mission, it became clear to me through conversations with administrators, supervisors, and allies that ARC's focus on community voice and benefits wasn't of significant interest to the powers holding the purse strings. What was of great interest, however, was student voice and benefits, particularly ARC's potential to engage students in community-based learning opportunities that enabled them to apply classroom studies in real world settings to build communication, teamwork, and problem-solving skills. ARC did, in fact, involve a handful of graduate and undergraduates in each project, yet the amount was clearly not enough if the program wanted to gain purchase within the academic system.

University administrators seemed equally lackluster about faculty engagement and contributions to the projects unless they culminated in "scholarly work." With the advance of public scholarship in the 21st century, such work theoretically includes digital productions published via online outlets

(Jay, 2012). In reality, UC Davis—much like other higher education institutions across the country (Ellison & Eatman, 2008)—primarily values publishing academic papers in peer-reviewed journals, which ARC hadn't focused on generating.

Interestingly, framing ARC's work as "community media" also seemed to put us at a disadvantage, mostly because the term necessitated a lot of explaining. As a result, I always found myself repeating and reworking my elevator pitches in university administration and public relations circles, amongst funders, with the press, and sometimes with potential collaborating partners. In contrast, everyone's ears perked up immediately if I called our work "community art." Universities have art departments, the press have art sections, and the arts field has specific funders making "the arts" much more legible to all these groups. Art is a well-known and understood category to use, even if the kind of art ARC was doing was different than what folks were imagining.

ARC's emphasis on community benefits, non-traditional scholarship, and community media framing not only seemed to lessen the program's value in key circles of support but also inundated me, as the project director, with tasks I had not anticipated. It came as a bit of a blow to realize that the combination of diverse jobs I'd purposefully taken on—teaching, facilitating, making media, managing projects—was an inordinate amount to do within one job, especially when my appointment was only 75% (and later reduced to 50%) time. Consequently, I ended up mostly facilitating and managing projects.[2] When I did get to create media, it was repurposing community-produced pieces into gallery exhibitions, television documentaries and social media channels. And while that was gratifying, it wasn't aesthetically rewarding because I needed to work within preset limitations of existing community-produced pieces and the artistic vision of the project generated by a community group. In other words, because of these contextual constraints, my creative voice was either absent, invisible or limited.

Looking back, I had devised a fabulously visionary program that blended my background, passion, and skills in a way that advanced the university's public mission while contributing to community change. But I was naïve about the context in which I was operating—a university bureaucracy with a different set of agendas and goals from mine. To remain viable within a university context as well as become more effective on the ground and personally fulfilled, I needed to make changes. With this in mind, I used my recent ARC project, *Restore/Restory*, as an opportunity to recalibrate and try some experiments in adjusting the design, implementation, and framing of ARC's methods and outcomes.

A Collaborative Public History

To set up the experiments I conducted, let me first give you a broad overview of the *Restore/Restory* project. *Restore/Restory* is a community media project[3] that tells the story of California's rich cultural and environmental heritage and builds connections between people and the place they call home. A collaboration between ARC and the Cache Creek Conservancy (CCC), the project tells the complex story of the Cache Creek Nature Preserve in rural Yolo County, California. The 130-acre parcel that makes up the Preserve has been home to Native Americans, European explorers, Mexican ranchers, Anglo farmers, gravel miners and—most recently—environmental educators. Agriculture, mining, groundwater extraction, damming, and other infrastructure development seriously degraded the ecological and cultural landscape. The Conservancy was created to restore the lower Cache Creek watershed. To date, restoration efforts have focused on enhancing the stream and surrounding habitat; the best example of that effort being the Cache Creek Nature Preserve. While the ecological transformation of the Preserve is well documented; its historical, political and cultural stories remained unrepresented. *Restore/Restory* filled this gap by working with diverse stakeholders to tell the public history of the site.

The *Restore/Restory* project brought UC Davis students, scholars, and me as the media artist together with a broad cross-section of Yolo County residents (including tribal leaders, miners, environmental activists, farmers, local historians, and policymakers) to tell the story of the Preserve from multiple perspectives. The project produced an interactive public history website and a site-based audio tour of the Preserve, featuring distinct voices and experiences at different places on the grounds. Visitors have the option of taking the tour at the Preserve using iPods, smartphones, or audio devices provided by the Conservancy or experiencing it via the project website, which also includes a storymap, digital murals, storyteller profiles, interview transcripts and an illustrated historical timeline. Through this rich mix of different representational methods, *Restore/Restory* inspired the conversations that still needed to happen among residents, educators, and policymakers throughout California on how we can simultaneously care for our watersheds, safeguard the local economy, preserve indigenous lifeways and protect the environment.

For *Restore/Restory,* I tested out some new organizing principles to streamline ARC's approach and model in a way that was easier to communicate to partners, participants, funders and the press. These principles included: collaboration, reciprocity, editorial engagement and multi-faceted interaction.

Collaboration: Previously, I spoke of collaboration in terms of a partnership with a local non-profit to design and implement a community media project. In *Restore/Restory*, I used the term to highlight and describe the multiple groups involved in the project, including various organizational partners, advisors, storytellers, students, scholars and myself as the project artist. This really helped bring home to all the different stakeholders the sheer amount of people involved, their various roles, the different types of expected outcomes, and the kind of resources needed (I never pass up a fundraising opportunity!).

Reciprocity: I had always set up projects so that they benefited multiple stakeholders. At the university, I found the field of engaged scholarship was closest to the work I was doing. In the academic literature, "reciprocity" is the word used for this strategy of creating mutual benefits. I incorporated the notion of reciprocity when talking about *Restore/Restory*, but gave it my own definition: what results when everyone involved gets something they want out of the project process or the media productions.

Editorial Engagement: Coming from a background in community media, my ethics centered on media-makers having editorial control on content, distribution and use of their work. But in those projects my role was confined to being the facilitator and/or project director. In *Restore/Restory*, I sought an equal—if not larger—role to see what it would happen if I took on the mantle of artistic director. I positioned myself as the lead artist who co-created work with all contributors, created some components of the project myself, and exercised editorial control over all productions. I developed the practice of Editorial Engagement, however, to give all project participants an opportunity to play a role in shaping or curating content. This practice allowed for flexibility in determining what role each stakeholder would play based on their interest level or concerns in combination with my artistic vision. In addition, I set up all MOUs, consent forms, and agreements to spell out that I had final say on all production work, all the possible places that work might be exhibited, and the right to share any work in non-commercial settings so that everyone involved was clear from the get-go on rights and roles.

Multi-faceted Interaction: Over the past five years, I have witnessed the rise in what is called "cross-platform documentary" or "trans-media projects." While there are different—and sometimes competing—definitions for what these terms mean, for me they both involve telling stories through a variety of channels (online, broadcast, mobile phones) in ways that are unique to that medium, presenting narratives that build on each other (e.g. they are not duplicative), and inviting audience participation. The new trend of Open Space Documentary identified by Helen De Michiel and Patricia Zimmerman (2013) takes these ideas even further, encouraging multiple mediamakers creating stories on a range of topics and to present them in dialogue with each other. For *Restore/Restory*, I tapped into these trends and added the idea of generating many different types of media art, sharing that media through diverse outlets, and enabling stakeholders to use the pieces in a variety of ways. My shorthand for this layered concept is "multi-faceted," signaling the intentional integration of multiple voices, topics, mediums, outlets, makers and uses.

On a more nitty-gritty level, I changed up whom I involved in the project and their role(s). In previous ARC projects, as the media artist I worked with community members to learn how to use media tools—photo cameras, video cameras, audio recorders—to identify assets or issues and propose solutions. In *Restore/Restory*, I worked with UC Davis undergraduate students, instead, through a series of courses in English, Technocultural Studies, and Design. These students were involved in different ways: researching local history, interviewing community storytellers, learning media production and creating a variety of media pieces for the project.

In contrast to other ARC efforts, for *Restore/Restory* I secured a graduate fellowship to involve a Ph.D. student in documenting, analyzing, and writing up the project process—providing the foundational work needed for peer-reviewed articles. I also worked more closely with participating faculty from the start to plan their involvement in a way that would lead to generating traditional scholarly writing on the project. Lastly, I referred to *Restore/Restory* as a media art project, called myself the project artist and spoke about our products as media art pieces.

How the Experiments Played Out

Restore/Restory turned out to be a tremendous success. Over the course of two years, I involved approximately 200 university and community members in chronicling our diverse and changing demographics, traditions and relationships with the land that is now a Nature Preserve. Collectively, we gathered about 25 hours of oral testimonies, 500 landscape photos, 100 archival images, and an assortment of maps, transcripts, policy documents, and artifacts that we used to produce a series of media arts pieces that could be shared with the public through different venues. In terms of collaboration, the project involved:

- A project advisory group made of residents from diverse backgrounds.
- Student media makers from different academic disciplines.
- Community storytellers from various walks of life.
- An organizational partner, the Cache Creek Conservancy, which manages the Preserve.
- An institutional partner, UC Davis, which helped to fund the project.
- A scholar cohort comprised of UC Davis faculty, grad students, and community scholars.
- Myself as the project director, collaboration facilitator, media instructor, and artist-in-residence.

With respect to my revised emphasis on reciprocity and editorial engagement, advisory group members got involved to tell a public history of the Preserve that reflected the wide range of peoples, animals, and plants that inhabited the place over time as well as document changing land use patterns. I facilitated the process in which the group generated project themes, prioritized story topics, identified community storytellers and then recruited them to participate in the project. Out of that process we produced a digital *Storymap of Community Memories* featuring 50 short, compelling audio narratives and accompanying storyteller print profiles (Restore/Restory, 2013).

Participating students, on the other hand, came to the effort in order to learn how to create digital media. I taught them how to record and edit short audio interviews, take photos, and—in collaboration with a participating faculty member—write up storyteller profiles. The roughly 100 students who got involved then produced the images, audio, and print pieces for the *Storymap*. As part of this process, community storytellers had the opportunity to review the student-produced media, request revisions, and give final approval to include in the *Storymap*. Our organizational partner, the Cache Creek Conservancy, asked to review all of the print profile pieces and made quite a few suggested revisions, mostly grammatical. The revisions were largely accepted, though storytellers and the participating faculty member who led the writing course had the ultimate say in making sure the writing stayed true to the conversational tone and spirit of the student-storyteller exchange.

Because ARC's organizational partner on the project, the Cache Creek Conservancy, wanted a professionally crafted audio tour to advance their outreach and education goals, I worked closely with the CCC board and staff, as well as advisory group members, to identify tour narrators, tour stops and tour content. As the project artist, I did the audio recording and editing and CCC and advisory group got to have two rounds of review and requested revisions. I produced, in return, an audio tour in which you can hear a diverse set of narrators (tribal chair, multi-ethnic rancher, farmer, gravel miner, ecologist) in dialogue with each other at different stops around the Preserve grounds to convey different—and often conflicting—perspectives on history, politics, and culture.

ARC's institutional partners, the UC Davis Humanities Institute and Center for Regional Change, wanted scholarly context to frame the stories so they could be used in teaching and research. To do this, I brought four university and community scholars together with advisory group members to produce an illustrated historical timeline that chronicles key peoples, events, and policies that shaped the land that is now the Nature Preserve. UC Davis partners and the participating faculty also hoped for publications to emerge from the effort. In response, I supervised a Ph.D. fellow in collecting data and worked with the student and other faculty to produce reports and peer-reviewed articles.

As the media artist, I wanted to bring in images, soundscapes, and stories that didn't surface in the other media pieces and I wanted to ground those in different habitats around the Preserve in a way that was the most opposite of a Google map as I could imagine. To do that, I produced a series of digital murals that present the Preserve's history through a mash up of archival images and contemporary landscape with audio stories and ambient sound recordings—some from the student productions, others from the audio tour recordings—embedded in them. Like the audio tour I created, the CCC and advisory group got to review and request revisions.

These multiple types of media, made by multiple authors for multiple uses, are presented through multiple outlets. All these productions are accessible online at restorerestory.org, where users can view work, listen or download audio stories, print out profiles or transcripts, as well as comment on anything they access and circulate it via their social networks. For those without ready access to the Internet at home, the Nature Preserve provides a public access kiosk. Thc audio tour is downloadable to smart phones and MP3 players as well as available on audio devices provided at the Preserve. To make the stories accessible to people who don't use the Internet or MP3 players, I organized on-the-ground public events at the Preserve and in nearby rural towns that combined food, music, and story-sharing activities to spark residents' engagement with their history, the land, and each other. Currently, I am working on a series of radio broadcasts so that the stories can reach NPR audiences.

Lessons Learned

Because I'm in the process of wrapping up *Restore/Restory* as I write this chapter, I am still reflecting on what I learned through my experiments. Here, however, are a few lessons that stand out:

- It is much easier to involve students than community members in community-based media projects. They have the time, motivation and—as digital natives—capacity to quickly learn new media tools. Working with students, however, doesn't contribute to building the kind of community capacity, pride and ownership of the results that advance ground-level change.

- Having a team member, in our case a graduate student, who is dedicated to project documentation, analysis, and report writing is invaluable. Project directors like me who wear multiple hats (teacher, facilitator, artist, fundraiser, project manager) are stretched too thin to chronicle project processes and outcomes in the systematic kind of way that lends itself to scholarly publications.

- The "arts" have more cachet than "media." Framing the project as community art and/or media art attracted much greater interest. To wit: *Restore/Restory* got more press coverage, foundation funding, and audience members at our public events than almost all of our former projects combined!

- Reciprocity needs to include me. Like many community media practitioners, I tend to privilege project collaborators' hopes and needs over my own. By making my role more visible as well as larger, for the first time in my community media career, I felt like I achieved the project goals (co-created with participants) and my personal aims.

- While I need a better term for it, "multi-faceted interaction" is the way to go in the 21st century, with the array of technologies available to create, access and share stories. Going this route offers a constellation of entry points for diverse authors and audiences to engage each other and leverages the power of collaboration and convening to create the kind of open spaces where, as Helen De Michiel puts it, "culture and social change meet in dialogue and synthesize new ways of thinking, imagining, and behaving" (De Michiel, 2011). However, multi-faceted interactions require a substantial amount of time and creative energy to enact successfully as well as a group of collaborators who are willing to trust the process.

- Phasing the work makes wearing multiple hats more feasible. In *Restore/Restory* I was able to play the role of teacher/facilitator, artist and project manager by foregrounding one role at a time. For the first year, I focused primarily on teaching and supporting student media production. In the second year, I dedicated my time largely to producing media myself. For the first few and last few months of the project, I was consumed with project set up and management, and continued to supervise the project throughout, but as a secondary emphasis. This type of phasing meant that the project took much longer than anticipated. Yet the result was worth it: I successfully juggled multiple roles within one job.

Unresolved Dilemmas

In a lot ways, *Restore/Restory* has been a real victory in terms of testing new ideas, taking on new roles and refining ARC's project model to be more legible to university administrators and the press. The experiment, however, also brought forward some new conundrums. The ones that keep niggling at me are…

Issues Trump Story Time. It is infinitely easier to get people, funders, and partners involved in media projects that are issue driven. Conversely, it's really hard to get support for projects that seek to involve people in using stories to build connections to each other and to the places they live. In other words, I can mobilize resources to save a place, improve a place, or change a place but not to bring people together to talk about a place in a way that strengthens their connection to each other, their history, and shared geography. That is problematic, because it's precisely that kind of connectedness that is necessary to motivate people to do the tough work involved in collectively affecting social change.

Participation and Production Values Butt Heads. The scrappy activist part of me is having a major wrestling match with the documentary artist part of myself. The activist part of me wants community members and/or students to be hands-on in all aspects of the media-making process but the artist part wants everything in a project to be well-crafted and beautiful. It is so much easier to create community media ***or*** student produced media ***or*** professional media; it's a constant and somewhat messy struggle when you try and combine them. Yet it's the combination that creates the richest, most mutually beneficial, and compelling products.

Editorial Engagement Is a Double-Edged Sword. Giving participants and partners editorial influence in content and form is time intensive and emotionally challenging, requires really good communication skills, and constantly tests your vision and your aesthetics. It is a hard combination to accept, especially when you are working with limited time and resources. Plus, editorial engagement doesn't always translate to accurate or inclusive media productions. Consider these examples: When the *Restore/Restory* advisory group came up with the topics, content, and storytellers for the storymap they left out key groups—like African Americans and Asian

Americans, who certainly are part of local history. Our organizational partner the Cache Creek Conservancy, which is funded by gravel money, wanted me to retract some of the environmentalist's points in the audio tour, even though when I fact-checked the statements I found they were accurate. And, the local tribe told me certain archival images I secured could not be used in the project if I wanted their blessing. In these ways, editorial engagement gives partners a stake in the effort but makes it hard to hold on to journalistic and artistic integrity within the project.

University Gigs Are a Mixed Blessing. Universities are a huge draw for me. They are filled with smart, passionate people doing interesting projects and are—even in this era of economic downsizing—filled with resources. They support the arts, generate useful data, convene public dialogue and offer venues for sharing culture, views, struggles and strategies for change. In short, my kinda place. But they are also stuck in the mud when it comes to recognizing diverse forms of "research" and have no formal structure for recognizing and rewarding the kinds of skills required to do engaged arts projects like entrepreneurialism, collaboration, facilitation, project management and holding the project vision throughout the bumpy life of community-based media endeavors. As a result, my talents are rendered invisible. And invisibility in the competitive university atmosphere equals death. To wit: the ART OF REGIONAL CHANGE was not refunded.

The Way Forward

It's interesting to be in this limbo space of wrapping up the *Restore/Restory* project and closing down the ART OF REGIONAL CHANGE program while pondering a potential future doing community media (ahem, I mean community art!) via university programs. I can't say I'm in a rush to create the next ARC, though I would sorely miss having a job that allows me to do the different kinds of work I love in an environment that really allows for experimentation and risk-taking.

Overall, I discovered that the university is a good launching pad for doing community media projects, but that such projects need to be fashioned in a way that is legible to administrators and is in synch with higher education's focus on student learning and faculty scholarship. I also realized that my role as a practicing artist needs to be more prominent within university-community media projects, not only to fulfill my own needs but because it is a strategic way to garner external funds and academic support. In addition, I found out that I can "have it all" in terms of doing media education, project management and documentary production, but that I need to do it in phases to be effective and avoid burn out.

Perhaps most important, the entire ARC experience reinforced the utility of constantly tinkering with one's methods and language for communicating what we do and why it's important, particularly within a university context. It's this continual process of testing and refining our practices that will enable us as practitioners to challenge and advance the community media field. And it's the ongoing process of conveying the significance of our work that will help campus administrators see the value of doing community media projects, the vital role professional staff play in implementing them, and how these kinds of programs are perfectly aligned with the mission of the public university (Goldbard, 2008; Fitzgerald, Burack & Seifer, 2010). Finding ways to get decision-makers to view campus-community media projects as not just one-off, feel-good electives but as a strategic avenue to realize the multiple goals of higher education is probably the only way we'll manifest the kind of support needed to build effective and sustainable university-community media programs. We need to find some champions and we need some powerfully framed arguments. For me, locating those advocates and making our case is the work ahead.

Figure 1. Community Media Characteristics

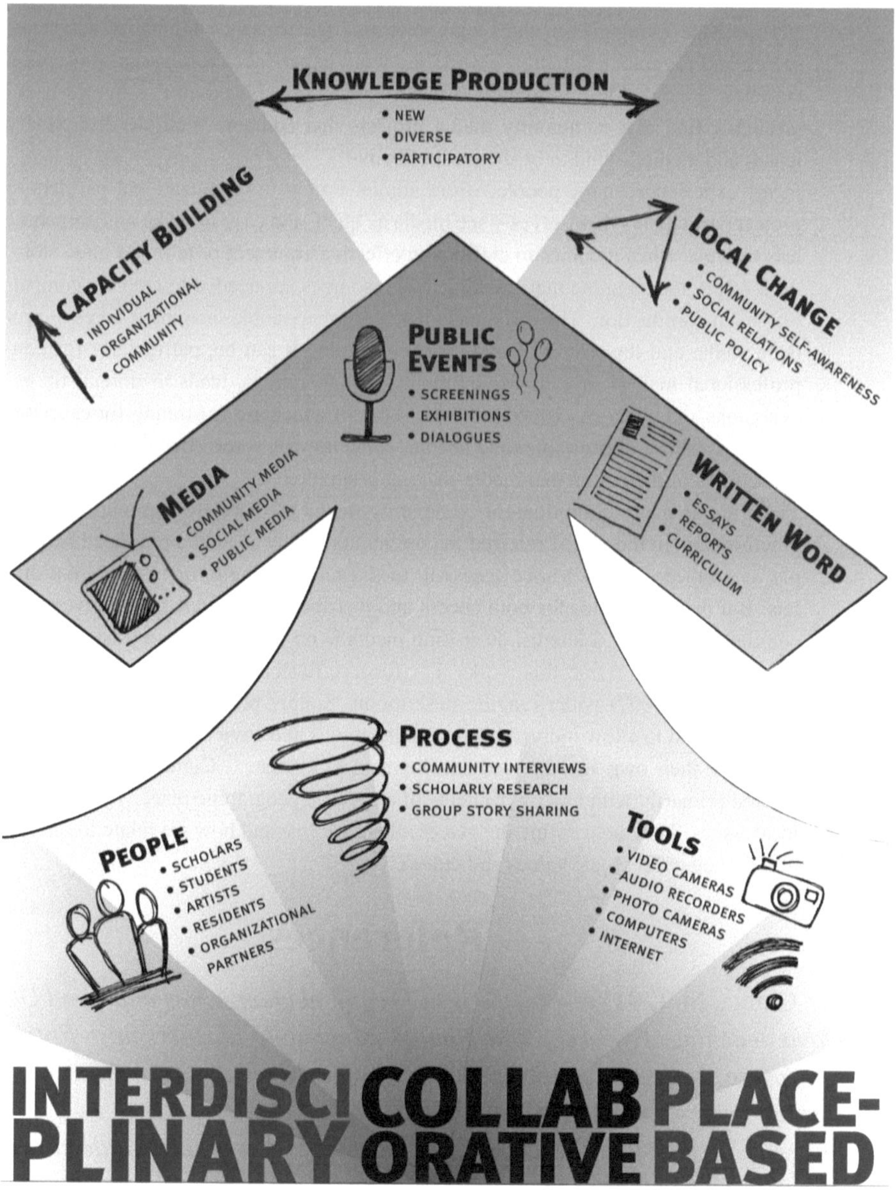

Notes

1. My graduate training is in the social sciences—particularly community action research and program evaluation—while my work experience crafting and presenting stories is grounded in the fields of arts and humanities. Based on this hybrid background, I find that community media projects that combine multiple disciplinary lenses and methods tend to be the most effective.
2. In my experience, many people—from administrators to organizational partners to project participants themselves—see media as quick and easy to make and somehow less rigorous when it comes to crafting an effective argument or telling a good story. As a result, they assume that less time and resources are needed to create a compelling media production. The disconnect between what people imagine it takes to produce media and the reality of how time consuming it can be, particularly for nonprofessional makers in campus-community collaborations, leads to unrealistic expectations and under-resourced projects—both of which are frustrating for everyone involved. Those of us in this field need to come up with some effective ways to disabuse folks of the notion that media-making is simple.
3. There are as many definitions of community media as there are community media practitioners. In the past, I referred to community media as media produced by people who otherwise don't have access to media tools, training, or transmission outlets. But the boundaries for both access and distribution continue to dissolve while community member's interest in making media is on the rise, causing me to reconsider how to best frame this work. For Restore/Restory, then, I use Johnson and Menichelli's (2007) wider-ranging description. Simply put, community media are media created to allow individuals to tell the stories and have the conversations necessary for their own self-directed development as citizens....Community media are created primarily with and by residents of a specific geographic place. They explore local issues. They help define the places where we live and how we relate to one another. They reflect local values and culture.

References

Chavez-Garcia, M. (2011). *How the art of regional change has improved UC Davis teaching, research, and campus-community partnerships: Potential future strategies.* White paper presented to university deans, provosts, and vice-chancellors, Davis: UC Davis.

De Michiel, H. (2011). Open space documentary. *A working guide to the landscape of arts for change. Animating Democracy.* Retrieved from http://animatingdemocracy.org/working-guide-abstracts#michiel

De Michiel, H., & Zimmerman, P. (2013). Documentary as open space. In B. Winston (Ed.), *The documentary film book.* London: British Film Institute.

Ellison, J., & Eatman, T. K. (2008). *Scholarship in public: Knowledge creation and tenure policy in the engaged university.* Syracuse, NY: Imagining America.

Fitzgerald, H., Burack, C., & Seifer, S.D. (2010). *Handbook of engaged scholarship: Contemporary landscapes, future directions.* East Lansing, MI: Michigan State University Press.

Goldbard, A. (2008). *The Curriculum Project report: Culture and community development in higher education.* Imagining America. Retrieved from http://imaginingamerica.org/wpcontent/uploads/2011/05/08.CP_.report.pdf

Jay, G. (2012). The engaged humanities: Principles and practices for public scholarship and teaching. *Journal of Community Engagement and Scholarship*, *3*(1), 51–63 .

Johnson, F., & Menichelli, K. (2007). *What's going on in community media?* Washington, DC: Benton Foundation.

Restore/Restory (2013). Retrieved from www.restorerestory.org

ross, j. m. (1999). *Community television training reconsidered: A model for increasing media literacy, civic engagement, and social capital.* Unpublished master's thesis, UC Davis, Davis, California.

Sholle, D. (April 1, 1995). *Access through activism: Extending the ideas of Negt and Luge to American alternative media practices.* Paper presented at the Union for Democratic Communication Conference, Austin, Texas.

Part 4: Pedagogies and Knowledge Construction

Chapter 8

The Teaching to Learn Project: Investigating Literacy through Intergenerational Inquiry

Rob Simon, Jason Brennan, Sandro Bresba, Sara DeAngelis, Will Edwards, Helmi Jung, and Anna Pisecny

Introduction

> *You must write, and read, as if your life depended on it.* That is not generally taught in school. *At most, as if your livelihood depended on it:* the next step, the next job, grant, scholarship, professional advancement, fame; no questions asked to further meanings. And, let's face it, the lesson of the schools for a vast number of children—hence, of readers—is *This is not for you.* (Adrienne Rich, 1993)

Appleman (2009) has argued that literacy teachers should not teach reading and writing as abstract skills, but rather as tools for helping adolescents make meaningful connections to their lives and make critical sense of the worlds they navigate. This is particularly important at a time when "new" literacy practices encourage an ethos of participation, engagement and "distributed expertise" (Lankshear & Knobel, 2007, p. 21), rather than transmission of knowledge. In the midst of far-reaching changes in the nature of literacy in the world, teaching adolescents' to read literature "as if [their lives] depended on it" (Rich, 1993) can be a means of exploring students' real world concerns, including broad social, ethical and identity issues (Beach, Appleman, Hynds & Wilhelm, 2006, p. 43). How can teachers approach texts in ways that invite connections to students' lives, cultivate critical perspectives, and encourage new social relationships?

In this chapter, we describe our experiences of reading young adult novels that explore social conflicts and identity issues with adolescents from a culturally and economically diverse community in West Toronto. This work is part of a broader investigation of teaching literature in a collaborative multiliteracies research community, the Teaching to Learn Project. In the spirit of what Campano, Honeyford, Sanchez & Vander

Zanden (2010) have theorized as "a stance of horizontalism," this community supports opportunities for teachers at various stages of professional development and adolescents to investigate issues in literacy pedagogy together, across generations, institutional boundaries and social hierarchies.

In the first section of this chapter, we situate our work in relation to practitioner research communities that take collaborative, intergenerational approaches to professional learning. We then describe the Teaching to Learn Project, including an explanation of how our group has developed and our approach to researching and writing collaboratively. In the remaining sections of this chapter we look at themes and issues that emerged from our exploration of teaching literature in six inquiry communities involving youth and teachers. Inquiries into young adult novels encouraged participants to investigate their beliefs and experiences as readers, teachers and students. These personal explorations became critical heuristics for textual interpretations, for broader social analysis, as well as for raising questions about the definitions and purposes of teaching literature in school.

Intergenerational Inquiry as a Means of Learning from Teaching

As Brauer and Clark (2008) have noted, in spite of rapid changes in literacy practices out of school, the study of literature in secondary schools remains oriented to acculturating students into a literary canon and particular ways of reading and responding to texts. These approaches are increasingly shaped by top-down policies, and are oriented to functional rather than critical purposes. In our own context, The Ontario English Curriculum encourages teachers to use texts as a basis for instructing students on "reading comprehension strategies before, during, and after reading to understand simple texts and some teacher-selected complex texts" (p. 59). This is one example of how a functional model of literacy impacts students and teachers, encouraging patterned choices of what students read, pedagogies rooted in skills-based understandings of literacy, and standardized forms of assessment. How do teachers entering Ontario literacy classrooms regard policy frameworks like this in relation to the complex literate lives of adolescents?

Questions like these rarely enter into literacy teacher education and professional development, which are commonly oriented to conveying externally derived knowledge into sites of practice (Cochran-Smith & Lytle, 1999, 2009; Simon, 2012, 2013a, 2013b). Inquiry-based teacher research communities can provide foundations for constructing more dialectical visions of learning in literacy education—positioning new and experienced teachers as knowledge generators, and connecting schools, universities and community-based initiatives (Cochran-Smith & Lytle, 2009; Kamler & Comber, 2005). As Lieberman and Wood (2001) have noted, inquiry communities can support teachers to become "active and interactive, developers rather than developed, passionate instead of passive" (p. 184). For literacy teachers, this can be a means of encouraging individual agency, more critical approaches to classroom instruction, and more horizontal notions of expertise (Campano et al., 2010; Simon & Campano, 2013).

Unlike traditional research that attempts to discern patterns and social practices, research by teachers often goes against the grain of inherited patterns to actualize forms of individual and social change (Simon, Campano, Broderick, & Pantoja, 2012). Many teacher research and educational activist communities have attempted to work across traditional hierarchies with the aim of reimagining practices and definitions of literacy, achievement, and learning, toward more socially just ends (e.g., Kamler & Comber, 2005; Rogers et al., 2009). Much of this work is grassroots and activist (Ghíso, Campano, & Simon, 2013), and involves navigating complex dilemmas in schools. As a result, teacher research is less commonly represented in traditional scholarly venues; the impact of inquiry communities is often locally oriented.

Cochran-Smith and Lytle (2001) have noted that teacher inquiry communities are commonly based on the assumption "that beginning and experienced teachers need to engage in similar intellectual work" (p. 53). For example, Kamler and Comber (2005) have documented how early-year and experienced literacy teachers collectively explore the problem of unequal literacy outcomes in their classrooms. Rogers et al. (2009) describe their work in The Literacy for Social Justice Teacher Research Group, a grassroots, teacher-coordinated professional development collective comprised of teachers "across the lifespan" working in collaboration with university-based educators and activists "to use literacy practices in ways that make changes in people's lives" (Rogers et al., 2009, p. 22). Campano et al. (2010) describe inquiry-based, school-university collaborations that support teachers, researchers, community members, and students to 'redistribute intellectual authority' (Campano et al., 2010, pp. 278–279) as a basis for intersubjective knowledge construction and institutional change.

These and other inquiry-based initiatives share a commitment on the part of educators themselves to take action and develop innovative approaches to literacy pedagogy (Ghíso, Campano, & Simon, 2013). As these examples suggest, inquiry communities can be a basis for literacy teachers to constructively disrupt preexisting power structures, critique policy initiatives and inherited practices, and develop more critical pedagogies (Cochran-Smith & Lytle, 2009; Simon, Brennan, & Edwards, 2013).

The Teaching to Learn Project

Within this tradition, the Teaching to Learn Project (TTL) is a research community we formed to explore and support inquiries by early-year literacy teachers and teacher candidates at the University of Toronto. TTL has become a forum for developing research collaborations across institutional and social boundaries, including work with youth from an economically and socially diverse faith-based organization that Anna co-directs. To date, adolescents from Anna's group have been involved in a number of research collaborations, including authoring literacy curricula with teacher candidates and the critical investigations of young adult literature described in this chapter.

As a community of teacher-learners we draw upon understandings of literacy as multiple, situated within social and political contexts, and meaningfully shaped by individuals (e.g., New London Group, 1996; Street, 1995), to take an inquiry stance on literacy policy and practice (Cochran-Smith & Lytle, 2001, 2009). Our explorations of teaching literature are informed by questions such as: Why teach texts? What counts as literacy "curriculum" in schools, and who decides? What does it mean to regard responding to literature as a social and cultural process? What do culture and context have to do with who, what, why, and how we teach? These questions sparked the inquiries into teaching literature we examine in this chapter, and were questions we returned to frequently as we analyzed our data and wrote collaboratively.

For this project we invited teenagers and teachers to choose texts from a list of young adult novels that explore social and identity issues including: Sherman Alexie's (2007) *The Absolutely True Diary of a Part-Time Indian;* Marjane Satrapi's (2003) *Persepolis;* M.T. Anderson's (2002) *Feed*; and Suzanne Collins' (2008) *The Hunger Games*. Participants were invited to discuss these texts in six inquiry groups in a pre-service literacy course Rob teaches at University of Toronto. Participants were asked to come to class prepared to discuss one surprise, one question and one passage of interest. Otherwise, the goals for these conversations were not predetermined. Our intent was to invite participants to use these conversations to explore their own concerns related to reading and teaching literature.

In addition to documenting these discussions, we were also participants in them. Each of us recorded and transcribed the conversation we were a part of, and we developed a collaborative approach to eliciting patterns and themes from these data. We worked in pairs to read (and reread) individual transcripts, reporting to the larger group about initial themes. These were discussed and cross-categorized. This process surfaced emic concepts that guided our analysis and writing. For example, a comment by one of the participating adolescents, Nina[1], "what teens are actually like," became a framework that helped us interpret how these texts became catalysts for exploring adolescent identity.

Each of us wrote analytic memos, which informed the group's analysis and helped us to organize data according to salient topics. We used Google Docs for our coding, which we also used to collaboratively author this chapter. Jason, Sara, and Anna transcribed and analyzed the *Persepolis* and the *Hunger Games* conversations. Rob and Sandro worked together on the discussion of *Part-Time Indian*. Will and Helmi worked on the *Feed* conversation. Each of these groups wrote initial drafts of the corresponding sections for this chapter. These were shared with the large group, and revised and edited jointly.

Researching and writing in this way proved time consuming, challenging, and sometimes messy. Learning how to research collectively involved negotiating seven readings of data and seven different approaches to writing. Rather than attempting to distill these multiple perspectives into what Bourdieu (1979) has described as "accounts of accounts" (p. 21)—simplified, abstracted representations of the social worlds we investigated—our methodology was essentially dialectical (Simon, Campano, Broderick, & Pantoja, 2012). We repeatedly returned to the questions and concerns that drove our inquiry, negotiating aspects of researching and writing about this work in the process of doing it.

While complicated, this process supported mutually developing and coauthoring our understandings. Each of us had a hand in the process at every stage—working side by side, rather than in hierarchical relation to each other—though Rob took the lead in organizing data analysis and writing, as for many of us, this was our first attempt at researching teaching in this manner. This process reinforced the value of working together across our differences, much as the conversations we document in the remainder of this chapter demonstrate the value of this kind of collaborative approach in literacy classrooms.

The Limitations and Potentials of Reading in School

> *There is this anxiety about putting anything that is true to you in the public sphere because you could be made fun of. Your views could be controversial. So there is a definite pressure to not infuse any of your work [with] something that is coming from a personal place. I think for me, personally, that would take away a lot of the joy that I find in writing and reading. (Aviva, teacher candidate)*

Before breaking into novel groups, we began with a shared a reading of "As If Your Life Depended On It" by Adrienne Rich (1993), which we quote from at the outset of this chapter. We used this poem to explore our experiences as readers in school. As Aviva noted in the above comment, rather than encouraging students' critical impulses or literary imaginations, adolescents often feel apprehension about sharing personal reactions to texts that may be viewed as "controversial" or in conflict with the pragmatic purposes of reading and responding to texts in school.

Alessandro, one of Aviva's peers in the MT program, reflected on this tension in relation to the last line of Rich's (1993) poem:

> [Rich] sets up two ways you can read: You can read, 'as if your life depended on it,' and that is unlocking all this potential—you are revealing yourself. But the other way to read is the school way, and that is for success. You can fail at that, and that is very, very dangerous. So "I don't understand poetry" is self-protection.

Echoing Aviva's description of the tension between conditioned school responses and more personal experiences of reading, Alessandro argued that students learn to guard themselves from critique. As Dennis Sumara (1996) has noted, "All texts are read in relation to the contexts of reading" (p. 1). School structures and curricula invite relationships to texts and among individuals that configure adolescents as particular kinds of readers, failing to account for the myriad ways in which they engage with literacy in their lives. Beneath the surface of schooled responses, Alessandro implied, individuals construct readings that can be personal and meaningful.

While elements of "school ways" shaped our discussion of Rich's poem and subsequent conversations in novel groups, individuals shared critical and personal reflections across their differences. One of the most surprising aspects of these discussions was how common boundaries and hierarchies were, to some degree, diffused in the ensuing group conversations. For example, the group discussion of Collins' (2008) *The Hunger Games* included moments of playfulness. Prompted by a teacher candidate, Louisa, who introduced herself by declaring "I'm Katniss," participants began by describing the characters they were most like. Rosalie, a teacher candidate, welcomed Elie, a high school student, to the group with the comment, "Elie, you're like our little Rue!" referring to the youngest participant in the Hunger Games. In the ensuing exchange, Elie interrupted Rosalie's critique to express her affinity with another character, Foxface, a "sly and elusive" girl who avoids combat:

Louisa:	What about Foxface?
Rosalie:	People like that annoy me. [Laughter]
Rosalie:	You just hide the whole time. She's hiding. She…
Elie:	You know what? Sorry, sorry. If I was in the Hunger Games, I would most likely be Foxface.
Rosalie:	You know what Elie? I'm not okay with that! [Laughter]
Elie:	My personality, I don't like encountering battles or whatever. So I just like to hide. I would just let everyone kill themselves.
Anna:	And be the last one standing. [Laughter]

This is an instance of how individuals read together but not necessarily in deference to one another. The exchange is marked by shared laughter. Elie, the youngest member of the group at fourteen, had described herself as shy. Here, she counters Rosalie, who in another context might have been viewed by her as an authority figure. Elie justified her appreciation of Foxface through a revelation of her personal approach to conflict and by highlighting the strategic validity of this approach in relation to the central conflict in the novel.

Unlike more narrow forms of textual analysis often encouraged in classrooms, groups approached these novels as "iterable" (Derrida, as cited in Sumara, 1996, p. 33). Authority was negotiated, and texts were opened to multiple interpretations, which sometimes involved consensus, but also disruptive readings and disconnections (Jones & Clarke, 2007). Texts became platforms for inquiries into the purposes and practices of reading and teaching literature. This formed a basis for social critique, as well as explorations of alternative relationships between teachers and students.

"What teens are actually like": Unlearning Assumptions about Adolescents

> One observation I had is the fact that through the whole book, I feel it's really realistic to what teens are actually like. "Cause I hate those books where it's like, this is what a teenager is actually like!" And they have them talking and you're like, "It's not like that at all!"—Nina, high school student

Noting the realistic depiction of the teen protagonist in *Absolutely True Diary of a Part-Time Indian*, Nina suggested that fictional characterizations often metonymically represent adolescents' complex identities. Building on our earlier conversation about reading in school, Nina's statement implied a critique of how texts can project identities onto young people. This observation cuts to the core of the relational politics in classrooms. How do schools become sites of representational tension? Whose interests, identities, and voices are represented? How are adolescents' literate identities negotiated, displaced, ignored or internalized?

Throughout the conversations, Nina and other youth poignantly described how experiences of schooling shape adolescents' academic and social identities and self-images. These youth repeatedly demonstrated a lucid awareness about the everyday dimensions of schooling, which are, as Collins and Blott (2003) note, "constitutive as well as regulative; the stuff out of which senses of identity are composed and recomposed" (p. 5).

Book group conversations surfaced various examinations of, in Nina's terms, "what teens are actually like." Groups explored teenagers' languages and literacies, their self-perceptions and self-efficacy, and the ways they valued—or did not value—school. For example, Caitlin, a high school student, and Alessandro, Susan, and Sofia, teacher candidates, explored how teens are constructed in Anderson's (2002) *Feed*, a novel that explores hyper-consumerism and the obliteration of autonomy in a dystopian future in which individuals have links to the Internet implanted in their brains. The group used an analysis of the novel's protagonist, Titus, as a basis for exploring teenagers' valuation of the purposes and practices of schooling:

Susan: Titus and his friends don't find any value in school. They hate it. They see no point in it.

Alessandro: [To Caitlin] Do all your classmates find value in school?

Caitlin: No. Well, it depends on who you ask. I'm friends with a lot of really intelligent students, and they don't really like school. [But] I see the value in it....

Sofia: Do you like this [conversation]?

Caitlin: No, this is fine. This isn't school. This is fun. But having to sit down and have some teacher lecture at you and say, "Okay, let's take up answers," and say four kids get to write answers on the board and you are just watching them. That's not really educational. I could sit at home and read the textbook and get the same information.

Susan: Or Google it on the Internet.

Caitlin: Or Google it...

Susan: The interesting thing is most students wouldn't be able to articulate that in the same way.

Considering that this conversation unfolded in a teacher education classroom, with a professor and many teachers, Caitlin may have perceived this to be the epitome of schooling. Yet her comment "This isn't school" suggested the possibility that interacting with teachers on a relational level that invited her opinions and interests—educational experiences that go beyond the deprecating mythos of the lecturing chalkboard teacher and passive learners—is more meaningful. As a result of the kinds of scenarios she describes, Caitlin notes that many students feel estranged in school or fail to see "value" in it. Caitlin's analysis recalls Rich's (1993) argument that the experience of school for many students is alienating, in spite of adolescents' intellectual capabilities and literate engagement outside of school.

Interestingly, Susan suggested that other teenagers might not have articulated this problem as thoughtfully as Caitlin did. In light of Caitlin's critique of the delimiting structures of schooling—and recalling Aviva's earlier observations about the risks of reading in school—this may have more to do with the lack of invitations commonly provided for adolescents to share their critiques of schooling rather than teenagers' lack of critical perspectives.

Throughout the conversations, youth thoughtfully articulated problems related to the ways that schooling often gets in the way of education. For example, echoing Alessandro's earlier comments, Nina, a high school student, used the last line of Rich's (1993) poem, "Or, you can say: 'I don't understand poetry," to describe how encounters with literature in school can be alienating for adolescents:

Nina:	This is just sort of an observation: I really, really, like the last line. It's so powerful, this thing among students, especially because I see it all the time. You know, we decide that we just can't understand it. It just doesn't make sense, and there is no point in even trying. I think this is really shown in this poem.
Rob:	So you think it cuts to the heart of an issue?
Nina:	For sure. An issue about the way that students are sometimes labeled. You might not be able to understand something, or might not get it so easily, and students believe it about themselves. They say, "I can't read poetry, or Shakespeare," or something like that. So it's sometimes hard to learn.

Nina's reflections regarding her own and others' struggles with literature in school, and her insights about how labels like "reluctant" or "struggling" reader effect students, has resonance with Caitlin's image of lectures that engage four individuals among a class of docile, disengaged students. Nina noted that school experiences like these aren't merely uninteresting, but may drive students to develop oppositional academic identities—to internalize perceptions about their lack of ability, leading adolescents, in Nina's words, to "believe it about themselves."

Conversely, Nina's response implied the intrinsic power that teachers and students have to foster their interests in a more supportive atmosphere. While these conversations about young adult novels were not, in any simple way, "open"—they were shaped by institutional norms, structures and expectations—they did provide more open-ended opportunities for participants to explore issues related to language and identity, and to collectively struggle with the multiplicity of meanings in texts, rather than settle on merely one reading.

For example, the *Feed* group used the hyper-teen language of the novel to explore the language practices of adolescents:

Sofia: [Teenagers] use weird words like "swag" and "wheels."
Alessandro: Swag and wheels?
Sofia: People have wheels now. That's a really cool thing.
Alessandro: Shoot. I don't know this one.
Sofia: Yeah, and "swag." So those types of words seem weird, but they're being used, right? Those are crazy, out-there words…[like] "I have wheels."
Caitlin: No one uses the word wheels? Or swag?
Susan: No.
Alessandro: Swag! You use the word swag?
Susan: Did you not hear me?
Alessandro: I heard you. But this is a real person.
[pointing to Caitlin].

Alessandro's surprise at this slang, and Caitlin's surprise at his discursive outsider position, suggests the conceptual and linguistic disparity between teenagers' and adults' worlds. Further, this conversation positioned Caitlin as a teacher and "expert" on teenage culture. This is an instance of how the horizontal rather than hierarchical nature of the discussion provided a basis for mutual learning but also disruptions of doxic beliefs, including interrogations of language, classroom norms, and assumptions about adolescents. As this conversation and earlier exchanges with Caitlin related to schooling suggest, teacher candidates used these interactions as opportunities to learn from adolescents about their cultural, linguistic, and institutional experiences. This formed a basis for using discussions of texts to better understand and connect with the individuals they were teaching.

"Where I'm From": Critical Investigations of Identity

Sally: Where I'm from—Saugeen Shores, right on the Saugeen River, and the Saugeen First Nations Reserve is right outside our town—they all went to school with us. "Tonto," I heard that being used.

Rob: You have? As a derogatory term?

Sally: Everyone was using the word "Tonto." They probably didn't know who it was. So that's what I mean, it's a generational thing but it's also, I think, depending on where you're from....You're from Toronto, right?

Nina: Yeah. I'm from here.

Sally: Maybe people from rural areas might know.

This discussion about the use of "Tonto" as a derogatory term arose from participants' readings of *The Absolutely True Diary of a Part-Time Indian*, a novel about a fourteen-year-old boy's experiences on and off of a Spokane reservation. Sally's "where I'm from" statement introduced the possibility that her own lived experience as a white, rural Canadian growing up near a First Nations community could inform her own and others' readings of *Part-Time Indian*. With her assertion, "Maybe people from rural areas might know," Sally claimed an epistemic authority grounded in her own cultural history (Campano, 2007). Sally used this experience as a conceptual framework to interpret the novel, providing the group with a means of textual (and extra-textual) analysis based not on claims to objective expertise but on lived experience.

Repeated numerous times during the discussion, "where I'm from" functioned not as a definitive means of interpreting the novel, but rather as a critical heuristic and an invitation for others to engage similarly. Grounding interpretations in "who and where I am from" produced a space in which all participants could, through the process of collectively interpreting the novel, critically explore issues of identity (Beach et al., 2006; Bean & Moni, 2003), to connect and contrast their individual experiences as a means of analyzing the novel and the world.

For example, this collective inquiry was evident in participants' exploration of the use of the racially derogative term "apple" in the novel:

Sally: That does happen, where I'm from. Any person from the reserve who goes to university or college are shunned and they are not invited back by the people on the reserve.... I have classmates who were really smart, really into school, got really good grades, but as soon as grade 12 was done, that was it. If they leave... they see it as, "Oh, you think you're better than us, you're trying

	to better your life? Our life's not good enough? You're leaving?"
Nina:	It's the "apple" thing.
Natalie:	The red on the outside, the white on inside.
Mae:	....It seems like everyone has a version of that. For Asians it's "bananas."
Natalie:	My aunts call themselves "Oreos." Right? Black on the outside, white on the inside. Everyone has....
Mae:	"Twinkies." The same meaning: White on the inside, darker on the outside.
Sally:	I never heard any of that. I've only heard "apple."
Nina:	I never heard of "apple."

Individuals used their experiences to reflect on the discursive process of racialization as a means of social and textual analysis. Nina, the only youth in this exchange, connected Sally's experience to the "apple" metaphor in *Part-Time Indian*, which provided an opportunity for others to use the text to explore their own experiences of racial stereotyping, labeling and assimilationism.

This discussion resonates with Christensen's articulation of critical literacy pedagogy, which involves interrogating texts through the lenses of students' lives, with the goal of moving students "beyond a description of society and into an interrogation of it" (Christensen, 1999, p. 56). Much as Christensen (1999) imagines curriculum as a dialectic between students' lives and the social worlds around them, in their discussions of young adult novels, participants interrogated texts from the vantage of their cultural identities and histories. Conversations involved complex negotiations of race, class, and culture, markers of marginalized identities, and issues related to cultivating a sense of individuality within complicated social circumstances, including relationships and institutional arrangements in and out of schools.

These explorations of identity as a means of interrogating the world were not unique to the *Part-Time Indian* discussion, nor were they limited to explorations of race. For example, Satrapi's (2003) graphic novel, *Persepolis,* a bildungsroman set in the religiously fueled Iranian Revolution, inspired participants to analyze their personal experiences of religion and its function in society. Teacher candidates raised critiques, suggesting that religion is, at worst, a state-imposed tool of social control, and at best an activity with little to no social benefit.

As a counterpoint to these critical perspectives, two of the participating adolescents, Mira and Justin, who participated in a church-based leadership group together, described their positive experiences with religion. While they acknowledged that their experiences were countercultural—"we all get into a circle, and we listen to a bunch of spiritual songs, and pray together…it sounds super lame"—they went on to explore the differences between their experiences of faith and those of the protagonist of *Persepolis:*

Mira: It's not even like, "Oh, I believe in Jesus!" It's not kind of like this religion, about, how you said, the government puts rules and regulations, stuff like that. It's more of what you feel.

Layla: It's more of a personal...

Mira: Yeah. It's a personal connection to God.

Justin: It's sort of like your relationship with God. It's like that.

Mira: And to each other. Because you really feel a lot better praying. For me, I feel a lot better praying when I'm with other people. I feel connected to others. It's just a really good experience.

This dialogue was risky in that it surfaced highly personal, faith-based experiences not commonly shared in classrooms. These adolescents countered the ways that religion was described in the text, as well as teacher candidates' critiques of religion, with personal experiences of faith. The text became a means for the group to explore individual experiences of the sacred, rather than merely making facile connections with the dogmatic, doctrinal characterization of religion in *Persepolis*, or allowing the conversation to be restricted by the notion that discussions of faith are off limits in the classroom.

Two teacher candidates, Nora and Aviva, took up Mira and Justin's invitation to express their own understandings of spirituality:

Nora: I come to like, as I get older, churches. And not even just churches, but what I call spiritual places. 'Cause I've traveled a bit, and I've been to Buddhist temples, Shinto temples, synagogues, mosques, and churches. I love these places, because these places are set aside so you can just be emotional—like you're talking about....

Aviva: And people conduct themselves in almost the same way, no matter where you go in a religious space. If you walk into a church, people acknowledge each other. Myself included.

In spite of differences in age and social location, exchanges like this one suggest that at some level, individuals regarded each other as peers. While not all participants responded to the unspoken invitation to use their experiences as a means of exploring texts, most participants across book groups offered insights from "where they were from" as a basis for critiquing the texts they analyzed and building connections with one another.

Though respect for individuals' knowledge in these intergenerational discussions created both a forum for exploration of the novels and a space for social critique, they sometimes surfaced problematic assumptions. Explorations of race in the *Part-Time Indian* conversation were rooted in analysis of the experiences of a fictional Spokane teenager as a basis for surfacing and interrogating racial stereotypes. For example, Nina, a high school student, asked the group if it is true that people on the reserve could not be given hand sanitizer for fear they would drink it:

Helmi: I'm sure some people would, but....

Natalie: But that doesn't....there are some Black people, some Hispanic people, some East Asian people who...

Sally: At our drugstore back home, you can only buy two bottles of Scope max. You can only buy two bottles of hand sanitizer.

This discussion surfaced a prevalent and problematic racial stereotype. The exchange was unsettling. Yet as Jones and Clarke (2007) have noted, dissonant encounters with text can provide opportunities for critical literacy pedagogy. Through the process of unpacking this racial stereotype, the subsequent conversation moved to address racially charged identity issues. Participants identified where they had encountered such stereotypes, how they have been used to malign and control others by reducing diverse individuals and communities to toxic caricatures. Later in the discussion, Helmi noted that refusing to allow minorities to be reduced to stereotypes can be a powerful means of redressing injustice and reclaiming authority: "If they're human, and they're whole, and they're three-dimensional, then that's a much more complicated story." As this exchange suggests, texts like *Persepolis* and *Part-Time Indian* can provide opportunities for complex issues and tacit assumptions to be surfaced and challenged, for issues of race, identity, and cultural stereotypes, to be historicized, critiqued, and countered.

Implications: Teaching to Learn

> In school I'm not really very talkative. I'd say that I'm reserved; therefore, I don't really share my thoughts in class. But after this experience I feel as though I don't really have to be afraid of anything. (Elie, high school student)

As a community invested in the larger project of advocating for and with young people, this work has suggested important implications for how we approach texts and teaching. Beach et al. (2006) note that literature can be a catalyst for exploring real-life concerns of our students because it provides "insights into their beliefs and values, [which] justifies the goal of having students make connections to and reflect on ethical and identity issues in their own experiences" (43). This process of engaging with meaningful issues through literature, as Sumara (1996) has suggested, drawing upon the hermeneutics of Derrida and Heidegger, also involves "self-interpretation" and "re-invention" (p. 33). As Elie and other participating youth noted, the experience of exploring literature alongside educators provided opportunities for reimagining their relationships to teachers and texts, toward actualizing more agential academic identities.

For us, the process of documenting and actively engaging young people's perspectives on language and literacy in the world and in school helped us, in some sense, to better understand "what teens are actually like," in Nina's terms. This was not a virtuous paradigm of meeting student's needs, merely "connecting" with texts or with each other through literature-circle discussions (Thein, Guise, & Sloan, 2011), or "discovering" diverse adolescents' critical capacities. These explorations with adolescents did, however, suggest implications for how we teach them, including how teachers structure classrooms, choose curricula, develop ongoing relationships, negotiate and manifest collective power, and ultimately invite students to be intellectuals (Campano & Ghíso, 2010).

Our experiences reading with youth suggest that teaching is fundamentally about mutual learning. If teachers are willing to learn how to listen (Christensen, 1999), there is much we can learn from students. As Aviva, a teacher candidate, noted in reflecting on her experience discussing *Persepolis* with youth, their conversation revealed adolescents to be "extremely mature, insightful and capable" in ways that called into question "who the 'teacher" is.' Aviva went on to argue that students "need to be treated as intellectual equals," representing a significant shift in epistemic authority.

Similarly, Louisa noted that her experience "further validated the fact that students know more than we think." Though as Ellsworth (1997) reminds us, individuals are never, in any simple way, reducible to roles they enact in classrooms, for Aviva, Louisa, and other teacher candidates, intergenerational inquiries into literature provided a forum for learning from students' perspectives and for imagining more dialogic approaches to teaching and research.

Correspondingly, youth noted that their perceptions of teachers were altered. For example, Nina "found it surprising how open [teachers] were to our ideas." Elie noted, "It was easy to relate to them, they weren't as different as I thought. I could really share my thoughts because I felt as if they understood what I was saying (or trying to say)." These and other responses from youth suggest that this provided space for them to develop relational connections with teachers. This does not mean that power differentials were ameliorated. Yet these conversations did present foundations for imagining literacy pedagogy as complex and oriented toward collective learning.

One of the most significant implications of this work was how these literature discussions provoked critical social inquiry. Across the six conversations, the novels and the world were explored from the immigrant experience, the adopted experience, the experience of wealth, the experience of poverty, the experience of faith and the experience of socioeconomically diverse and marginalized communities. No reading was claimed as definitive. Rather, individual experiences were offered as facets by which the world—and the respective novels—could be interrogated. Outcomes of these conversations were broad; learning intersubjective.

As Christensen (1999) notes, classrooms and communities are animated by unfinished struggles. This work has invited more questions than it answered. At times, in trying to present a coherent narrative of complex conversations—both in our data, and about it—we may have elided some of the dilemmas and complications that arose for us. For example, while some social and professional boundaries were indeed diffused in these interactions—throughout our data are instances of students and teachers responding to each other as peers, negotiating ideas collaboratively, as well as examples of how students took intellectual or even pedagogical responsibility in these conversations—authoritative practices sometimes reasserted themselves. Rereading the data, we encountered troubling moments. We have represented some of these, for example in the risky conversations about race inspired by *Part-Time Indian*. We found that the opportunity to unpack moments like these together helped us to make sense of them.

In spite of these struggles and contradictions—and perhaps as a result of them—this project has led to a deepening awareness of the importance of cultivating pedagogies that disrupt some of the inherited norms and hierarchies that shape university and school literacy classrooms. Approaching teaching and teacher education through collective inquiry encouraged each of us—teachers and students alike—to question our assumptions about our own and others' abilities and roles, and to value an ethic of mutual responsibility for learning. Rather than uncritically entering into discourses that reproduce hierarchies of knowledge, working across social, cultural, and institutional boundaries has productively altered some of the "familiar contours" of literacy pedagogy (O'Reilley, 1993, p. 37). This has challenged our understandings of literacy, our practices as teachers, and our regard for the array of adolescents' imaginative and literate insights.

Note

1. Here and elsewhere, all names other than those of the authors are pseudonyms.

References

Alexie, S. (2007). *The absolutely true diary of a part-time Indian.* New York: Little Brown.

Anderson, M.T. (2002). *Feed.* Cambridge, MA: Candlewick Press.

Appleman, D. (2009). *Critical encounters in high school English: Teaching literary theory to adolescents* (2nd Ed.). New York and Urbana, IL: Teachers College Press and National Council of Teachers of English.

Beach, R., Appleman, D., Hynds, S., & Wilhelm, J. (2006). *Teaching literature to adolescents.* New York: Routledge.

Bean, T., & Moni, K. (2003). Developing students' critical literacy: Exploring identity construction in young adult fiction. *Journal of Adolescent and Adult Literacy, 46*(8), 838–847.

Bourdieu, P. (1979). *Outline of a theory of practice.* Cambridge: Cambridge University Press.

Brauer, L., & Clark, C. T. (2008). The trouble is English: Reframing English studies in secondary schools. *English Education, 40*(4), 293–313.

Campano, G. (2007). *Immigrant students and literacy: Reading, writing, and remembering.* New York: Teachers College Press.

Campano, G., & Ghíso, M. (2010). Immigrant students as cosmopolitan intellectuals. In S. Wolf, K. Coats, P. Encisco, & C. Jenkins (Eds.), *Handbook of research on children's and young adult literature* (pp. 164–174). New York: Routledge.

Campano, G., Honeyford, M. A., Sanchez, L., & Vander Zanden, S. (2010). Ends in themselves: Theorizing the practice of university-school partnering through horizontalidad. *Language Arts, 87*(4), 277–285.

Cercone, J. (2009). We're smarter together: Building professional social networks in English education. *English Education, 41*(3), 199–206.

Christensen, L. (1999). Critical literacy: Teaching reading, writing, and outrage. In C. Edelsky (Ed.), *Making justice our project: Teachers working towards critical whole language practice* (pp. 53–67). Urbana, IL: NCTE.

Cochran-Smith, M., & Lytle, S. L. (1999). Relationships of knowledge and practice: Teacher learning on communities. In A. Iran-Nejad & P. D. Pearson (Eds.), *Review of Research in Education, 24,* 249–306. Washington, DC: American Educational Research Association.

Cochran-Smith, M., & Lytle, S. L. (2001). Beyond certainty: Taking an inquiry stance on practice. In A. Leiberman and L. Miller (Eds.), *Teachers caught in the action: Professional development that matters.* New York: Teachers College Press.

Cochran-Smith, M., & Lytle, S. L. (2009). *Inquiry as stance: Practitioner research in the next generation.* New York: Teachers College Press.

Collins, J., & Blott, R. K. (2003). *Literacy and literacies: Texts, power, and identity.* Cambridge: Cambridge University Press.

Collins, S. (2008). *The Hunger Games.* New York: Scholastic Press.

Cummins, J. (2009). Transformative multiliteracies pedagogy: School-based strategies for closing the achievement gap. *Multiple Voices for Ethnically Diverse Exceptional Learners, 11*(2), 38–56.

Ellsworth, E. (1997). *Teaching positions: Difference, pedagogy, and the power of address.* New York: Teachers College Press.

Ghíso, M. P., Campano, G., & Simon, R. (2014). Grassroots inquiry: Reconsidering the location of innovation. *Language Arts, 91*(2). 105-112.

Jones, S., & Clarke, L. W. (2007). Disconnections: Pushing readers beyond connections and toward the critical. *Pedagogies: An International Journal, 2*(2), 95–115.

Kamler, B., & Comber, C. (2005). Turn-around pedagogies: Improving the education of at-risk students. *Improving Schools, 8*(2), 121–131.

Lankshear, C., & Knobel, M. (2007). Sampling "the new" in new literacies. In M. Knobel & C. Lankshear (Eds.), *A new literacies sampler* (pp. 1–24), New York: Peter Lang.

Lieberman, A., & Wood, D. (2001). When teachers write: Of networks and learning. In A. Lieberman and L. Miller (Eds.), *Teachers caught in the action: Professional learning that matters* (pp. 174–187). New York: Teachers College Press.

New London Group (1996). A pedagogy of multiliteracies: Designing social futures. *Harvard Educational Review, 66,* 60–92.

O'Reilley, M. (1993). *The peaceable classroom.* Portsmouth, NH: Heinemann.

Rich, A. (1993). *What is found there: Notebooks on poetry and politics.* New York: Norton.

Rogers, R., Mosley, M., Kramer, M. A., & The Literacy for Social Justice Teacher Research Group. (2009). Designing socially just learning communities: Critical literacy education across the lifespan. New York: Routledge.

Satrapi, M. (2003). *Persepolis: The story of a childhood.* New York: Pantheon.

Simon, R. (2012). "Without comic books there would be no me": Teachers as connoisseurs of adolescents' literate lives. *Journal of Adolescent and Adult Literacy, 55*(6), 516–526.

Simon, R. (2013a). "Starting with what is": Exploring response and responsibility to student writing through collaborative inquiry. *English Education, 45*(1), 115–146.

Simon, R. (2013b). Literacy teacher education as critical inquiry. In C. Kosnik, J. Rowsell, P. Williamson, R. Simon, & C. Beck (Eds.), *Literacy teacher educators: Preparing teachers for a changing world* (pp. 121–134). Rotterdam: Sense Publishers.

Simon, R., Brennan, J., & Edwards, W. (2013). *Investigating literacy through intergenerational inquiry.* Paper presented as part of symposium, "Writing ourselves into the work: Critical reflections on community-based digital literacies, practitioners' knowledge and experiences." American Educational Research Association Annual Meeting, San Francisco, CA.

Simon, R., & Campano, G. (2013). Activist literacies: Teacher research as resistance to the "normal curve." *Journal of Language and Literacy Education, 9*(1), 21–39.

Simon, R., Campano, G., Broderick, D., & Pantoja, A. (2012). Practitioner research and literacy studies: Toward more dialogic methodologies. *English Teaching: Practice and Critique, 11*(2), 5–24.

Street, B. V. (1995). *Social literacies: Critical approaches to literacy in development, ethnography, and education.* Harlow: Pearson Education Ltd.

Sumara, D. J. (1996). *Private readings in public: Schooling the literary imagination.* New York: Peter Lang.

Thein, A. H., Guise, M., & Sloan, D. L. (2011). Problematizing literature circles as forums for discussion of multicultural and political texts. *Journal of Adolescent and Adult Literacy, 55*(1), 15–24.

Chapter 9

Finding Voice: Building Literacies and Communities Inside and Outside the Classroom

Josh Schachter and Julie Kasper

Introduction

> *Each waterfall starts with one drop of water.*
> *—Martin, FV student from Mexico*

What does it mean to find one's voice? We—Julie Kasper, a public school educator, and Josh Schachter, a teaching artist–created Finding Voice in 2006 at Catalina Magnet High School in Tucson, Arizona, as a literacy and visual arts program for refugee and immigrant youth in English Language Development (aka, ESL) classes. Catalina has the largest number of refugee students in Tucson Unified School District, and Arizona has the 8th-highest rate of refugee resettlement in the U.S. Through research, photography, writing and speaking out about critical social issues in their lives and communities, students develop their second language, literacy, and 21st century skills (Partnership for 21st Century Skills, 2013). Students direct the moves each class makes and the issues explored, and they decide how the work is shared and with whom. Finding Voice provides immigrant and refugee youth in a traditional public school setting—who are otherwise constrained by a four-hour model of English study required by Arizona state law—with critical opportunities for academic development, civic engagement and artistic expression.

Because Finding Voice students come from across the globe, our project strives to address matters common to all of them, such as the lack of opportunities for refugee/immigrant youth to build communication skills, to voice their perspectives about issues impacting their lives, and a growing disconnect between Tucson's refugees/immigrants and the community at large.

Many refugee students struggle academically due to language and cultural barriers, compounded by a feeling of isolation in Tucson and discrimination at school and in their community. Finding Voice provides space and time and teaches skills students need to generate change—for example, in the form of thought-provoking works they create and then share with the community through exhibitions, digital stories, community forums, publications, public installations, our project website (Finding Voice, 2013), blogs and theater, to name a few. We—Julie, Josh, and the students—co-construct knowledge and share experiences that shape our individual and collective voices.

Case Study: Finding Voice Project Work, 2007–2008

Hold onto your work with two hands.
—Mariama, FV student from Sierra Leone

That is certainly what we had to do during only our second year of collaboration—hold on with both hands. Since we were still very much engaged in the process of figuring out what exactly we were doing as a collaborative team, 2007–08 challenged us as individuals and as a project to mature quickly. Due to the pivotal nature of 2007–08, we thought we would offer a brief window into our pedagogical and collaborative processes that year.

Figure 1. Finding Voice students meeting with medical professionals, social service agencies, civic leaders and others at a community forum to discuss pressing health issues in the students' lives and communities.

During the 2007–2008 school year, Julie, as the classroom teacher, and Josh, as the artist in residence, worked with 30 Advanced English Language Learner (ELL) students enrolled in English Language Development classes. During the fall, students developed foundational skills in literacy and photography. They focused their project work on health issues in their community, hosting a health forum in December of 2007, which drew over 100 community members, including school personnel, community leaders, parents of youth in the program, and many health care providers from around Tucson. The forum resulted in further discussions among TUSD health professionals, problem-solving sessions with refugee service organizations, and health internships for students. During the spring semester, the students chose to explore issues of war and immigration. They wrote texts, read, discussed, took portraits of each other, and ultimately created posters that were displayed in Tucson's bus stops. The students discussed potential audiences for the work (the governor, immigrants, Border Patrol, principals, courts, peers, teachers, and others) and formats to reach these audiences (photo exhibits, banners, YouTube, local radio, television, etc.) before deciding (after much heated debate) on the bus stop public art/civic engagement project. The 2007–08 year culminated with the installation of the posters and a community celebration attended by families, community leaders, school staff, project supporters, alumni, and others, at which students presented their writing and photographs.

In tandem with the 2007–2008 class-based work, we continued the previous year's project work, entitled: "Home? Teen Immigrants & Refugees Explore Their Tucson." We worked with city and federal political leaders to publish a book of the "Home?" writing and photographs, and to exhibit the students' work in the U.S. Senate building in June 2008. Six students presented at a Congressional Briefing in the U.S House of Representatives, where they spoke to the staffs of nearly 20 congressional offices and service agencies about their refugee, immigrant, and educational experiences and related policy implications. We also spoke about the importance of rethinking evaluation strategies in our education system, and about providing adequate funding for arts education. The year was filled with multiple opportunities and challenges that led our small grassroots project (with very limited funding and only two very part-time coordinators) to evolve into a nationally recognized and highly publicized program. The 2007–2008 year transformed our thinking and relationship as teachers and collaborators, as well as how we understood the potential of Finding Voice. We saw what we were capable of; we learned more about what mattered to the students and what they brought to Finding Voice; we struggled and experienced being overwhelmed and exhausted; we took note of areas of conflict and dissatisfaction; we celebrated unforeseeable successes; and we incorporated innovations into our preparations for another year. Six years later, we can still see the influence of the 2007–2008 year in our patterns of interaction, the design of our co-construction process, and the very project that is Finding Voice.

Figure 2. Sadaf, a Finding Voice student from Afghanistan, presents her personal story at a Congressional Briefing in the U.S. House of Representatives.

Permeable Boundaries: Balancing Acts, Tensions, & Co-construction in the Finding Voice Project—A Dialogue

Julie: One of the greatest challenges we face in the Finding Voice Project is working within a traditional high school setting where the expectations of students raised or indoctrinated in it—with a few exceptions and pockets of light—are low, a system that fosters passivity and is disconnected from

> *When I crossed the line, I couldn't go back...*
> *–Layth, FV student from Iraq*

"real-world" applications and engagement. This is true not only of U.S. public school systems, but many others worldwide, including those in refugee camps. Coupled with still pervasive grammar-translation methods used in English language instruction both overseas and by teachers in the United States, students come to my classes and to our project with an expectation that memorizing lists of vocabulary words or manipulating structures grammatically without context will lead to success and language development. They also expect to not be asked their opinions and to not be welcomed to share their ideas or question the teachers. They have rarely engaged in an inquiry-based, problem-solving, or project-based curriculum and are largely used to doing discrete skills study, a new worksheet or chapter each day, with little connection between those units of study and little to no application, analysis, synthesis, or evaluation. And then there's the reality that, coming from very distinct linguistic and cultural backgrounds and having intense life histories, our students are incredibly diverse. There aren't a lot of shared cultural norms, values, or routines. Given these facts, I must spend the first few months of every school year building a community of learners, establishing new norms for learning and working, and introducing them to a more communicative, academic and real-life content-driven, project-based approach to language learning.

Josh: In your classroom we encourage them to speak up, speak out, and share what's going on in their own lives.

Julie: Sure. And we can't ignore, in a project titled Finding Voice, that the students we're working with are facing severe constraints in terms of voice, both because of their linguistic biographies and their various immigrant statuses. They can't all run out and speak up and be seen and heard the way you and I, or other students and their families, can. So, we're also walking lines between worlds and values in terms of our goals, certain socio-political realities (such as racism, immigration status and laws, curricular constraints, etc.), and the students' own expectations, but we're also working to shift those "realities" and our students' expectations through skills development, confidence and local community building, civic engagement...

Josh: Yep, it's tricky to build skills and expectations and encourage the students to share their voices based on the realities they face while not at the same time setting them up for unrealistic outcomes. I think your willingness to be flexible and take thoughtful risks to connect our students' voices with the larger community allows us to find a pretty healthy balance. Not to mention the courage it takes for the students to put themselves out there.

Julie: I don't believe teaching happens in a closed-door classroom. I don't believe learning happens in a closed-door classroom. That's not productive; it's not meaningful.

I think Find My Voice means that we have to find the leader we have inside...
—Esteban, FV student from Mexico

Josh: I believe, and youth development research supports, that true transformation requires long periods of consistent engagement. I feel like this kind of sustained work is not being done as much, because frankly I think it's harder. It's easier for me to go into a classroom and get students jazzed for a few hours or days about a subject because it's new, I'm new. That's more about exposure and creating curiosity and excitement. But to do it for eight months requires a whole other kind of commitment, persistence: a marathoner's mindset versus a sprinter's. I feel like this long-term work supports the kind of change I want to see in the world. The other work has valid goals, but it's not going to achieve the depth of impact and sustainability.

Julie: And maybe that's what distinguishes our project from a lot of multiliteracy projects and a lot of community-based projects. It's not a weekend or summer program. It's sustained hard work. Our goals are about transformation of individuals and systems. We're trying to help students realize that their voices are powerful and can make a difference in their communities. We teach them how and help them to navigate—and maybe even shift—complex social and political systems. And once you engage with that, the thinking and processes of doing such work stay in your head.

Josh: Totally. Sometimes I think if I'd gotten a degree in psychology rather than environmental management it would have served me better in this work. But—like we tell students—all our experiences inform how we see, read, and interact with the world. Who would have thought that an aspiring primatologist would find his way to digital media and literacy development? I guess the part about working with primates hasn't changed. But seriously, when I look back, I think tracking lemur behavior twelve hours a day was as good a foundation as any. What better way to learn the importance of critical observation and attention to detail? After all, these skills are fundamental to being an effective documentarian, artist, activist, student, teacher and informed citizen. Not surprisingly, much of my pedagogy focuses on critical observation and encouraging youth and communities to examine the lenses through which they see the world and sharing those lenses with others. As Marcel Proust said, "The real voyage of discovery consists not in seeking new landscapes but in having new eyes." The process of documenting our own lives and communities provides us with both a window and a mirror through and in which to look at ourselves and others around us.

Similarly, I think my grounding in ecosystem management and social ecology has played a key role in how I see, photograph, and analyze issues, relationships and equity in the world. As an educator and activist, I constantly challenge folks to observe and document their lives within a larger context and to engage in social change work with a clear understanding of how biophysical and social systems shape the health of their communities. Paulo Freire's contextually based work has also shaped how I approach social change, both as an educator and artist. But if it wasn't for community artist Wendy Ewald, I would never have seen and fully realized the link between community, literacy and photography.

Julie: If I had to explain my own teaching philosophy, or my approach as an educator, I would have to start by saying that for me teaching is activism, an artistic process, and a necessarily collaborative venture. I see myself as a community activist, and I see education as the best way to engage with and transform my community. Driven by the words of choreographer Bill T. Jones, I strive to create a world I want to live in. That world is one in which all members of the community are given room to speak and share, have skills to listen with empathy and interest, and have developed a voice—a sense of self and skills to support articulate expression—that they use to engage academically, socially, politically, economically and creatively with everyone around them. For me, this necessarily leads to language instruction—and particularly to English language instruction—for some of the most disenfranchised in our communities. Given that I started my teaching career in 1995 overseas, in Japan, it's not surprising that I work from a place of recognition that access to a dominant language is access to power, but also that access to various languages brings access to new ideas, new cultures, new relationships, and new possibilities. After completing my Master's at Teachers College, Columbia, and while working with immigrant teens in a tough urban environment, I also knew that language instruction could not happen in a grammar or vocabulary vacuum. A bubble of nonsense, of disconnected, discrete learning activities, cannot lead to fluency, nor can it develop a sense of inquiry, curiosity, discovery, understanding, or human concern and compassion, which I believe are at the heart of lifelong learning and personal and social transformation. Thus, my teaching is more like what Noam Chomsky refers to as "laying out a string along which a student can explore and progress in her own way," as opposed to filling and indoctrinating young minds.

Josh: Despite our disparate backgrounds, I don't think we could keep doing this work if our values, pedagogical frameworks, and passions weren't pretty much aligned. Not to say we don't butt heads. But the fact that we are willing to take a stand and at times agree to disagree speaks to the trust we have built and values we hold.

Julie: We've had to develop a relationship beyond this work in order to sustain the work and ourselves.

Josh: It is definitely a balancing act. Sometimes I'm juggling four or five projects at once, and with our co-construction framework, scheduling is challenging. Especially since we don't know in advance what we're doing every week or every year, since the students' input drives our process.

> *...by myself I wouldn't be able to find all the answers, but with a team it's much easier.*
> *—Jemael, FV student from DR Congo*

Julie: Given that, I wonder if it would be worthwhile to outline which aspects of the work we collaborate on and which we don't. For example, I do the work of grading and that form of evaluation alone. I also do the day-to-day planning, though of course we do some larger vision planning and some individual lesson planning together. You, on the other hand, do a lot of the community outreach and negotiations without extensive input or support from me. It's true we collaborate on the large picture items, and we collaborate on daily matters when we're working on them together...but there is quite a bit that we do individually, as well. I think many people think of collaboration as everything being shared and all decisions being made by consensus, but that's not always the case in our collaboration.

Josh: For sure. As a photographer and arts educator who had primarily worked in an afterschool setting prior to Finding Voice, I guess I initially saw my role as a guest artist in your classroom. In the beginning, I focused on developing a photography curriculum that supported literacy development. After the first year of work together, I think we both saw the potential impact of our collaboration. As the scope of our work expanded, the need for more community engagement, grant research and writing, website development, etc., developed. And due to my passion for community engagement and background in that domain, it seemed that my responsibilities grew in those areas. To a large extent the success of our collaboration came from a willingness to trust that each of us would get our parts accomplished while constantly communicating to ensure that we were moving forward together.

Julie: Yeah. I'd like to think it was about our interests and skill-sets. I think that was part of it. But I think a lot of it came down to schedules—like what we were capable of doing. I was at a breaking point in terms of how much more writing and things I could do, so at a point when we needed a grant done, you took it on and you were successful. I think that established some confidence, and maybe that shifted some things. Now, I would like to meet with more of our community partners like you do, but my schedule doesn't flex. So it's partly passions and skills, but it's also just…

Josh: ...reality. Well, and that's perfect because that's where my identity gets thrown into the mix. When the work requires that I serve as a community liaison for a few months, or as website manager, I have to let go of my identity as a photographer or photography teacher. But it's hard to let go sometimes—especially when the funder sees me as the project's "artist." I think that adds a little pressure. If I'm not doing art or arts education in the traditional sense, is it going to be a problem? Am I failing as an artist and teaching artist if I'm mostly serving as a facilitator between the project and the community?

Julie: For me, as "the teacher," I have the same concern. There are days where we're not hitting an Arizona State ELD Writing Standard dead on. I know how what we're doing is connected to those standards and what it's leading towards, but should anybody from the State walk in on that day, for example, will *they* be able to see it, too? So it's a matter of being flexible, knowing my evaluators might have questions for me some days...This flexibility is really important in our co-construction because there are teachers who wouldn't be able to let go of their "standards," either personally or because of the system they're in, or their position and sense of vulnerability in that system. And there are artists who wouldn't be able to let go of their "art" to work on things that are happening.

Be Sincere.
—Hari, FV student from Nepal

Julie: Even before I started doing this, when I first started teaching, I modeled thinking, questioning, and problem-solving in the classroom. I don't understand why more teachers aren't doing it. So you're rolling along with a lesson and it's not working, what do you do? You can't always figure it out. I mean, sometimes you can, but you've got 20–30 people there with you at that moment. Why not ask them about next steps? "You guys really don't seem to be engaged here, or you seem to be confused, or I'm confused, so what's next?" Why not engage their minds in that pedagogical process?

Josh: Right, because that's part of the learning. That's as valuable as the content itself. It's learning the process of moving forward. But many teachers aren't able or willing to engage in that kind of honest dialogue because to do it you have to let go of control and at times be vulnerable. Not everyone wants to take those risks. It raises the question of how much should a teacher give students control over a project?

Julie: It's important, I think, to have that vulnerability and that openness, but also to have a really concrete structure. Students need to know that somebody's there leading them, somebody who knows where they're going, need to be going, or want to be going, and is going to get them there. They need to have that strength, sense of direction and purpose, and urgency. I feel like I'm able to bring those pieces because I'm willing to construct curriculum and design projects with and for my individual students each year, but I also know where we need to get to in terms of state standards, college and career goals, etc., and I'm 100% committed to getting there. I make that clear and transparent to the students, too. You know, "we're doing this as a means to get where we're going." Also, you and I have a positive reputation now, which makes it easier to establish that sense of purpose and trust.

Josh: That's a good point. We have really built our social capital in the school and community—with students, administrators, funders and community partners.

Julie: But it's definitely a balancing act, because you can swing too far to the other side by letting the kids control everything. This is one of the tensions that plays into curriculum and pedagogy. We're accountable to the State of Arizona in terms of English Language Arts and English Language Development standards. But even if we weren't in the school structure, you and I have definite ends in mind, non-negotiables that we want the young people we work with to achieve, so it requires openness and flexibility, but also tight structure and clear goals and full commitment all at the same time.

Julie: I think it's important for us to point out that not every decision is made together. Part of our structure is trust in each other and in our students to get some things done and to decide some things independently. Most people consider group think and the consensus model to be ideal. There's a lot of value in consensus building, but does it really achieve some greater ends than what we're able to achieve by trusting each other to make decisions separately?

> *This is where I fit in.*
> *– Briana, FV student from the Republic of the Marshall Islands*

Josh: Yeah, and I think you have to pick your battles. When are the battles really about ego and when do they challenge your underlying values?

Julie: Right, and that's true with the students, too. So there are points where we put our foot down, not to stop the process but to prolong and deepen the discussion before decisions are made. It's a question of what's the most equitable or democratic system for our decision-making. And our decision-making processes vary every year.

Josh: Definitely. It's always tricky to determine when to engage the youth in a decision and when we just need to make it ourselves and move forward, particularly with the time and other constraints of a public school environment and the changing student chemistry in our classes each year. Some of our decision-making processes are consistent, but it doesn't seem that we have a fully systematized decision-making process. I don't know if it should be more or less, but maybe it's good just to acknowledge this.

Julie: Well, I think the things that *are* systemic now are two-fold. One, students decide on the topics or the content for each project. If we give them an umbrella topic, they choose an individual focus within it, and often they even select the umbrella topic(s), as they did in 2007–2008. So they definitely have choice in the decision making there. Then, two, they generally decide on the product (within our constraints of time, money, know-how, and community partnering abilities). Those are the two pieces they control, and those are two really hard pieces for us, because every year we have a topic we want to pursue (food, for example) and every year we have really cool product ideas, but we let go because the content must be their own and the products must reflect their thinking, learning, values and goals. As for other stuff—such as actual assignments and day-to-day activities and other pedagogical and curricular concerns—maybe it is problematic that students aren't more directly involved, but then it goes back to that question of having choice and voice and vulnerability, but also having structure. As a trained educator and as an experienced facilitator of learning and problem-solving leading a learning community, I see it as my responsibility to provide that structure.

Thinking about all this, and thinking about our attempts at consensus building, I remember that in 2007–2008 we chose two broad topics (health & wellness/war & immigration) specifically because we *couldn't* reach consensus. We really wanted to focus the learning and the student energy around one topic, and we tried to get there, but we had a passionate and adamant group of students, and we really didn't want to force something on anyone that wouldn't let them tell *their* story. And we didn't want anyone to feel left out.

In the end, it was the right way to go because the students really did take ownership of those two projects. There were days, do you remember, where you could literally hear a pin drop when someone was showing their photographs because it was intense stuff and it meant so much to them individually and collectively.

> *I feel comfortable taking pictures so people can visualize my thoughts.*
> *—Hamida, FV student from Somalia*

Josh: How many people would be willing to document their home life and health issues and then share those images at a school or community-wide event? That takes immense courage and trust in the process. Sometimes I worry that the power differential between us as educators and them as students "pushes" them to participate. I particularly felt this when we asked the students to document health issues in their lives because their images and words revealed very personal family health challenges like depression, alcoholism, etc. Their art represents their daily reality.

Though we are sensitive to this and aware of the lure of voyeurism, it still concerns me. Compounding this problem is the expectation by the funders and the public that the students' work be honest, powerful, and intimate. If we want folks to rethink some stereotypes about refugees and immigrants, the work needs to be emotionally compelling. Having said that, I think we have found that if our process feels safe, transparent, and authentic, the work will reflect that honesty, and each student will find his or her comfort level for sharing.

Julie: That comes up in the writing, too. There are certain kids who don't want to write about certain things, and we have to work through it or around it, but…

Josh: Absolutely. For me, one thing that has been an exciting aspect of our program is the opportunity for families to engage in the creative process when our students undertake photography and interviewing in their homes and neighborhoods. Though we know this can also be a challenge, since many of the parents and families we work with are struggling to make ends meet, and participating in a photography session understandably may not be a priority…

Julie: Yeah, when they do—and increasingly they do collaborate—the photography creates so many opportunities and bridges… But sometimes we struggle to make it work.

Figure 3. Finding Voice students, Christian (left) shares his digital photo with Abdikadir during a photography workshop.

Josh: I think it's something we often discuss: What role is digital media playing in our project? To what extent is it moving the process forward? Can it just support the process of language, reading, and writing development? If so, will it be OK with our art funders if digital media is a small aspect of our final product? How do we balance our multiliteracy goals?

Julie: Every year we're reconfiguring that, aren't we? Sometimes it works and sometimes it doesn't. And sometimes we shift right in the middle because it's not working. It's become clear to me that for students with really low literacy skills and very basic English language skills, the photography aspect of our work is a gift since it provides another means of sharing ideas and participating in rigorous debate about social concerns.

Josh: But because time is limited and our primary goal is to develop the students' traditional literacy skills, I sometimes find it hard to provide enough foundation in visual literacy for the students to effectively communicate visually. Most of our students have had little to no formal training in photography, and as a result many see photography as a "point and shoot activity" that doesn't have a language and a process of revision—in effect, the whole process you go through with the writing. For some students, it's almost as if photography is a mechanical process. What you see is what you get.

This is complicated by the fact that the students' relationship to photography and the role it played in their home countries sometimes differs from how we are using it in Finding Voice. From what they say and from what I've seen firsthand in my travels, photography was primarily used for portraiture or to document formal events. So to shift from that frame of reference to asking them to tell a story about their own daily lives, at times through visual metaphor, understandably might seem foreign and potentially irrelevant. So how do we honor and incorporate their frame of reference for photography into our process while challenging them to explore new ways of seeing and documenting the world?

Julie: And then we compound that challenge of visual representation by inserting our own voices into the learning process and the production phases of project work. How much should we say, knowing that the students are going to take that in and knowing that our voices have a lot more strength than the students' own internal voices—at least early in the school year? And how much do we trust that they're going to let us know when we've pushed them too far or we're simply off-base?

Believe in yourself to make people believe in you.
—Amna, FV student from Kuwait

Josh: I think peer critiques play a critical role in ensuring that their voices don't become mirrors of our own. But peer critiques take time. Before 2009, when we had two-hour class periods (versus one-hour now), we had more peer critiques, self-critiques and fieldwork instruction. As a result, the students were able to make more informed photography editing decisions. This also created more opportunities for revision.

Julie: In terms of the written texts, we do so many revisions that students have plenty of room to accept or reject things. Also, they're really invested in reworking text in a way they're not invested in reworking photographs because they're concerned about being able to write well and pass state exams. But it's tricky in the writing, too. The best approach—what I would prefer to do—would be to sit with each student individually, for as long as needed, to discuss their ideas fully, ask questions to help them consider writing approaches, and coach rather than direct revision. However, that isn't realistic given the way a school day is structured. I try to do some of this through questioning and dialoging in the margins of students' papers, but when there are twenty students who want to talk with me during the same class hour about what I noted on their papers, it's not feasible. Still, if I measure growth over the school year, I definitely see them progress from doing or accepting everything I suggest to questioning my revision or editing comments. By the second semester, I have students come up to me and say, "I don't want to delete or change this because…" after reading my comments on their paper. At that point they're really in control of that revision process. My voice is only one among many, including their own, that they consider when making decisions; it is not *the* voice deciding for them.

Josh: So there's sort of two approaches: a more inquiry-based editing process versus a more directed or teacher-led approach. Which raises the question of the value and role of listening during the editing process. I remember when I was looking at Lydia's photo of a light fixture in spring 2008, and how I just wanted…needed… to rush through her photos so badly because there were so many other photos and lots of other students needing one-on-one mentoring. And honestly, her light fixture photo to me was aesthetically unremarkable. But for whatever reason I slowed down and I asked her why she'd taken that photo and she explained that each light represented the hope in each house in her neighborhood, and that the darkness between the bulbs was the fear and danger she felt in the neighborhood.

Hearing her explanation made me realize that if my aesthetic lens takes precedent over her voice, then we lose. We lose sight of the goals of our project. And so negotiating the pressures of time while honoring students' voices through deep listening is tricky, both throughout the creative process and in the production design phases of the project. During these processes it's also challenging not to be too influenced by community expectations. The community is assessing the youths' work based on their own cultural norms, their stereotypes of refugees and immigrants, and their expectations about what youth art and refugee/immigrant art "should" look like. And frankly, there's a lack of value that many adults attach to youth voice and art. I think that is why we both put a lot of resources towards presenting the students' work professionally. How we present their voices shapes how seriously their voices are received and interpreted.

Due to this awareness, as well as time pressures each year, we often take more of a leadership role during the final production phase. Our political context has also impacted our production process. Remember in 2007–2008, we designed the bus stop posters—of course with student input, but not with their leadership in this particular case—and then presented them to the bus stop ad agency. After reviewing the work, the ad agency executives indicated that the posters had too many words and that they wouldn't be willing to print and install them. Totally disappointing and frustrating. Based on this information, you and I examined the word count on existing bus stop posters and determined that some posters had many more words. We both knew at that point that it was likely not a word count issue but a political issue regarding the poster content—student stories about war and immigration. Then we shared this information with the students and asked them how they wanted to proceed. Did they want to let go of the bus stop poster idea, argue for keeping the posters as they were, or compromise by shortening the text? I'm really glad we turned the decision making back to the students. In the end, after much debate, they decided to shorten the text and proceed.

Julie: And that was an extremely difficult and frustrating task. Just as selecting only one photograph to represent themselves had been challenging, selecting a short phrase, not even a complete sentence, to stand in for an extensive poem or three to four-page essay was truly painful. It made me question the product we were creating on some levels. The students themselves saw this "product" as being the one true way they could engage the entire community, rather than "preaching to the choir," and were adamant that we make it happen.

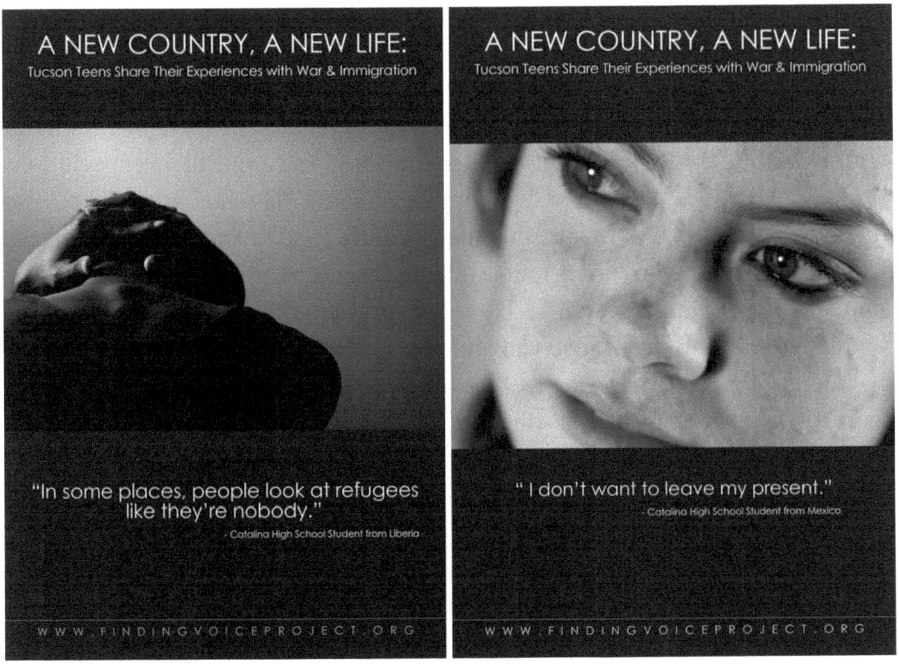

Figure 4. Finding Voice youth wrote and took portraits of each other based on their personal experiences with war and immigration. The youth decided that they wanted their work shared "on the streets" and as a result we created and installed 4 x 6 posters in over 22 bus stops throughout Tucson for a year.

Josh: Which raises the question: To what extent do you distill a work to reach beyond the choir? When does that distillation process compromise the integrity of the students' voices? We had to make some tough calls.

> *Our voices can only be heard if someone is listening.*
> *—Suleiman, FV student from Afghanistan*

Julie: For example, our funders—whose central mission at that point in time was about empowerment of youth, youth voice, and youth activism—questioned the value of the bus stops and denied the additional funds required for this student-initiated action. They argued that such a display was not really activism and that its impact would not lead to changes in the community.

Josh: We disagreed with them on several fronts, not the least of which was that the bus stop poster process taught the students about navigating local politics in one's community, the negotiation process, and the value of compromise without compromising one's values. Though, in retrospect, we could have involved the students more directly in the negotiation process, as I really took the lead with the negotiations due to time and transportation constraints.

Regardless, we both felt the stakes were really high. The students were super invested in the posters. And frankly, there was and is already a cynicism and skepticism among some of the youth about whether their voices really do matter. Whether adults really want to hear them. If the posters did not move forward, we were just feeding this skepticism. In this divisive political context, it's pretty hard to make any change. So it was about not setting them up for disappointment while being real and honest about the political challenges of our work.

Julie: And not setting ourselves up for disappointment, either. I mean, I share that cynicism with them to some extent.

Josh: So I guess it's sort of balancing that realism with hope. If you get too cynical, then it might paralyze you. So how do you do community engagement and evaluate that work in a realistic way?

> *Start as micro and end as macro.*
> *—Snehapriya, FV student from India*

Julie: I think our expectations have shifted over the last couple of years in terms of the students' mental states, their thinking processes, and the skills they walk out with, versus what we're actually doing in Tucson that's visibly different or that effects concrete or immediate change. And I really feel like the 2008 project in some ways helped me make that shift, because the bus stop posters went up and nothing really happened except that the kids felt incredible. They felt like they were visible, and that was the whole point—that's what they wanted: to feel visible. It made me think that I have this whole other agenda of what I want, but why should it be about what I want? It's not. If the students just wanted people to know they were there and to know their stories, they did it. They succeeded in meeting their objective.

Josh: For sure. Remember when Andrea sent you that email after seeing her bus stop poster?

> *Hi miss- miss about 3 weeks ago i went to my poster to take pictures of my poster and a woman asked me for my autograph !!!!! i was so exited!!! she was crying!!! thank you !!!*

Julie: Talk about a measure of success! Stories like that make me think of Shukuru starting a debate club at his university and researching grants for his youth arts organization in Phoenix, Laxmi having the confidence to audition and perform in a major theatrical production, Zeljka thinking about setting up a non-profit of her own one day, or Christian recently enrolling in an ESL teacher training program in Mexico. These indicate success in ways that state exams, public surveys, and other dominant measures miss. Such stories reflect personal transformation of skills and values that youth are carrying forward into their communities, transforming those communities.

References

Finding Voice Project (2013). Retrieved from www.findingvoiceproject.org
Partnership for 21st Century Skills (2013). Retrieved from www.p21.org

Part 5: After the Project

Chapter 10

Visions Beyond the Bricks: Reflections on Engaging Communities to Support Black Male Youth

Ouida Washington and Derek Koen

"Do you think you're a smart kid? Yes, I'm a smart kid..."

We sat in the mid-town New York office of a potential funder, anxious to show the fine cut of the film we'd been working on for almost a year. We didn't have much experience with philanthropy, where social-issue work like the film we'd produced found a lifeline, nor did they as funders know what to expect from a film project. Much of our work thus far had focused on helping non-profits use media to tell their own stories, so now for us to come with a project we had developed on our own was new, bold, and nerve racking for us.

As we dimmed the lights in the conference room, we began sharing the film and the voice of a young Black male begin to echo in the room: "Do you think you're a smart kid?" the interviewer asked. "Yes, I'm a smart kid...I am a smart kid!" Fifteen-year-old Shaquiel answered as he walked down the hallway of his new school. As the 30-minute film played from the laptop on the table, we looked up to see the program manager becoming very emotional. I think that was the moment they knew and we knew that this film would connect directly with communities who needed to hear this call. The reaction from the people in that room changed the way we looked at the film and how we as filmmakers would move forward. Our little film landed at the center of the growing national initiative for Black male achievement and was our first hint that we had an obligation beyond just producing a film to make sure as many people as possible could see it. This knowledge was both exciting and scary, and was a pivotal moment for us. It was also the start of a process that has seen many inspiring moments but has also revealed many challenges that test our will, patience and resolve.

Introduction

We are filmmakers. We saw a need and felt the pull to use film to tell a story of Black male youth that moves beyond surface discussions. Our film *Beyond the Bricks* (2009) blurred both personal and community lines by focusing on how all of us, as members of various communities, can work with Black male youth and support them around holistically increasing their educational outcomes. The film follows African American students Shaquiel Ingram and Erick Graham as they struggle to stay on track in the Newark, NJ, public school system. Fifteen year-old Shaquiel is a bright student who enjoys writing poems and playing the trumpet, but finds himself a ward of the court system when he can longer take the "chaos" of his local high school and stops going to class. Erick, a nineteen-year-old high school dropout, realizes that the freedom he sought from his former daily school routine is not all it's cracked up to be. Unemployed and unable to find a job, he spends most of his days bored at home and watching TV. In danger of becoming just another couple of statistics on the "school to prison pipeline," the boys find a lifeline with support from compassionate community leaders and alternative education programs that address the root causes of their problems with staying focused in school.

We had no idea that this film and the way it got taken up in communities around the country would be the beginning of a whole other life for us. As we wrote this chapter, we began to think: if our work has a digital life that can be repurposed and remixed, what are the implications of that for our understandings of the life of community-based projects? How do we think through what happens "after the project?" How do we think through and experience the new challenges that arise once our community-based project seemingly takes on a life of its own? How do we think through and experience the dissonance that happens in our own experience of the project once it takes on a life of its own? How do we make sure to not lose sight of our overall goals for this work? Our goal in this chapter is to take you with us as we work through our reflections on these questions and the challenges that they make visible.

As we took up the challenge of developing a plan for a national tour for the film, it was critical for us to shift our identities from only being filmmakers to being filmmakers and advocates (and soon after, program developers). This shift in thinking was not an easy one, but it was necessary as we began to also think of ourselves as activists in our communities. Through listening to community responses to the film, we saw that the work needed to go beyond simply sharing the film; we needed to follow up the viewings of the film with truly working with communities to take action to support Black males. Subsequently, this shift in focus also revealed to us that the underlying challenge to achieving what we know needs to be done for our young men and in the larger movement for positive social change is a willingness to act—this realization was both frustrating and understandable. After much struggle and anger, that realization became the principal motivation for us to find out what we could do beyond the film and the tour to help make a difference in the lives of young men and their communities. Since traveling with the film and developing Beyond the Bricks Project, Inc. into a non-profit organization, we have faced many transitions, but there are three major challenges that seem to be constant as this film and our work has taken on a focus around community engagement. These three challenges have emerged over the four years since we completed the film and we think they represent some of the fundamental issues that are inherent in trying to foster a prolonged social movement.

The three challenges we will discuss in this chapter concern first, building effective collaborations around this community-based project—a project that centralizes the concerns and issues facing young Black men in American society. Second, we will explore the challenge of developing a program that fulfills our mission to truly help young Black males understand and live their potential, while also encouraging their educational prowess. Finally, as we moved more and more toward building an organization around our work, we began to experience ramifications of a third challenge of obtaining consistent funding to support all of our efforts. In this chapter we are not presenting a blueprint for doing this work; we are instead trying to lay out the challenges we have and are facing to build community around doing this work of taking action and supporting social change in our communities. Through these challenges we have accepted that this is an ongoing journey for us and there is no turning back now.

"A Rising Tide Lifts All Boats:" Building Effective Collaborations Around the Beyond the Bricks Film

Though *Beyond the Bricks* was created as a showcase of our work as filmmakers, it was also created as a tool for increasing awareness. As we were finishing the film we began to shift our distribution strategy to more of an outreach strategy, so the film festivals and hoped-for PBS broadcast morphed into wanting to engage audiences on a much more personal and communal level. The film needed to be in front of the folks who most probably are not watching PBS, and who would not be at the film festivals. This film carried a message for the people who were working with these young boys every day, or had influence and contact with them and their families: the teachers, principals, parents, community organizations and members, state workers, policy makers, philanthropic organizations, public officials, local business people, and the young men themselves. This film highlighted a community issue and every aspect of that community needed to see and better understand what these boys were facing. This knowledge was at the heart of our strategy to reach folks on the grassroots level, connecting with communities through organizations they already knew, through schools and churches. This approach also surfaced several "hidden" challenges in mobilizing around this film that we hadn't anticipated.

Why Black Males? Most of the pre-film screening locations had us working with organizations and people in cities where we knew no one and in sectors that were unfamiliar to us. We researched, sent out emails, and made phone calls to these very diverse local groups, seeking organizations we imagined would be natural allies and that would have a vested interest in helping young people meet their potential. This formula for identifying potential collaborators proved to be more difficult than we expected and could rely on. It also surprisingly raised one of the most perplexing and frequently asked questions of the work so far.

We'd made some contacts in one of our Midwestern locations and had pulled together some key organizations for a conference call and a representative from one of the leading foundations there joined the call, along with community organizations and the public library, which had agreed to provide its main branch as our venue for the film screening (we talk more about the screenings in the next section). After we had talked about all the logistics and had a plan of outreach for each of the organizations, the foundation representative said she had one final question. Why Black boys? At that moment, after all the discussion, I (Ouida) was very angry that she even could ask a question like this. Of course it was prefaced by, "It's something I know that my bosses and board will want to know." I remember thinking, "We are sitting here, in this city, whose Black population is over 80%, whose education system is crumbling, whose unemployment rate was one of the worst in the nation, and you have the audacity to ask 'why Black boys?' If this is the work you are claiming to do, if this is the effort to support the work of others who are looking to find solutions to the ills facing the city and most importantly its young people, and after this conversation and the materials I've passed on…if you don't know the answer to that, then the foundation is disingenuous in its statement to support schools and children."

I didn't say that, of course. What I did say has become our fixed answer to this question, a question that still gets asked, "A rising tide lifts all boats, and by focusing on addressing the issues facing the lowest performing students, consistently Black males, we inevitably assist all students." This seemed to make sense to her as she repeated it and was something she could take back. Ironically, by the time the town hall event took place, the foundation, who did participate in the screening, announced from the podium that they were beginning their own initiative to support Black and brown boys and they would use the success of our event as a kickoff for more public forums and discussions. They noted that they were taking on this work because they understood that by supporting these young men, they are able to help other students and communities. The person who had been on the call was not there, but we simply took it in stride because, in the end, a major foundation had found its way to spearheading an effort that brings necessary support to young Black males, and that initiative still continues today. This would turn out to be another critical moment for us, as it was the evidence that helped to solidify for us that a movement was at hand. However, we needed to make sure we were not just talking about doing, but that we were actually doing this work.

Moving Beyond Talk. In the previous section we mentioned the film screenings that we set up around the country. We moved forward with the national 10-city town hall tour, and the key challenge that emerged was that when we were able to reach these potential collaborators in a city, most did not know of or had never communicated with the others. Folks were/are working in silos even though they were all interested in addressing common issues highlighted by our film. So the town hall became a testing ground for how these organizations would collaborate to act as one group first to make an event happen, then beyond that to collectively keep the work going. It was difficult, but we learned as we went along that it would take a lot of prodding. We eventually became the glue that held things together, at least until the day of the event. We created a framework for the event that folks could use to think about how they wanted to execute the town hall meeting. During the tour, we carried most of the costs and were simply asking the folks on the ground, those who had agreed to be collaborators in each city, to outreach to their constituents about the event, reach out to and secure local panelists, facilitate workshops in which they were already versed and think about ways in which they could continue the work beyond the event day.

The initial reaction to this concept was generally overwhelmingly gung-ho from everyone involved. The enthusiasm over the phone was gratifying. We were making it happen! Our task now was one of getting people to go beyond talking about it to actually following through with what they agreed to do. This challenge began to shed light on why so many kids are in the sad predicament we uncovered in completing our research for the film. Folks talk much more than they do. Consider this example: we met some young community organizers during a convening put together by the funder institution for grantees. Everyone spoke very highly of one of these young people, a youth leader from a town in the state. We were very interested in talking with him and were able to have a conversation at this convening about some of the challenges that young Black kids were facing in his city. As a southerner myself, I (Ouida) thought it might be very poignant to begin our tour in a state very much characterized by its brutally racist past and slow forward movement, so I reached out to the young leader, who met my call with wonderful excitement. He was on-board to do whatever we needed because "this film, this conversation about solutions was greatly needed in this town." We heard that sentiment quite often from folks we reached out to and who reached out to us. This young man thought that with his and a partner's connection to a local college, we could easily have a venue partner for the event in no time. I was ecstatic to hear this because the local college he discussed had its own historic community organizing story, so what better place to kick off the tour.

Then after that phone call we would not be able to speak with him again for more than a month, even when we set up conference calls—he would miss them, and the time was fast approaching to pull this off. I ultimately made a trip down to meet him and see what I could do to move things forward quickly. His partner, who I met for the first time during this visit, would eventually be the one to take the reins and make the event happen, and we were extremely grateful because I'm not sure if it would have happened without him. The young man that so much praise had been showered on during the funders meeting, and who had told me he would pull crucial pieces of the local work together didn't do any of what he had committed to, yet showed up at the event ready to help. He would later divulge that in addition to personal issues, the established organizations that he gathered to support him, and that had participated on conference calls, did not come through with what they said they would support him with. It had disappointed him and he was unsure of how to share that with us. We learned in that moment the way that community mobilization bumps up against good intentions and life in general. We are still working on this issue in our work around this film and new projects—how do we move beyond talk in light of good intentions? How do we provide reasonable support to folks in local contexts who, like us, are developing skills in mobilizing diverse individuals and organizations? This experience would not be the last place where the "commitment to do" was a challenge to us or to the community with whom we were working. Our willingness to do the work is directly connected to the challenges of working together.

Thus far we have participated in over 70 screenings and town halls, and the solutions to addressing the issues faced by Black male youth that are discussed in these screenings are consistent: better trained teachers, exposure to 21st-century technology, out-of-school opportunities that enrich their experiences, and other more immediate ideas like churches connecting older men in the community with young men who need guidance and mentoring. However, we still have not found the formula to get people to collaborate more effectively to take action on these suggested solutions. We developed the tours and screenings to engage other partners around the country with the vision that they would make a concerted effort to implement action plans created by their communities. However, few actually continued the work of keeping the plans moving forward in the cities. This has been one of the big disappointments about the work so far. People talked, and some even preached about what needed to be done, but after their speech, very little happened. Why hadn't folks kept their pledge? We have learned that change is hard but it has to start somewhere.

On the other hand, we were very inspired by the collaborators who did move the work forward, and we did what we could to continue to support their efforts. It became clearer to us that the most important dynamic that was missing for far too many was WILL. Yet, we are learning that having the will to do the work is great, but when it bumps up against larger institutional structures, what are the next steps?

Listening to the Boys Themselves: Challenges of Building a Program that Supports Black Males Where They Are

The creation of the Produce! Create! Innovate! (PCI) Community Producers Program came out of what we heard from the young people during the town halls. They challenged the community members who were present at the town halls to have the will to create spaces for direct change in their lives. Though there is a plethora of out-of-school youth programs, they were mostly geared toward younger children and offered little else than homework help and a place to congregate. The young men who were participating in the town hall events, who were primarily thirteen to nineteen years old said that young people generally had nothing to do after school. So we constructed the PCI program to actualize our mission and address what we were hearing from young people around the country.

Blurring the Lines between Beyond the Bricks and the Beyond the Bricks Non-Profit to Add the Stories

At this point in our reflection, we want to talk briefly about The Beyond the Bricks Project (BTBP) non-profit that simultaneously emerged from the experience of the film. BTBP is a media and international community engagement organization that promotes and encourages support for increasing educational and social outcomes for school-age Black males. Many of our young men were and are still in crisis, and there needed to be a concerted focus to change the trajectory for these children. At the time we began the film research, few researchers and scholars were publishing work concerned with Black boys specifically, and more often than not, those who were writing about them were focusing on what was wrong with them. Politicians, policy makers, institutions, even parent groups were also not really paying much attention to the troublesome signals, even as the discussion of education reform became a hot-button issue. And though the conversation around bettering the public education system came with special initiatives and ideas to assist those who are hurting the most—ironically still there was very little focus on the group who have consistently been at the bottom and had been the lowest performing students in 36 states according to the *50 State Report on Black Boys* by the Schott Foundation. The report also stated that Black males had an on-time high school graduation rate of less than 50% nationwide. The unemployment rate among Black men 16–34 was and continues to be staggering.

So we were determined to use that burgeoning discussion to attempt to insert the real-life stories of young men who were living these statistics and yet beating the odds. It's a seemingly overwhelming issue that can ultimately be a story of hope. As we listened to stories from the young men during the tour, it was striking to hear the repeated narrative of young men who simultaneously accepted and rejected the thought that they needed to be the all too familiar image or "caricatures" of a Black man, in order to really be a man.

How Do We Move Beyond Talk to Doing Something? When we began to think about what else we could do, we wanted to develop a program that engaged these young men in a way that was a continuation of our work using the power of media as a tool to tell true stories of young men, and that reframed the prevailingly negative narrative regarding who Black boys are. We went through many machinations of how this could operate and finally decided the best idea was to give the camera to the young men themselves this time. The program was shaped and reshaped over several months and the final 400-page curriculum was packed with not only media literacy and community components but digital and physical literacies, and with ideas on STEAM (Science, Technology, Engineering, Arts and Math). We knew there was a lot in there and we felt like all of it was important. The test was to get it out there. The focus group we tested let us know we were on the right track and with support from the Kellogg Foundation we launched the PCI program in three universities: Columbia University Teachers College in New York City, Jackson State University in Jackson, MS, and Georgia State University in Atlanta.

Though we did not have the time to complete the program, along with other issues, 60% of the young men who began the program remained involved. The feedback was overwhelmingly positive, with many seeing it as progressive out-of-school programming. This feedback kept us going into the second year to continue piloting the program as we developed other areas of the project. The goal was to go at the work on several different levels, which presented another challenge: making sure we are developing what we are doing in a way that meets the needs of the young men. What we have learned so far is that more time is needed to execute the PCI curriculum and the program needs to be longer. We are also increasing the STEAM components to work as an integral part of the curriculum. We look to meet this challenge by seeking out relevant research and by listening closely to the young men and our collaborators. We anticipate this to be an ongoing challenge and the one we are most anxious to work on because we want to give the young men and their communities something that will most benefit their lives.

Navigating How to Build Collaborations with Universities. While we are excited about this outcome of the town hall meetings and how the PCI program is being received, the challenge of building collaborations and partnerships within university settings is something we are learning to navigate. Our out-of-school media literacy and community advocacy program for teenaged Black males is a model that engages universities and colleges in collaborating to implement our curriculum on their campuses. The initial reactions were enthusiastic from the faculty we engaged, but there were times when it seemed like their commitment waned in the face of others in the university system that were less than enthusiastic about this program being on campus. The constraints on the faculty and us were numerous and highlighted the tensions between universities as businesses and universities as community members, among other tensions. Trying to navigate these tensions became a very time-consuming effort because we are a small organization trying to build a relationship with large institutions, whose bureaucracy can be daunting and seemingly unnecessary when it comes down to it. Once we had our first strong commitments we made the effort to legally formalize this relationship as a way of holding all parties accountable to what we had agreed to do. This incidentally proved to be yet another example of the will of individuals impacting outcomes. These collaborations were also further weakened because of another major challenge, which I discuss below—the lack of consistent funding, which made it very difficult for faculty collaborating with us to run the program at their university to prioritize our program, as we do not have the financial clout to have influence.

Funding the Cause: The Challenges of Obtaining Consistent Funding for This Emerging Work

The final challenge that has presented major hurdles for us is around funding. The lack of funding to increase Black male achievement is one that has limited our ability to do our work as well as we would like. Having adequate funding for your vision is something most non-profits know and learn that they must constantly go after—it's a never-ending cycle. It is a difficult reality that we are still figuring out how to navigate. We are finding that the work we are doing falls into different-than-the-normal areas of funding from foundations and others that regularly provide support for programs. From media to programming, it's like a new world for us and we are fast learning that we have limited options when seeking out traditional grant support. Black male achievement was, and in a lot of cases is still, not on the agenda for funding institutions. We still have to convince them that this is a viable concern that needs their attention but we keep hearing that old question—why [just] Black boys?'

Going back to creating the film that started all of this work, the funding topic challenge has been with us from the moment we took our first proposal to a funder who understands the power of film and directs an extensive division dedicated to it, and is also a Black male. He understood the plight all too well, but was skeptical of his ability to "sell" it to his boss and the board; in speaking with him, our frustration was palpable in the room. We received less than half the funds we requested. This would prove to be the first test of our own will to move forward and make the film anyway. Our second test came following the funders' meeting discussed at the opening of this chapter. Though they really liked the film and it spoke directly to their issues, they gave us funds for only the 6 cities they were interested in rather than the proposed 10 that we had identified. And because we had already begun to engage organizations in our chosen cities we had to think very strategically about how we could leverage these funds to get to all 10 cities.

This determined spirit and mindset has been a big part of our success, but it has also stretched us too thin at times because there just aren't enough funds or staff to be our most effective, both in the task at hand and in human capital to spend seeking more diverse sources for funds. Black male youth, especially teens, are rarely considered vulnerable, and that makes it a tough sell, because it seems that everyone, including philanthropists, have all but given up on them.

Refusing the Deficit Construction. We believe what we have learned thus far tells another story—that it's not too late, but more importantly that Black male youth aren't the kids who are painted into that image that most people hold of them. They are instead children who still need us to carc and nurture their potential. The ironic thing is that if we were looking for funds for kids who are on drugs or are spending considerable time in the juvenile system—labeled as "at risk"—we would have more access to funding. There is, however, a more concerted effort to bring the topic of Black male achievement to more philanthropic organizations but it continues to be framed by many in a way the perpetuates the deficit mindset. Because our goal with the project is to reframe that image of our children we cannot give over to this way of thinking; it undermines the issues and successes in all the work we have and want to continue to do.

Conclusion: Moving Onward

Shaquiel, the young man at the beginning of our chapter, has now graduated from high school and will attend college in the fall. The second year of our PCI program has ended and we are planning the third year. We have learned much about the complex relationships between community-based media projects and the assumptions we all have about this work. We asked a series of questions at the beginning of this chapter. These questions guided us as we reflected on our work so far. We are in-process and it is our hope that you found yourself thinking about your own work as you read this chapter. We raise more questions than answers but hope that the discussion of the process brings about actions as well.

We have to find ways to meet our most fundamental challenge: we must find the will within ourselves and within those with whom we collaborate to make sure that this most important humanitarian issue does not fade into a cause that had a brief lifespan, but make sure that the young men we are working with become the leaders we know they are. Our ultimate aim is that this movement to help young Black males succeed is seen as enhancing the movement to build brighter futures to help all of our children.

Chapter 11

Seeing the Synergy in the Signals: Reflections on Weaving Projects into Social Movement Mobilizing through Community Radio

Kofi Larweh and Jonathon Langdon

Introduction

Wana:	*... So if I may ask, who are the elders choosing to take the position [of the head of our clan]? We are still searching but no one has been decided on yet. It shall be well...it definitely will be well, but don't you think Songorteytse's first daughter may be a good choice? The girl he had with that lady who stayed in that mud house close to the forest.*
Nomo Gbleetse:	*Yeah...yeah...yes I think I remember her.*
Wana:	*Yes, that is the girl I am talking about. Her name is Yohupeeor...Yohupeeor is the daughter's name...*
Nomo Gbleetse:	*Is she not the one schooling in Accra or so?*
Wana:	*Exactly, she is very humble and very-very respectful. I will be very happy if you will consider allowing a female to take the chief trustee position because I believe the gods had prepared her specially to bless us through her.*

Nomo Gbleetse: *Oh...oh Wana, it is a good idea that you are bringing, though but do not forget that it is the over-all chief of the Songorbiawe clan. If you have forgotten, let me remind you that this position has since time immemorial been occupied by males, so why are you suggesting a female? Will this be possible?*

Wana: *Oh yes, I know, but the issue here is this: those who we will say qualify for this position are the same people who are misbehaving and making up stories to cover themselves up. Are we going to stoop that low to getting people with ill manners to rule this clan? No way; that cannot work. You [elders] really need to digest this issue better before things get out of hand. And do not forget that this is the one unto who all assets and properties of our noble clan is going to be trusted to. Think...think and think well my elder.*

Nomo Gbleetse: *Ok I have heard what you said, but...*

Wana: *Let me leave you with this: whenever the hen lays its eggs, it protects and incubates it for good twenty-one days before it hatches. Her care does not end there, it continues to care for the chicks till they come of age. Within this period, mother hen provides food for its chicks, protects them from the hawk as well as serpents. Whenever it feels any danger, it quickly gathers its chicks under its wings. Whatever food she finds, she opens it up and scatters it for its chicks. Aw emales (mothers) are better care providers.*

Nomo Gbleetse: *Wana, you have really broadened my catching net, and I promise that in a few days time, the chiefs and elders will be meeting, so I will sell*

> *this suggestion to them and whatever the response will be, I will inform you. Thanks so much for all you have shared with me. These are the advices we need day in day out from you [elderly women]. Thanks so much once again, and I pray the gods bless and keep you longer on this earth for our sake.*
>
> —Okor Nge Kor, Episode 10, "Trusteeship: Males or Females?" (translated from Dangbe and transcribed by Jemima Larweh)

We begin this chapter with the above excerpt for two salient reasons. First, this excerpt, from an ongoing radio drama being produced by Radio Ada, a Ghanaian community radio station that draws inspiration directly from the tense context we will describe below, asks critical questions about what trusteeship, leadership and power mean in this context. Second, the above excerpt confronts patriarchal norms around leadership that have emerged as an issue throughout the host of other ongoing projects that support the challenges this program is highlighting to the Ada society. In this sense, this program is where the action is, as thousands of Dangbe speakers tune in to the station to listen to the program every week, but this action is possible because of a different approach to project thinking that blurs the lines between efforts, discarding such consumerist notions as "attribution," and rather builds a layered, and multi-pronged array of activities that all add up to impact power-relations around a key livelihood resource in the Dangbe-speaking area of Ada. In effect, it contributes directly to what we describe below as a growing literacy of struggle in Ada.

Therefore, this chapter is not so much about what happens at the end of a project; it is rather about reconceiving the conception of projects as discreet containers of activities, and instead seeing them a porous set of moves that "bump up" against other sets of moves. In illustrating how this reconception has shaped our way of working, we wish to show how deepening this awareness, and engaging in collaborative and mutually supportive (even if differently focused) projects can lead to the multi-pronged approach hinted at above that is plural in nature, and synergistic in its effects. In such an approach, attribution is not possible (Okor Nge Kor cannot say it alone has changed the thinking of Adas on such issues as women's leadership in the community) but locally owned and derived change is.

This chapter begins with a description of the context, as well as presenting our understanding of what the central terms of literacy and digital literacy mean in the Ada context. The chapter then goes in-depth to describe the synergistic effects of this multi-pronged approach between a number of ongoing efforts, the Okor Nge Kor drama[1] quoted above, a social movement learning research study[2] looking at activism related to communal access to the livelihood resource at the center of the above drama, and a new project supporting the revitalization of the Songor salt cooperative.[3] Throughout this piece, we will aim to draw back the curtain to reveal our thinking, as two people (amongst many) associated with the design of some of these projects. In order to do this, we followed the path cleared for us by Paulo Freire and Miles Horton in their talking book, *We Make the Road by Walking* (Horton & Freire, 1990), in that we sat down and talked through how we understood the concepts at the center of this work. These conversations were recorded and transcribed,[4] and are drawn on extensively below.

The Salt of Life—Contexts of Struggle in Ada's Songor Lagoon

To situate this chapter in an in-depth examination of its context would demand a fairly exhaustive historical account. Geographically speaking, Ada, and the Songor Lagoon at the center of Ada's salt production, are located roughly 150 km east, along the coast, from Ghana's capital, Accra. While the majority of Ghana's coastal peoples derive their livelihoods from fishing and farming, the people of Ada have, for at least the last four hundred years, derived a major component of their livelihood from salt (Ghana Export Promotion Council, 2009). Ada's Songor Lagoon is a natural salt-yielding lagoon, and in the past (prior to British Colonialism and subsequent independent nation-state formation) the resource was managed through custodian relations that maintained the resource, but did not restrict access to the lagoon, even for those from outside the Ada area and ethnicity who wished to "win" salt (Manuh, 1992). In previous work (Langdon, 2009; Langdon, 2010) Jon, drawing on Kofi and others, has detailed how this custodian arrangement was founded on a mutual defense pact, as the overlap of water and land implies overlapping responsibilities of care. Although pre-colonial wars were fought to defend the custodianship of the resource by the Dangbe (the people of Ada), Amate (1999) argues it is only with the advent of the British that the unity of the people in defending the collective access and maintenance of the resource was put under pressure. Much like Geschiere

(1993) has documented in the case of the British in Cameroon, the colonial officers used their positions as mediators between different internal factions to deepen internal tensions—a hallmark of the British divide-and-rule process (Mamdani, 1996). Although much more could be said about the continuation of the exploitation of internal divisions by the Ghanaian central government after independence, it is enough to say there is not a single government that has failed to use this colonial approach to destabilize the unity of the Dangbe people. Much of the contemporary tension around the resource stems from this ongoing lack of unity, even as much of the contemporary movement to defend the communal access to the resource circles around rebuilding this unity.

Without delving too deeply into recent history, Manuh (1992) describes how the building of Ghana's Akasombo Dam severely impacted the natural flooding process associated with the lagoon, located down river from the dam. This interruption of the natural flooding process had disastrous effects on the salt formation process, and, as a result, a faction of traditional authorities entered into an agreement with two companies in the late 60s/early 70s to help replenish the salt formation processes. Subsequent to salt reforming in the lagoon, partially as a result of work done by one of these companies, a major conflict erupted between artisanal salt winners and the company doing this work, as it now claimed all salt that formed in the lagoon to belong to the company. This was in addition to the salt the company itself was producing at its factory site. In short order, tensions erupted between the company and the community, with the company using police and the military to harass and brutalize the resident Dangbe populace. These localized tensions were occurring even while national tensions also grew, resulting in a revolution in 1981 that brought in a socialist-leaning military government. Although this dramatic shift did not redraw outright the situation in the local residents favor, it did provide an opening by which local salt winners could legitimate their position in the eyes of the central government by forming cooperatives (Ada Salt Cooperative Committee, 1989). The emergence of this body helped to reconfigure the terrain and eventually led to the cancellation of each of the companies' leases. Finally, on the eve of Ghana's return to democracy in 1992, the military government passed a law holding the resource in trust for the Dangbe's and the broader people of Ghana (Radio Ada, 2002).

Since then, the communities around the Songor Lagoon have been trying to push the central government to do more to increase the production of the resource, while also fighting any government plan to alienate the resource from them—a difficult struggle to say the least. While a relative stalemate has existed in the lagoon since the establishment of the law, where the central government has not come through with the funds to truly enact a Master Plan (Government of Ghana, 1991) put forth to make the lagoon highly productive without excluding community artisanal production from this process, the government (which has democratically changed hands three times since 1992) has also not been able to leverage an outright sale of the lagoon as a mineral exploitation concession as a result of continued Ada activism. However, this stalemate was also in place throughout a period of relative disinterest by those whom Akonto Ampaw calls the national political class[5] in salt production. This has all changed since the 2008 discovery of oil in commercial quantities in Ghana. As Affam and Asamoah (2011) have noted, with an already existing high demand for salt throughout the sub-region, and the prospective huge demand for a domestic petro chemical industry in Ghana, the prospects for Ghana's salt industry are bright. Unfortunately, this kind of attention often brings with it solutions that mean the end of artisanal salt production (c.f. Hinestroza, 2001). At the same time, a localized challenge has also surfaced, where local Adas, often supported by outside and/or inside elite interests, have constructed small salt pans, called Atsiakpo, around the lagoon, making collective access to the resource very difficult. It is under these changing conditions that activism in Ada has taken on a new life, and it is around the growing sense of the threat from within and without ahead that a number of the projects described below were mobilized. Two key actors in these mobilizations are the movement defending collective access to the Songor, the Ada Songor Advocacy Forum (ASAF), and the Dangbe people's community radio station, Radio Ada. We feel it is important to say a bit about each of these before we go on.

The Ada Songor Advocacy Forum (ASAF) is an umbrella forum of groups and individuals within Ada committed to defending collective access to salt resulting from the Songor Lagoon. The membership of the movement ranges from the now revitalizing Songor salt cooperative, including representatives from each salt winning community around the Lagoon, sympathetic traditional authority figures, local elected assembly persons, a number of local civil servants (many of whom are activists from the last large-scale struggle around the resource), as well as Radio Ada. The movement also includes some external allies, such as Jon and members from nationally based NGOs, who are in support of and in solidarity with ASAF's collective cause. The Songor salt cooperative revitalization work, whose members are now close to 500, has rooted the movement effectively in the salt-winning communities. This is an important growth as the forum started as an educational strategizing group in Ada's biggest town, where the literacy of struggle began to emerge, before rooting itself more concretely in the interests of those most affected by decisions concerning the resource. At the same time, though, the participation and initial hosting of the forum by the community radio station has ensured that much that emerges from these meetings has been broadcast with community check-ins—a process that anticipated the later rooting of the movement in the revitalization effort.

Radio Ada, Ghana's first community radio station, went on the air February 1, 1998; it broadcasts from 5 AM to 10 PM every day, only in Dangbe; as mentioned above, it is run by volunteers, some of whom are long standing (roughly 30 in number), and some of whom come and go fairly quickly; a gender-balanced group of local district civil servants seconded to the station act as an administration team, drawing from the Non Formal Education Department, the National Disaster Management Organization, the Ministry of Culture and the Department of Community Development and Social Welfare. The station, grounded as it is in community radio philosophy, describes itself as the voice of the voiceless; at the same time the station aims to promote Dangbe culture, which often means working with those in traditional authority positions who may want to maintain the status quo, even while the station may challenge this status quo with shows such as Okor Nge Kor. The key underlying principle here, though, in contrast to commercial radio, is that the radio be embedded in community-centered agendas, and as such, community member views are constantly sought to evaluate and enrich this agenda. McKay (2003), for instance, documents how the station processes and programming were reconfigured through an engagement with male fishermen and female fishmongers, leading to better understanding between the two groups, and programming that met the needs of both, while promoting dialogue between the mutually interdependent groups. In this, Radio Ada takes its work beyond just programming, and actually contributes directly to the strengthening of supportive relations between the different facets that make up the Dangbe community, while still putting marginalized voices at the forefront of these processes. In other words, it is not just a communication tool, but is in fact an important player in building the Ada community.

Joining the Literacies Discussions—Contributions from Ada

While it is easy to drink deeply from the cup of literacy theory in entering the discussions at the center of this book, much like the issues we raise about project containment below, too deep a delving into theory is likely to contain and frame our understanding of the issue. Instead, we wish to chart another path. There is a proverb in Ghana that says, "the one cutting the path cannot tell if it is straight." With this proverb in mind, we submit our thoughts here for others to evaluate the path we are taking here to see if and where we may have taken a wrong turn. In other words, although we acknowledge the importance of Gee's "social turn" in literacy studies, and the way it led to the emergence of the new literacies school of thought, we present here a different path; one that may be parallel to this "social turn" in that it strays widely from instrumental definitions of literacy, but the starting point of this path is the literacies emerging from Ada experiences. Also, while this departure can draw a common lineage to Freirean (1969) concepts of critical emancipatory literacies, it is still embedded in the intricate epistemics and material reality of the Dangbe and Ghanaian context.

In the context of the above struggle, a definition of literacy has emerged as being literate in the various dimensions of understanding the issues confronting the Adas. For Kofi, in our conversation about this notion, he said,

> The literacies here, the best way of looking at it, is to see the communication models that have emerged. One key is Akpetiyo's[6] form of literacy, where she is using her natural voice and the talent of using Dangme idioms and expression to layer people and direct their attention to her music and lyrics. That is one, and it has a strong feeling because she is using the culture, the sound forms that make her presentation attractive.

While Akpetiyo may not display the typical literacies associated with orthodox and colonized educational norms, such as reading and writing in English, her deep literacy in the signs and meanings of the Dangbe people have made her songs a powerful commentary to the people of Ada about the issues of the Songor. Here is an excerpt of a translation of one of these songs:

> *Hark Almighty, put on the sun light; I say Almighty Radio Ada, put on the sun light forever. Whatever is under water through you comes to light. Whatever is underground through you comes to light. [...] Chorus (implying; "what do you think my people?" And they: respond "we agree."* (Applause).
>
> *Look behind us, there comes Government after us Okor People. I repeat, turn and look behind Dangme People, Government is catching up with us. But what is the issue? Atsiakpo is consuming the whole Songor. And all attempts to stop it have proved futile, the fire rages on. Government could not help but to step in. They told our Elders, they are going to take over Songor, to quell conflicts so that we live in peace. Radio Ada heard of this development, took on their broadcast armour, mobilized us; we entered the communities and started informing the people; we are spreading it. [...]*
>
> *What someone does not know; I say, what one doesn't know, someone knows! (Repeat emphatically). (Audience response): What someone does not know; what one doesn't know, someone knows! What someone does not know; I say, whatever one doesn't know, someone knows! (Repeat emphatically). (Audience response): What someone does not know; what one doesn't know, someone knows! Hail Goodwill; (response) come Goodwill!* (Applause).[7]

Here, Akpetiyo's call for people to come to know the situation is at once a call for listeners to become critically literate of the situation in the Songor, and an indictment of those who know but do not share the knowledge. In this sense, literacy is as much about gaining fluency in a new knowledge context, as it is displaying the appropriate community-building attitude towards this knowledge. For the purposes of this chapter, Akpetiyo is also an apt example to draw on as she herself has shown a growing digital literacy, in the way we conceptualize it here. More on this connection in a moment as it is first necessary to elaborate how we understand the "digital turn" in literacies, as Kate Mills (2010) has put it.

Recent discussions of digital literacies often focus on the explosion of social media use globally (especially in areas with strong Internet infrastructure, such as North America, Europe and parts of Asia) and ignore what many call the digital gap of contexts in Africa and parts of Latin America

(Chinn & Fairlie, 2007). While it is apt to pay attention to, and critique, the dominance of the rise of Internet and digital platforms leading to an explosion of new modalities of communicating, the effect of digital technologies in other contexts, such as those in Africa, is at least as revolutionary as Internet-based social media. Therefore, while acknowledging the gap between these contexts, it is crucial to pay attention to the way in which Africans are revolutionizing their own digital age literacies. From this post-colonial perspective, African contexts must be understood as a part of the digital age as much as are the downtowns of New York or Toronto. It is true that the percentage of Internet users may remain lower than in other contexts, but other forms of digital media use have exploded across the continent—most notably use of the cellular phone (Overa, 2006). Not only are Ghanaians and other Africans using cell phones (or mobiles) to remain connected to one another, a growing number are using them to conduct banking transactions, and access email on an ongoing basis. The growth of users across all walks of life also clearly indicates a growing digital literacy of many whom traditional literacy programs would have classified as illiterate. Akpetiyo, who has had a mobile for the last year, is indicative of this category—people program her phone to call those she needs to touch base with, including Radio Ada, and otherwise she receives calls. The impact of this continent-wide transformation cannot be underplayed, as mobiles have featured prominently in, for instance, the Egypt's Tahrir Square revolution (Allagui & Kuebler, 2011). In Ghana, mobiles were an effective deterrent of electoral fraud in the 2008 elections (Rotberg & Aker, 2012).

Importantly, for the context of this chapter, it is not just the impact that mobile phones are having on communications in Ghana, but their combination with one of mass media's now older and relatively inexpensive technological forms, the radio, that has created a vibrant, pluralistic, and often emotionally and politically charged media context. The call-in show is a well-known phenomenon that often breeds controversy and political propaganda. And yet, in Ghana it also is incredibly pluralistic, as national radio shows receive calls from across the country, equally from small towns only recently able to access the mobile network, to big cities with professional "serial" callers that make their living on different radio phone-ins. The impact of this highly effective combination has, in fact, become the subject of public debates over what should and shouldn't be said over the airwaves. Prof. Kwame Karikari, at a recent forum on the right to communicate held in

Accra, argued forcefully that private radio sensationalism needed to be checked, and what has been dubbed the "politics of insults" needs to be curtailed, not just by radio stations, but by political parties themselves.[8]

At this same symposium, Prof. Karikari, as well as Akoto Ampaw, underscored the important difference in the country between sensationalist private stations, and a small, but distinctive community radio sector that has never engaged in these kinds of practices. This does not mean that community radio in Ghana does not connect with the proliferation of mobile phones to enrich its programming, its just that it is put to other uses. For instance, Radio Ada conducts regular community check-ins on current affairs; draws on listeners for contributions to collectively define what political and traditional trusteeship mean; conducts programming evaluation processes; and, even reaches out to listeners through proverb and poetry contests. These are in addition to typical call-in shows that are structured around particular themes. In contrast to commercial stations that thrive off of insult and controversy, the strategic use of mobile phone pluralism by Radio Ada has helped to deepen the sense of widespread ownership of the station, and collective debate and discussion through listening groups, check-ins and other approaches. In fact, this difference between commercial and community radio is grounded not just in approaches, but in epistemics, as was discussed above. In a further elaboration of our understanding of literacy, Kofi notes how literacy is relational rather than a commodity:

> We are also using another form [of literacy]; you may want to call it gossip, but it is our traditional way of spreading what is new. People have started talking of "hey, have you heard, I went, I had an experience which is different from what we have been doing," and you can tell that the sort of meetings we [Radio Ada and ASAF] hold are different from other meetings because they leave indelible marks on their minds, so the way the meetings are conducted is like using all the people who are there to go and carry out the message again. There are some ways of handling information, whatever you hear you keep it to yourself and you just shut your mouth. There are others, they are a trigger; you hear and you feel that, hey, it empowers you to show others how much you know, how much you care, how much you are part of a certain system and so the driving force is there [to spread the knowledge].

This idea of literacy as a collective asset, being spread to others, rather than as a commodity to be used for personal gain is a strong theme in the interlocking projects described below. At the same time, the way digital formats have allowed for this approach to literacy to move beyond those who come for meetings to those who listen to and engage with Radio Ada's programming reveals the positive side of the democratizing impact of Ghana's cell phone proliferation. Returning to the example of Akpetiyo, Jon describes how her mobile has made her part of a literate leadership of the movement and the station:

> The fact is that you have a radio station that is broadcasting one hundred percent in Dangme. That is taking all the news in Ghana and translating it in Dangme, you have international news in Dangme, and you have local news in Dangme.
>
> And you have telephone participation in Dangme. What are the implications: you can bypass traditional forms of literacy and go to the kind of literacy that is about collective dialogue. So someone like Akpetiyo who doesn't speak English well becomes a transformational leader; she is not encumbered by those past structures that excluded her from leadership, like language, like a formal literacy and other things. Her literacy in the language and her literacy with her mobile phone to call in and contribute to a phone-in about dynamics around this Songor issue, allow her to be a very vocal and key transformational leader in this whole thing. So in fact, someone at an ASAF workshop, he even said it last year. Beyond all the learning we are doing [about the struggles of the past], the single biggest and most important thing that has changed is Radio Ada. If not for Radio Ada, we couldn't be having this learning dynamic. So I think its critical to understand that and the ways that, that kind of removal of the language barrier and allowing people to truly converse is whether you're a mechanic, whether you're a salt winner, you're the MP whatever, you can all talk; that alone is deepening the kind of literacy and understanding that people have for these things.

Yet, Radio Ada's use of digital technology is not limited to mobile phone use. In fact, the revolutionary effect of digital recording and editing processes has had an equally dramatic effect on the radio station's practice. As a volunteer organization, having access to easily used mp3 recorders, as well as easy-to-learn editing software is a key way to build pluralist programs and include many in all aspects of the creation of programs. The searchability of these data formats, as well as the growing availability of large memory storage devices makes archiving and ensuring longtime and easy access to programs much easier than in the past. And yet, much like the discussion above, it is less the availability of these technologies and more the use they are put to that matters in this context. Digital recording technology in the hands of Radio Ada volunteers is deepening not just the literacy of these volunteers with the technology, but broadening the range of voices that can be sourced and broadcast for programs. When one adds in the key dimension of language to the picture, having access to easy-to-use, edit-and-store audio technologies helps not just in the preservation of a language but its dynamic interplay over an entire language-speaking group.

Synergies Across Projects

The people-centered approach we both describe above helps us start from a particular standpoint that sees projects not as containers, discreet from the world, but rather as one angle of actions designed to contribute to an agenda emergent from communities in Ada. The end goal of all of these different approaches is a multivalent literacy of struggle, where broad-based discussions and mutually constituted understandings of the struggle bump up against one another and enrich people's literate connection with and ownership of the issues at stake.[9] In beginning from this standpoint, multiple projects focused on a similar problematic: shifting from either competition, or duplicating of efforts to instead synergizing with each other, interlocking, deepening and multiplying the effect. Elsewhere, Jon has worked with Blane Harvey to describe this open and synergistic approach in two participatory action research projects in the Ada context (Langdon & Harvey, 2012). Here, we aim to describe a series of different overlapping projects that start from the open and synergistic standpoint. We will expand upon their mutual effect, paying particular attention to aspects that reveal the growth of literacy as we have described it above, as well as the aspects of this that connect with digital literacies as we have understood them. Most importantly, we will elaborate our own evolving learning and thinking throughout this process, pulling back the curtain on this synergy to share how we have understood it. For instance, we have both come to the conclusion that locally owned change is the only process that can truly reconfigure power relations, and that any singular project approach will have little long-term effect. Kofi explains this best:

> The temptation is to look at projects as a stand-alone or one-off activities, and then we tend to measure immediate outcomes and outputs to see whether it is successful or not, but the lessons we are getting this time around is that there are so many interconnection of activities and the manifestation of issues that one is dealing with… when you are dealing with one, if you do it well you will come across another one; in other words, one issue begets another, so what we are doing is to look at it holistically through the systemic research approach. For us to say that, "oh this is happening because of this and that" and so if their activity is not attaching itself to some of the root causes of the manifestations we are trying to address, what happens is that we think that the intervention has failed or we haven't gotten what, but some

> will have delayed effects depending on how endemic or how entrenched the issues that we are dealing with are. If we have even one person understanding the change that is necessary and the fellow owns it, it is a big leap because the person lives in the community and works at it.

To begin to illustrate the synergy we have seen emerge in the work with the ASAF as well as Radio Ada it is useful to return to the quote from Okor Nge Kor that opened this chapter. The quoted section exemplifies the interconnection between an ongoing research project, following movement and community radio organizing around collective access to the Songor resource, and the radio drama. Dcspitc thc fact that the Mwananchi project that funds the Okor Nge Kor program is not involved in the community-mobilizing processes of the movement that the research is documenting and contributing to, each of the community meetings was used to generate feedback on the programs and new thematic angles. For instance, the community of Luhuor insisted that the program reveal the depth of chiefs' involvement in the ongoing Atsiakpo process. This is the very issue that leads Wana to argue that all male leadership candidates are implicated in this anti-social behavior and therefore it is time to turn to women instead. This later shift in programming to emphasize women's leadership has then had a synergistic impact on movement organizing, as recent Radio Ada and ASAF processes have begun to focus on Queen Mothers and women's leadership[10] as a key entry point to work with the traditional authority figures to realign them along the lines of the communities they purport to represent. Akpetiyo is reflective of this emerging focus, as her songs and her emergence as a leader of the movement are central to the evolving literacy of struggle.

Similarly, a key member of the ASAF, the cooperatives, recently received support for mobilization work that dovetails the ongoing broadcasts of the station and other collective education processes of the movement. They are deepening discussion at the community level of the cooperative concept, as well as enriching popular understanding of the Master Plan. The cooperative builds on its own processes of collective literacy building as well, which Jon describes here:

> There's innovations happening; the co-op, for the last year and a half have been using text messaging to spread the revitalization message, to hundreds, they have a whole texting list and they send it to all… So the kind of way that the digital side has fused with some of the existing organizing and message creation processes to support them.

This process, coupled with the outreach that emerged from Radio Ada broadcast forums during July 2011, where the cooperative concept was reintroduced, enabled the membership to grow to its current level of 450 members in 10 communities. Unlike in the previous incarnation of the cooperative, where no cell phone network existed, and no community radio worked to build processes for collective community decision making, a key tool in this revitalization is information proliferation and literacy building. Synergistically, this has meant that information gathered through the research project has been given out to community members through cooperative activities, many of whom are seeing government plans for the resource for the first time, despite being over 20 years old. Kofi describes the impact of this interlocking synergistic effect, where it is the people's agenda, and not project outcomes that drive the process:

> Take the radio for example; the radio understands that we are not there only to report things, but whatever we report we are a part of it and so we are deeply involved. Take the cooperatives; they have been looking for an opportunity; take the Queen Mothers, they are saying that individually they don't, they have a fight, a war, and they don't know who to help them, so being part of what we are doing now gives them a very big opportunity and so they are ready to take up some of the activities.…So we are getting different ownership groups emerging and conferred as the project moves on. So for me what it simply means is that this project is never going to end because it is part of the life of the people. This is the way I see it going, and the different competences that the different projects are bringing on board in terms of capacity building and resources, it is making things move even faster for us. You (Jon) can tell, yourself, the stage we worked to before you left (in August 2011) and where we are now and the different caliber of persons who are even talking as if they started it all, so that is it.

Kofi's reflection here reveals the inner work both of us have been engaged in, deepening and broadening the literacy of struggle associated with the Songor. While Kofi has been engaged in bringing different "ownership groups" into the work, Jon has been engaged in developing a solidarity network of support grounded in this same literacy. In fact, as Jon notes, it is the contemporary digital age that enables this:

> You know, then you have Aketiyo, I mean the fusion with technology; you have her singing the traditional way and coming up with these fantastic lyrics, but you also have Radio Ada capturing it, on digital, recording it, broadcasting it and then even sending the broadcast, sending the recording to us in Canada so that when we're talking about the movement, we play her song and we give the translation. This

> connects directly with people, and suddenly the literacy of people's struggle is conveyed in this different context, building a new source of solidarity.

These different modalities of work on a literacy of struggle, refusing to be held captive to a project-based mentality, create a synergistic and interlocking effect that broadens understanding and ownership of the struggle for defending collective access to the Songor Lagoon. Both of us have learned much through this process, where there is a constant learning curve, as government moves are constantly evolving, even as internal elite interests also take unexpected twists and turns. The strength, though, of this diversified and yet interconnected approach to movement building and broadening is that it is flexible and premised on people building their own understanding and agenda. To build this agenda in a truly participatory way means taking a multi-layered approach, where dialogue is a constant feature, and we all build each other's literacy in the process.

Conclusion

There are two contributions we have aimed to make to digital literacy projects in this chapter. The first of these is the path we have cut to reveal what we have termed here a "literacy of struggle" of the people of Ada. The second contribution is our reflections on the strengths of a multivalent approach to project work.

In terms of the concept of a literacy of struggle there are six interlocking components to our evolving understanding. First, it is not based so much on becoming literate in a particular skill set, but rather it is an attitude of constant learning and growth of understanding of the Songor struggle. Second, this growth is based not on a banking idea of learning, but rather on the mutual acquisition of and contribution to understanding that is based on a process of dialogue—in fact, the very process of discussion deepens learning for all involved. Third, becoming literate is not a commodity, but is rather premised on deepening collective ownership of issues and of understandings. Fourth, digital communication technologies are an important enhancive component of this type of pluralistic literacy, as they allow marginalized language groups such as the Dangbe people to broaden collective discussions of the issues they face, even as they determine how these technologies are useful to them. Fifth, this literacy form invites ownership though action, as it implicitly commits people to the struggle. Finally, sixth, pluralistic literacy allows for understanding to be defined and enriched by marginalized voices, as opposed to elite ones.

In terms of our reflections on project processes, there are five realizations we have come to. First, externally derived interventions will rarely produce effective and power-challenging local change—this does not mean outsiders can't contribute, but that this contribution should be in solidarity with and along lines defined internally. Second, any interventions must be rooted in the constantly evolving people's agenda, where both the understanding of the issues and the way forward come from collective discussion. Third, this agenda needs to be grounded in a literacy of struggle that is locally rooted. Fourth, a multi-pronged project approach allows this literacy to emerge in a complex way, where no one external donor or agency can attribute local change to their intervention. Here there three subsequent thoughts: a) the many issues at play and their entrenched nature mean they need to be tackled from many angles; b) multiple angles also lead to a reaching out to different groups and thereby inviting a growing spread of ownership; and, c) multivalent nature also allows for flexibility to adjust to the evolving nature of issues as well as the shifts in the people's agenda. Finally, fifth, this locally owned approach actually allows for external solidarity to be appreciated, rather than it reverting to colonial power hierarchies.

Notes

1. Production of this program is supported by the Mwananchi Ghana Program.
2. Supported by a Standard Research grant from Canada's Social Science and Humanity Research Council (SSHRC).
3. Supported by the Business Advocacy Fund.
4. Transcribed by Leah Jackson and Stephanie MacKinnon
5. Ampaw used this term repeatedly at the IDEG forum described below (see previous endnote).
6. Akpetiyo is a praise singer from Matsekope, one of the Songor communities, and she has emerged as the face and voice of the ASAF and the movement's struggle.
7. Translated and transcribed by Kofi Larweh.
8. These comments were made at the Institute for Democratic Governance (IDEG) symposia on "The Right to Know and the Power to Regulate the Airwaves: The Way Forward," held on June 18, 2012.
9. Choudry and Kapoor (2010) make a strong case for all research (and project) work with social movements to be articulated by and responsive to movement membership.

10. The implications of this are profound. First, while the Queen Mother position, well recognized as an important mediating position in other contexts in Ghana, is a recent addition to Ada traditional governance structures, there has been a flurry of Queen Mother enstoolments, even as tensions within the male-dominated Ada Traditional Council is resulting in court cases and destoolments. Second, the growing acceptance that women's leadership may represent another route to articulating local needs has resulted in both the main political parties nominating female parliamentary candidates for the 2012 elections, with the newly victorious NDC female MP now being part of cabinet. While these developments cannot be attributed to Okor Ng Kor and the work of ASAF to foster discussions on who is most affected by the current crisis in the lagoon (women and children) as well as who is most often left out in discussions about it (women and children), they have certainly helped.

References

Ada Salt Cooperative Committee (1989). *Who killed Maggie?* Accra: Ada Salt Cooperative Committee.

Affam, M., & Asamoah, D. N. (2011). Economic potential of salt mining in Ghana towards the oil find. *Research Journal of Environmental Earth Science*, *3*(5), 448–456.

Allagui, I., & Kuebler, J. (2011). The Arab spring and the role of ICTs: Editorial introduction. *The International Journal of Communication, 5,* 1435–1442.

Amate, C. O. C. (1999). *The making of Ada.* Accra: Woeli Publishing Services.

Chinn, M. D., & Fairlie, R. W. (2007). The determinants of the global digital divide: A cross-country analysis of computer and Internet penetration. *Oxford Economic Papers, 59,* 16–44 .

Choudry, A., & Kapoor, D. (2010). Learning from the ground up: Global perspectives on social movements and knowledge production (pp. 1–13). In A. Choudry, & D. Kapoor (Eds.), *Learning from the ground up: Global perspectives on social movements and knowledge production.* New York: Palgrave Macmillan.

Freire, P. (1969). *Pedagogy of the oppressed.* New York: Continuum.

Gee, J. (2009). Digital media and learning as an emerging field, part 1: How we got here. *International Journal of Learning and Media, 1*(2), 13–23.

Geschiere, P, (1993). Chiefs and colonial rule in Cameroon: Inventing chieftaincy, French and British style. *Africa*, *63*(2), 151–170.

Ghana Export Promotion Council (2009). Salt strategy for Ghana's salt sector: Final report. Accra: Ghana Export Promotion Council.

Government of Ghana (1991). *Master plan for salt production in Ghana.* Accra: Government of Ghana.

Hinestroza, J. (2001). *Cargill's salt mine development causes social exclusion and pollution at northwest coast of Lake Maracaibo, Venezuela.* Retrieved from http://www.mindfully.org/Industry/Cargill

Horton, M. & Freire, P. (1990). *We make the road by walking: Conversations on education and social change.* Philadelphia: Temple University Press.

Langdon, J, (2009). Learning to sleep without perching: Reflections by activist-educators on learning in social action in Ghanaian social movements. *McGill Journal of Education/Revue des Sciences de L'éducation de McGill*, *44*(1). Retrieved from http://mje.mcgill.ca/article/view/2946/3049

Langdon, J. (2010). Contesting globalization in Ghana: Communal resource defense and social movement learning. *Journal of Alternative Perspectives in the Social Sciences*, *2*(1), 309–339.

Langdon, J., & Harvey, B. (2012). *Blurring the boundaries of collaboration in Participatory Action Research.* Paper presented at Canadian Association for the Study of International Development conference, Waterloo, ON.

Mamdani, M. (1996). *Citizen and subject: Contemporary Africa and the legacy of late colonialism.* Princeton, NJ: Princeton University Press.

Manuh, T. (1992). Survival in rural Africa: The salt co-operatives in Ada district, Ghana. In D. R. F. Taylor and F. Mackenzie (Eds.), *Development from within: Survival in rural Africa* (pp. 102-124). New York: Routledge.

McKay, B. (2003). Enhancing Community over the Airwaves: Community Radio in a Ghanaian Fishing Village. M.Sc. Thesis. University of Guelph.

Mills, K. (2010). A review of the "digital turn" in new literacy studies. *Review of Educational Research, 80*(2), 246–271.

Overa, R. (2006). Networks, distance and trust: Telecommunications development and changing trading practices in Ghana. *World Development*, *34*(7), 1301–1315.

Radio Ada, (2002). *Radio Ada oral testimony documentary: Resource conflict—The Songor Lagoon*. Ghana: Radio Ada.

Rotberg, R. I., & Aker, J. C. (2012). Mobile phones: Uplifting weak and failed states. *The Washington Quarterly 36*(1), 111–125 .

Afterword

Dana E. Salter and Heather M. Pleasants

Getting Here

Heather: *I vividly remember my first forays into community-based digital storytelling work. I'd been working with Eugene Matusov's "La Red Magica," class and research project in an amazing place called the Latin American Cultural Center. I wanted to strike out on my own, and force myself to learn some things from the ground up—I wanted to know about using IEEE 1394 cables and Hi8 and about what would happen when kids had control over their literacy work with what was then "new" media in out-of-school environments. In 2006, after connecting with other community-based media workers at the Gathering of Digital Storytellers at MIT, I felt like I had found my tribe—a diverse group of artists, scholars, activists, researchers—all invested in using media within community contexts to address a variety of issues. Over the next few years, I looked forward to the stories, questions, and ideas generated in after-session coffee meetings that were had in other similar professional meetings; even establishing a "virtual happy hour" with a good friend across the miles to continue talking through ethical, conceptual and practical dilemmas. However, it wasn't until after listening to Lissa Soep talk about her work with Youth Radio at a dinner after her 2010 American Educational Research Conference talk that two things crystalized for me—the first was that there was a side to the story of community-based multiliteracies and digital media work that wasn't a part of the discourse, a side that conveyed the complexities, challenges, and possibilities of this work that folks had been discussing "offline" for years. The second thing was that there was a growing group of people with years of experience, across diverse contexts, who were uniquely prepared to address this.*

Dana: *I was in the middle of writing my dissertation and had just taken a program manager position at a national non-profit. In both places, I searched for research, articles, websites—any resource that talked about, for lack of a better expression, "what went wrong" in community-based multiliteracies and digital media products in critically reflective ways. I found fantastic reflections and research on process and practices, but discussions of problems and tensions were relegated to the margins of this reporting of the work. I understand why. Rhetorically speaking, the journal articles, book chapters, websites, etc. shape how the projects are viewed by a diverse audience that can include the participants themselves, future potential funders, organizational supervisors, to name a few. Therefore, I toyed with the idea of figuring out how to carve out a space with the journal articles, book chapters, websites, etc. for exploring and discussing "what went wrong" when the work we do bumps up against the assumptions and realities we bring to and experience in community-based multiliteracies and digital media products in ways that both thoughtfully reflect on process, while also being mindful of possible rhetorical consequences of these conversations. It was at this moment that Heather and I connected.*

This book is an initial step in an ongoing quest to carve space for reflections on process in community-based multiliteracies and digital media work. We are not trying to naively position this book as being the first to note the complex interconnections between community-based multiliteracies and digital media projects. On the contrary, we hope that as others read this book and have knowledge of others who are thinking along the same lines, we will connect and build an increasingly larger space for this kind of research and reflection. Our aim is to situate this book in calls for pushing the boundaries of the analysis and reporting of this work, and to highlight people who are talking, writing and thinking through what we miss when we obscure conversations of process (however messy) from discussions of community-based multiliteracies and digital media work. As discussed in the introduction, looking at the uncomfortable boundaries and borders of this work—where so much of this work rests—helps us continually reconceptualize the broader personal, local, and global implications of the work we do. We conclude with some thoughts related to our methodology as we worked with the authors of the chapters in this book and next steps for creating more space for projects like this.

A Note on Our Methodology: Identities and Roles within Community-Based Work

The chapters in this book are firmly situated within the perspective/assumption that who we are is deeply connected to the choices we make about the work that we do. Though seemingly obvious, this point is not often highlighted within the research and writing about community-based multiliteracies and digital media projects. We have encouraged the authors in this book to acknowledge and foreground the connections between their personal identities, experiences and philosophical perspectives and the work in which they are engaged. We have also asked them to reflectively consider who they *are* within their work. We believe that this kind of reflection should not be relegated to an afterthought, methodological note or prologue within representations of products and outcomes within community-based multiliteracies and digital media work. Rather, we see the authors' personal stories and critical reflections as essential to advancing the development of knowledge, with the potential to push both theory and practice forward.

It is essential because acknowledging who we are—our identities—and the role these identities play in how we approach multiliteracies and digital media work provides us with an opportunity to bring a caringly critical eye toward our practice. It allows us to engage with questions like: "What does it mean to me to work to create change or 'do good' in this way?" and "What are the real limits of what I can and could be doing through this work?" Many authors in this volume directly address these kinds of questions, whether through thinking about the ethics of engagement (Hill; Lee & Miller), through considering the role of personal biography in crafting an organizational ethos (Nucera & Lee) or through negotiating the pain and possibilities inherent in disrupting boundaries between insider and outsider status (Lewis & Fragnito).

Because community-based multiliteracies and digital media work is, by nature, oriented toward the representation of selves and communities of people, unpacking our identities is also essential to understanding what social, cultural and experiential knowledge (and baggage!) we might bring to our work with others who may be different from us. As authors in the book articulate, our statuses relative to immigration, ethnicity, language, health, gender, etc. have important connections to the possible stances we can and should take within our work. Related questions include ones like: as middle-class people of color, what sensitivities should we bear in mind in working with people of color who do not make a living wage? How do we bring humility, supportiveness and authentic engagement to our work with diverse communities of people? What definitions of authenticity do we call up, given our situatedness within particular social and cultural identities?

Exploring the identities we bring to our work is also essential because it assists others in understanding what it "looks like" to grow and develop the expertise, emotional intelligence and habits of mind that are essential in this kind of work. Community-based digital literacies and multiliteracies projects require the people leading them to have a complex constellation of skills and abilities including, but not limited to, being able to talk effectively with people occupying different positions and roles within the diverse communities; having the listening and empathetic skills needed to reach media-makers and storytellers where they are; having various kinds of technological expertise across multiple platforms, communication devices and media-making applications; and having writing/communication skills across multiple domains, including grant writing, public relations, communication of the results of their work in articles, blogs, newsletters or book form. While there may be commonalities across the experiences of authors included in this book, there are many paths into and through the work they do—and as discussed earlier, these paths have not often been discussed.

Contributing Knowledge and Next Steps

By means of this book, we have sought to create a space for conversations to be started among those who have been doing multiliteracies and digital media work in communities for a relatively long period of time, and those who may be at the beginning of conceptualizing projects in order to support specific communities; with those who work in formal educational settings and those who work in the most informal of contexts; with scholars who situate themselves within the academy and scholars who operate out of community-based organizations. We have put this book together with the idea in mind that the voices of individuals—such as the authors in this book—*must* be a part of the broader conversation about the significance of digital literacies and multiliteracies projects for advancing social justice. What the chapters in this book collectively remind us all is that we must seek to create for ourselves an understanding of, an enactment of, and articulations of communities of practice that provide a mooring even while we work to create movement in our lives and the lives of people with whom we work. Community-based program directors, teachers and scholars who do digital literacies and multiliteracies work possess a depth of knowledge that comes from multiple sources. Centralizing the practices and praxis-based knowledge of these individuals and groups of collaborators is necessary for a full consideration of what it means to be a scholar, creator and conveyor of knowledge within this area of work, as well as for our thinking about the contributions that community-based multiliteracies and digital literacies programs and projects can make to diverse people around the world. As the competition for the financial resources needed to support this work becomes more intense, and as conversations about how to think about who deserves what resources and why become more heated, it is our perspective that the ideas, conceptual frameworks and lived experiences of individuals who create and direct community-based digital literacies and multiliteracies projects should be a more visible aspect of how we understand what has been accomplished and what we might seek to achieve in the future.

However, there are barriers that must be overcome in order for more work of this kind to be included in public discourse. When we first approached the scholars and practitioners who would eventually join this book project, many declined. And yet, overwhelmingly, most indicated that they had been wanting to write about the "behind the scenes" aspects of their work, or about some of the challenges they had faced, about their growth and the growth of people involved in their programs, or about their concerns regarding the value of their work relative to the resources available to support and sustain it. Some authors expressed that they had been hoping to find the time to write about their work for years—but that they were not "academic" writers and so turned down our invitation. This motivated us to find creative ways to help provide time and thinking space for each of the authors who did agree to contribute to craft their chapters. Our motivations lay in providing an opportunity for each author's story to be told, but also in allowing ourselves the chance to use methodological and representational strategies that respected and honored the unique contributions and challenges faced by the authors within their work and the presentation of their knowledge. We encouraged the authors to tell their untold stories, in the forms that seemed most consistent with their practices and their approaches. As a result, collaborative dialogue and storytelling feature prominently within the text.

A prevailing challenge within digital and multiliteracies scholarship is the tension between producing work that moves rapidly into public spaces, and creating the time to move from a "fast-fast" orientation to a reflective mode for processing what we are learning and why this knowledge is important to us, and perhaps, to others. Case in point: at the final stage of creating this book, we came across a call for chapters for an academic book that focused on the challenges of conducting research "at the speed of technology." The increasing pressure to produce more work, more quickly is not a new tension; classroom teachers, doctors, public health workers and other working people who are also researchers and writers have been dealing with this challenges for decades. The question has been, and continues to be, how can we "do" and also find the time to think reflectively—and write critically—about what we do? The authors in this book have provided a model for how this may happen, and though many of the authors have published work in a variety of online and print publications, an unanticipated but welcome result of this book has been a repeated conversation about how the process of working on this book has renewed their interest in and optimism about writing that represents their knowledge in ways that are meaningful to them and relevant to a variety of audiences. We hope that those who read this book are similarly affirmed. We welcome—indeed, encourage—further questions that may emerge as a result of reading each chapter and the book as a whole. We hope that our book both presents partial answers, and raises additional important questions in regard to the ethics involved in thinking through the integrity of process and product. We further hope that these answers and questions might inform our collective knowledge—even while changes in technology, politics and access continue to shape how we do our work and what we do with it. Most importantly, we look forward to continuing to write ourselves into the story of our work, and into the story of community-based multiliteracies and digital media scholarship.

List of Contributors

Jason Brennan is a doctoral candidate at the Ontario Institute for Studies in Education of the University of Toronto, works as an occasional teacher with the Toronto Catholic District School Board, and holds a part-time administrative position at Ryerson University. Apart from his research in practitioner inquiry and teacher education, his current projects investigate the imbricated cultural and relational literacy practises of youth in and around digital environments, including video games. He continues to be heavily involved in practitioner research communities, including the one featured in his chapter, as well as an online teacher-researcher inquiry group. He has been a member of the Teaching to Learn Project since its founding in 2011.

Alessandro Bresba has a Master of Theological Studies from Boston University and has taught religion, ethics and philosophy in San Francisco for four years. He earned a Master of Teaching at the Ontario Institute for Studies in Education of the University of Toronto, where he explored the incorporation of critical inquiry and the role of doubt in religious education. He joined the Teaching to Learn community in 2011. He is currently a high school teacher within the Toronto Catholic District School Board.

Sara DeAngelis teaches high school English at an independent school in the Greater Toronto Area, and literature with the Faculty of Continuing Education at Seneca College for Applied Arts and Technology. She received her Master's of Teaching at the Ontario Institute for Studies in Education of the University of Toronto, and has a Bachelor of Arts degree in English from York University. Sara has been involved in the Teaching to Learn Project (TTL) since 2011. Her research interests include art integration and exploration in the English classroom as a means of expression and therapy for students.

Will Edwards is a teacher researcher working in a community college in downtown Toronto. Will has been a member of the Teaching to Learn community since its inception in 2011. He participates in practitioner inquiry communities to further his understandings about the complexities of his practice. His recent studies invite immigrant students and adults with non- traditional academic pathways to co-author literacy curricula. He is currently pursuing his PhD in the department of Curriculum Teaching and Learning at OISE/UT.

Skawennati Fragnito makes art that addresses history, the future, and change. Her pioneering New Media projects, including CyberPowWow (1997–2004), Imagining Indians in the 25th Century (2001), and TimeTraveller™ (2008–2013) have been widely exhibited across Canada, the United States and Australia. She has been honored to win imagineNative's 2009 Best New Media Award as well as a 2011 Eiteljorg Contemporary Art Fellowship. Her work has been collected by the Canada Art Bank, the Aboriginal Art Centre at Aboriginal Affairs and Northern Development Canada and private individuals. Skawennati graduated with a BFA from Concordia University. A founding member of the First Nations artist collective, Nation to Nation, she has been active in the Artist-Run Network and sat on the board at Galerie Oboro. She is co-director, with Jason E. Lewis, of Aboriginal Territories in Cyberspace, (AbTeC) a network of artists, academics and technologists investigating, creating and critiquing Aboriginal virtual environments. Please visit www.skawennati.com to see more.

Pip Hardy has always liked to be on the crest of a wave. Despite becoming a vegetarian in the early 1970s, she managed to get a degree in English Literature, and soon started teaching courses in women's literature and women's studies. She moved on to work with homeless and unemployed people, helping them gain useful life and job-seeking skills. Pip eventually went to work at the National Extension College—a radical experiment in second-chance education for adults, designing and developing open and distance learning programmes intended to help people become more reflective and effective practitioners, whatever their job. In 2003, Pip co- founded the Patient Voices Programme in the hope of reminding all those who design and deliver healthcare of our shared humanity and the need for kind, dignified, respectful, patient-centred care through the creation and sharing of digital stories of health and illness, hope and hopelessness, care and lack of it. The Programme is now one of the largest and longest-running digital storytelling projects in the world. Pip is currently working on a PhD looking at the potential of digital stories to transform healthcare.

Amy Hill is a trainer and consultant on the ethics and practice of strategic storytelling and participatory media for health, development, and human rights. After spending twelve years coordinating women's health and violence prevention projects throughout California and learning the mechanics of video production while working on a series of documentary films about HIV/AIDS in Ethiopia, she founded Silence Speaks (www.silencespeaks.org), an international digital storytelling initiative that since 1999 has employed oral history, facilitative filmmaking, and popular education strategies to support the telling and public sharing of life stories documenting injustice and promoting individual, community, and policy change. She currently manages Silence Speaks as an initiative of the Center for Digital Storytelling (www.storycenter.org). Amy holds a BA in British & American Literature from Scripps College, and a Master's degree in Gender Studies from Stanford University. She lives in Berkeley, California, with her partner, Thomas Paul, and their daughter, Fana Luisa.

Helmi Jung is a teacher who specializes in how second-language acquisition can create opportunities for student expression and self-awareness. Helmi was a founding member of the Teaching to Learn community and has relocated to Nova Scotia. Her recent experience in a private school in Toronto focused on empowering students to take control of their learning by inviting them to design curriculum they found personally engaging. Helmi is currently pursuing a French-based career in Halifax.

Julie Kasper is a graduate of the University of Arizona and Teachers College, Columbia. She is a National Board Certified teacher who has been teaching ESL/ELD for over 16 years—in Japan, NYC, and now in Tucson, Arizona. She works with very diverse English Language Learners from around the world who range in age from 14–21, the majority of whom have refugee status in the United States. Julie co-founded the Finding Voice Project with Josh Schachter in 2007 as a way of better integrating the arts and technology in interdisciplinary, project-based literacy instruction and with the hope that traditional barriers between the classroom and the community could be dissolved so that a more responsive, connected, and engaging learning environment could develop.

Derek Koen is the co-founder of Washington Koen Media, Inc. and the co-executive director of the Beyond the Bricks Project. He began his career with Amen Ra Films East, producers of HBO's *Disappearing Acts* and the documentary chronicling the life of the professor and scholar Dr. Yosef A.A. Bjen-Jochannan, affectionately known as "Dr. Ben." Koen was production coordinator for the Harlem-based documentary film company Roja Productions, working on the PBS series *Matters of Race*, award winning documentary *Citizen King*, *Bones of Our Ancestry*, and others. Derek is an experienced digital videographer and editor with credits that include music videos, commercials, short-form documentaries, short films, and an Internet sports talkshow, as well as producing and directing the feature film *Ghetto Fabulous*.

Jonathan Langdon has been working with social movements in Ghana for the last 10 years, and with the movement in Ada since 2008. At the same time, he has also worked with those who challenge Eurocentric knowledge systems in order to reconfigure whose knowledge counts in discussions of development (i.e. who is considered literate). In all of this work he is preoccupied with the ways in which people contesting power relations learn. His work has been published in *the Canadian Journal of Development Studies*, *Studies in the Education of Adults*, *the Institute of Development Studies Bulletin*, *The Journal of Alternative Perspectives in the Social Sciences*, and the *McGill Journal of Education*. He also edited the collection *Indigenous Knowledges, Development and Education* (Sense, 2009). He is an assistant professor in the Development Studies Program and Adult Education Department at St Francis Xavier University.

Kofi Larweh is a broadcast journalist, trainer and adult educationist. He was the first station coordinator (manager) for Radio Ada (the first community radio station in Ghana) from its inception February 1998 until March 2009. Preferring working with marginalized groups in their self-motivated liberation efforts, he abandoned teaching mathematics at the Teacher Training College to become a community activist and a founding member of the Ada Songor Advocacy Forum (ASAF). He has been working with Dr. Jonathan Langdon for the past 10 years and is co-author for the paper "The Thumbless Hand, the Dog and the Chameleon: Enriching Social Movement Learning Theory through Epistemically Grounded Narratives Emerging from a Participatory Action Research Case Study in Ghana," a David Jones Award winner at the 2013 Standing Conference for University Teaching and Research on the Education of Adults, held in Glasgow.

Jenny Lee is a co-director of Allied Media Projects. She was instrumental in relocating Allied Media Projects from Bowling Green, OH, to Detroit in 2007 and has since facilitated the growth and evolution of the conference nationally while deepening its roots in her hometown of Detroit. In 2009 she led the process of founding the Detroit Digital Justice Coalition and securing a $1.8 million stimulus grant for the coalition through the Broadband Technology Opportunities Program of the American Recovery and Reinvestment Act. Jenny graduated from the University of Michigan with a degree in Comparative Literature in 2005.

Edward Ou Jin Lee is presently involved as community organizer and board member with AGIR (Action LGBTQ with Immigrants and Refugees), located in Montreal, Québec / Haudenosaunee (or Mohawk) Territories. Presently a doctoral candidate at the McGill School of Social Work, Ed's research explores the social organization of queer migrations and the everyday experiences of LGBTQ migrants with precarious status.

Jason Edward Lewis is a digital media artist, poet and software designer. He founded Obx Labs, where he devises new means of creating and reading digital texts, develops systems for creative use of mobile technology and uses virtual environments to assist Aboriginal communities in preserving, interpreting and communicating cultural histories. He co-directs Aboriginal Territories in Cyberspace and Skins Workshops on Aboriginal Storytelling and Video Game Design. Lewis' creative work has been featured at Ars Electronica, Urban Screens, ISEA, SIGGRAPH, and FILE, among other venues, and has been recognized by a Prix Ars Electronica Honorable Mention, several imagineNATIVE Best New Media awards and four solo exhibitions. He's the author/co-author of five chapters in collected editions covering mobile media, video game design, machinima and experimental pedagogy with Native American communities. He is currently associate professor and program director of computation arts at Concordia University, Montreal.

Liz Miller is a professor in Communication Studies at Concordia University in Montreal and an award-winning documentary maker whose films and trans-media projects offer new and critical perspectives on social movements and media. Miller offers training in video advocacy and digital storytelling to a wide range of human rights organizations. Her documentary films, *Novela, Novela* and *The Water Front* have been exhibited and broadcast around the world and used to impact policy and educational initiatives. Her collaborative media project, Mapping Memories: Participatory Media, Place- Based Stories & Refugee Youth a book/DVD/website, is used to raise awareness around refugee rights. Her most recent film, *En la casa* follows a visionary women's rights group working to end sexual violence at home, in bed and in the streets through their powerful blend of TV drama and grassroots organizing. Miller is on the board of the International Association of Women in Television and Radio.

Diana J Nucera is a co-director of Allied Media Projects. She attended the first AMC in 1999 as a 17-year-old independent artist and joined the national advisory board in 2006, while on staff as a video arts instructor at Street Level Youth Media in Chicago. Diana joined the AMP staff in 2008 to produce the first ever "How-to" track and coordinate the Hands-on Media Lab of the Allied Media Conference. She has since evolved the AMC Media Lab into a year-round training facility out of which AMP offers its Detroit Future Media Workshops and other community educational programming. Diana has led the development of AMP's earned income strategy, managing training contracts with local institutions including the UAW International and Highland Park School District, as well as various non-profit clients. Diana provides direction and support to all AMP trainers, the Detroit Future Media Workshops and the Detroit Future Schools Program. She participates in fundraising and strategic planning for all areas of AMP programming. Diana is an accomplished cellist who has performed with internationally-renowned artists such as Matthew Barney, in addition to being a core member of multiple local music projects.

Anna Pisecny is an Ontario Certified Teacher. Her qualifications include English and history in the intermediate/senior division, along with qualifications in special education and English as a Second Language (ESL). She graduated from the University of Toronto, receiving her Honours Bachelors of Arts degree. She then continued her education at the Ontario Institute for Studies in Education at the University of Toronto (OISE/UT) where she completed a Master of Teaching degree. Currently, Anna is teaching English within the Toronto District School Board. Over the past several years, Anna has been a participant in the Teaching to Learn project, a collaborative research community of teachers, teacher candidates and youth at the OISE/UT. As part of the project, Anna has participated in a series of research projects that explore literacy across various communities. Anna's current research interests involve investigations in literacy with an emphasis on social justice.

Heather M. Pleasants is a writer and ethnographer and is the director for community education in the Center for Community-Based Partnerships at The University of Alabama. Dr. Pleasants coordinates the Parent Leadership Academy and the Our Voices, Our Lives Program, and is involved in supporting the development of community-based research projects that address educational issues. Since completing her first digital story in 2003, Pleasants has been engaged in ongoing research that explores how youth and adults use multiliteracies and digital media as tools for personal expression, reflexive identity work and social change. Pleasants is a graduate of the University of Michigan-Flint (B.S. in psychology, 1992) and Michigan State University (Ph.D. in educational psychology, specialization in language, literacy and learning, 2000).

jesikah maria ross is a documentary artist who collaborates with schools, non-governmental organizations and public media stations to create participatory media projects that generate community dialogue and development. She recently wrapped up a five-year stint as the founding director of the UC Davis Art of Regional Change, a university-community engagement initiative which brought scholars, students and artists together with social action groups to produce place-based storytelling projects that catalyze community change. She is currently the community engagement specialist in Capital Public Radio's multimedia documentary unit The View From Here, where she is involving regional youth and community partners in telling their stories about high school dropout via the community media blog RView209. She has worked around the globe launching youth media initia- tives, exhibited work in street galleries as well as state museums, and served on the board of national organizations focused on the intersection of media and community development. Find out more at Praxisprojects.net.

Dana E. Salter is the founder of DES Education Consulting, and the community service specialist at Georgia State University's Alonzo A. Crim Center for Urban Education Excellence. Salter has been a community-based program organizer and program director, literacy and writing teacher, curriculum designer, and educator for over 15 years. She has done this work within and outside of the United States (Canada, South Korea, Turkey). She obtained her undergraduate degree from Rutgers University and holds a Masters in Education from Penn State University. She is currently completing her doctorate at McGill University (Canada).

Josh Schachter is a visual storyteller, educator and cultural organizer who has collaborated with organizations throughout the U.S. and globe to document critical social and environmental issues. His images have been published internationally in books, magazines and films in venues ranging from the *New York Times* to the *Navajo Times*. Josh earned a master's degree in environmental management from the Yale School of Forestry and Environmental Studies, where he explored the role of youth photography in building community. Over the past 15 years he has collaborated on community-based media projects with youth, teachers, neighborhood groups, and nonprofit organizations in places ranging from New Delhi to Nigeria. In 2010 Josh received PhotoPhilanthropy's International "Grand Prize Community-Based Activist Award" and in 2009 was the recipient of the "Arizona Teaching Artist Award for Innovation" from the Arizona Commission on the Arts. You can learn more about Josh's work at www.joshphotos.com and www.findingvoiceproject.org.

Rob Simon is assistant professor of multiliteracies in education at the Ontario Institute for Studies in Education of the University of Toronto. His teaching and research investigate how schools can better support the learning and life chances of diverse adolescents, documenting the social and political contexts of literacy teaching and teacher education from the perspectives of practitioners and youth. His current projects include investigations of youth out-of-school multiliteracy practices such as Pokémon and Minecraft. Recent publications include an edited volume on literacy teacher education, *Literacy Teacher Educators: Preparing Teachers for a Changing World.* He is the principal investigator of the Teaching to Learn Project, a Connaught- funded intergenerational research community made up of teacher candidates, early-year literacy teachers, and youth.

Tony Sumner's story began, not in the sunny brightness of the California of Pip Hardy's childhood, but in the leafy green lanes of rural Hampshire (old, not New!). The plotline meandered through Physics and Astronomy before chapters set in the aerospace industries of the Falklands crisis and the computer industries of the Silicon Fen boom years. As the millennium changed and our two protagonists met, he was likewise drawn into the development of open, distance and e-learning materials before digital storytelling became part of his own story, and set the scene for the sequel. Tony is now embarking on a PhD to consider the opportunities for using new technologies, such as digital storytelling, to promote reflection and develop insight. Pip Hardy and Tony are both Fellows of the RSA.

Ouida Washington is co-founder and co-executive director of Beyond the Bricks Project (BTBP) with partner Derek Koen. Her role as co-founder and executive producer of WK Media, a video production and media company focused on creating high-impact media that promote socially responsible messages, initiated the "Beyond the Bricks" film, which spawned a media and international community engagement non-profit organization focused on increasing educational and social outcomes of school-age Black males. BTBP has four activity streams to achieve its mission; Media Production, community engagement, direct services, and research. Through its direct services work BTBP developed a media literacy and community leadership curriculum, which is implemented through partnerships with universities and community organizations around the country. Ouida has enjoyed a diverse career as a film and video producer, and began her socially responsive work with her role as director of the CAS Intel Computer Clubhouse, a creative technology program for children 11–19 yrs.

Index

new literacies
AND DIGITAL EPISTEMOLOGIES

Colin Lankshear & Michele Knobel
General Editors

New literacies emerge and evolve apace as people from all walks of life engage with new technologies, shifting values and institutional change, and increasingly assume 'postmodern' orientations toward their everyday worlds. Despite many efforts to take account of such changes, educational institutions largely remain out of touch with the range of new ways of making and sharing meanings that increasingly mediate and shape the lives of the young people they teach and the futures they face. This series aims to explore some key dimensions of the changes occurring within social practices of literacy and the educational challenges they present, with a view to informing educational practice in helpful ways. It asks what are new literacies, how do they impact on life in schools, homes, communities, workplaces, sites of leisure, and other key settings of human cultural engagement, and what significance do new literacies have for how people learn and how they understand and construct knowledge. It aims to challenge established and 'official' ways of framing literacy, and to ask what it means for literacies to be powerful, effective, and enabling under current and foreseeable conditions. Collectively, the works in this series will help to reorient literacy debates and literacy education agendas.

For further information about the series and submitting manuscripts, please contact:

Michele Knobel & Colin Lankshear
Montclair State University
Dept. of Education and Human Services
3173 University Hall
Montclair, NJ 07043
michele@coatepec.net